CHECKMATE

CHECKMATE

The Many Myriads of Life

ARUN NAIDU

PARTRIDGE

Library of Congress Control Number:		2018963380
ISBN:	Hardcover	978-1-5437-4710-2
	Softcover	978-1-5437-4709-6
	eBook	978-1-5437-4711-9

Print information available on the last page.

To order additional copies of this book, contact
Toll Free 800 101 2657 (Singapore)
Toll Free 1 800 81 7340 (Malaysia)
orders.singapore@partridgepublishing.com

www.partridgepublishing.com/singapore

CONTENTS

NEW PHASE IN LIFE

Dedicated To Jessica

Behind every successful man, there is a woman

For me

Front of my success is my lovely woman

My Darling Jessica,
You are my Dearest Love of my life,

Life together we have traversed
A maze together we dispersed

Many a moment of despair
Quietly we stitched them in repair

Challenges plenty at us thrown
Through the dark clouds the sunrays shone

The beacon of faith in each other we borne
Destined to be together always, never alone

With you in my life every moment is Showtime
Every day of our lives will always be a Valentine!

Lovingly Yours Always

One and Only

Arun

Disclaimer

This is an autobiographical work written as an ode inspired on true life experiences. Names, characters, businesses, institutions, places, events and incidents are products of author's imagination used in a fictitious manner. Names, place, date and time are but an indication as the story evolves. The writer has woven the identities of the characters involved throughout these labyrinths of autobiographical events highlighting real plight of the society we live in where relationship is but relative.

Any resemblance to actual persons, living or dead, or actual events is purely coincidental.

Author's Note

The following autobiographical story CHECKMATE is spun as an ode to the many myriads of life. It gives a kaleidoscopic insight in life of an ordinary individual Aarvan our main protagonist.

How his trust and faith over years gets abused, betrayed and desecrated by family, friends, colleagues and bosses altering several times path of his destiny, so often always finding him at life's crossroads.

The author likens life to game of chess. Typically, a mind game requiring foresight of rival moves in advance in planning your defense or offense.

Life similarly in passage crisscrosses in loops of straight, oblique, back and forth, even in two and half jump where survival becomes primal as an immediate need. Constantly checkmated in one's progress in life by powers with vested interest creating a situation of helplessness and hopelessness.

However, difference being; in game of chess eventually there is only one winner but in real life there are no winners but so-called winners are equal losers.

Author likewise also draws similarity to feral world of beasts in jungle. Whether grasslands in tropics or bush of the Savanah, the inhabitants of prey and predator live to survive another day constantly in fear of when or where does it get its next meal or becoming the next meal.

Domination for territory, right to mates, stealing and scavenging a kill as might is right, holds all the cold similarities in human world.

Here of course the only dissimilarity separating them from us Homo sapiens is animals do not overkill.

Their world is called the jungle and ours is called society? But in reality, we live in civilized jungle that is even more ruthless, intimidating and scary; Man, just kills!

Whether family, friends, businesses or corporates relations are relative just to a point, thereafter it just does not matter!

The biggest barrier defined in success as winners or losers is emotion. Unfortunately, history too glorifies winners despite all its criminal expulsion. And in actual their crimes lay suspended and buried for the dead don't talk!

The angel and demons that rule heaven and hell is but our own conscience!

CHECKMATE in true sense is our CROSSROADS in real LIFE!

Who am I?

The journey of a new life begins even before birth
In a union of love in time somewhere on earth
Testing period now begins for a new life getting a berth

Choices none in knowing your eventual worth
But in challenges since, there is no dearth
A chance no doubt in a hearth full of mirth

Against few million seeds an egg I fertilized
Destroyed competition for life I capitalized
But in life many a situation to be analyzed
Demonic emotions shackled my core to be capsized

So many encounters thrown and so many to stun
Feelings tear your core weighing you down with force in ton

Stripped you will be of all life necessities bare
Having achieved their fare, they will walk away without care

In our earthly journey this harsh reality is so true
Simmering differences petty always in latent ready to brew

So often asked, it is but a cliché
In solitude I ask myself too for my fears to allay
In a civilized world were civility has no say
Lost and lonely when you feel betrayed

Why am I not beyond all the irrelevant sentiment?
As a miniscule gamete I was beyond any predicament

Now my identity is my name, gender, race and nationality
Adding to it the gross ignominy of religion banality
A case in point, place dependent is also my caste defining community
Am I just another ID tagged by all the above triviality
High expectation to fulfill the burden of legacy in all its brutality

But I don't give a damn and couldn't care less for its political crudity
Yet why do I still feel so incomplete something missing in criticality
An insatiable mystic truth that I seek so desperately!

A voyage in existence formed in doctrines so contradictory
Honesty, truth, trust and faith high pillars of extreme morality
But in identity, none finds a hallowed place so apparently

I am who I am yet I don't know who am I?
inheriting these gifts of inequality, I don't wish to buy
A fictional, fantasy of multi-dimensional personality
Exists a fine line between sane and insanity

About me, I am yet figuring out my veracity
So, who am I really, is this just me in reality
A trifling particle in an infinite space of cosmic immortality!

Chi and Be

Instinct only companion to me
Strengthen my chi and be!

Of sound body and mind mostly blessed
Seek but in others how they are dressed

Slaves we are to a lustful mind
Bellyful Desires of a material kind

No Kin or Kith nor friends or foe
Dare my march lest I hoe

Oh! What world has come to be!
Angels & Demons Fight Within Me!

Tears of Anguish flood torrential rain
Oh please, oh please, save me this emotional pain!

Closed eyes imagine a world beyond strife
A cry for help and its back to life

Try to save everyone from despair
Pushed into abyss holding on my dear hair

What's willed to happen will happen;
Long paths winding, perilous and dampen;

Fraught labyrinth so cryptic and mysterious
The journey septic, lonely and dangerous;

Impossible nothing! Possibilities rain,

Making all difficult for someone's rightful gain

How many kills to cheat and win?
Too many sacrifices to be supreme!

Hope doesn't fail with age
But hope again will inevitably fade

Fall I will fallen I will not be
I shall rise every time you felled me

No forces so great put me to pin
For I will rise every time to win

Now I see the essence of a true mend
Only I and I alone am truly my only best friend

Instinct only companion to me
Strengthen my chi and be

Prologue

Destiny and Fate

What is right and wrong
This is but an enigmatic song

Two sides of a coin you toss
Heads I win, Tails your loss

Life a destiny true, an existence where real choices are few
No choice in parents, kith and kin, friends or foe as life begins anew

Personality, sexuality, looks, color and built inherently is genetic
Defining factors of society deeply conditioned in a fixed bandwidth

Religion, order and power measured also by status in wealth
Now added to your profile as entity certified at birth till death

Unfortunately bestowed by dogmatic rituals deep in tradition
To bedevil a poor soul in burden without choice in an imposition
Life's voyage a coiling path of crossroads but never in true redemption

But then in life, you do make your own choices as well
Decisions whether rational or not always only circumstantial
Destiny of choice, fated in heaven or hell only and only time to tell

Crossroads in lifetime, harsh test of nerves, always at every bend
Experiences in happiness but momentary, pain always in stipend

Negotiation a way of life for a bottle of milk an infant will cry
Growing up in childhood, demands in teen seeks in another sacrifice
Sinister and chilling an adult, willing in any to just roast and fry

Give and Take a phrase in make
Take we surely do, Give we reluctantly fake
Because we all do just want to take in rake

Harsh reality game of life, with twist and turn always enigmatic
Like in chess, if careless not in check, have you at best in panic
In control of settings, helplessly trapped by several mindless lunatics

Destiny to shape sometimes in your hands to be pragmatic
Self before others, always be in wary of any melodramatic

Destiny in real life is what you carve for your sake
Options in a choice you make yet only one in chance you take
Your fate locked in lady luck whether you make or break

Checkmate!

Chess is a symbolic game of war
Engaged intensely at clubs, homes and even at a bar

Played by the rivals on board of 64 squares
On framework of rules and time one has to care

Four divisions', infantry, cavalry, elephantry and chariotry,
All at disposal to protect your threatened territory

Amateurs, Professionals, Connoisseurs alike
Slug it out no sweat, with the aplomb of elite

Warring factions trade in their ammo
The silence around as loud as a crescendo

Battle on alert and quietly predatory
Astute yet crafty mind wins each glory

Waiting for the moment to open a gate
Check, check, until checkmate

Life is but just like a game of chess
Like an infantry you onward press

Hurdles many want you totally in a mess
Bruised and hurt brave you are nonetheless
Friend becomes foe a rival so sore
Foe you know but Friend pains you to the core

Challenge only not emotion, in will to spur you on
Mount the cavalry the knight will charge head on

Experience in time makes you capable and stronger
Now you are confident of changing the order

Slowly and surely you climb the ladder
Chipping away at the stratum of disorder

Against all odds finally on top
Look down upon your harvested crop

Safeguard your position from a deadly drop
The war has just begun to stay right on top

There are many in wait for an open gate
If not careful, check, check and checkmate!

Chess a war game enacted on a coffee table
Amateurs, passionate connoisseurs spin many a fable

Brows burrow narrow deep in thought
Scanning board to drive rival to naught

End unknown until the mistaken move of fate
If not careful, check, check and checkmate!

Life too is a serious game and all in black and white
Either as bishop, knight or rook in Open Square to fight

To be a king one day, focus on queen within your sight
Not with the power of brawn but brain to create an opening light

A pawn often ignored as small, is the one to give a major fright

Life's no different for a common man
A sphinx like game of chess to fan

Stacked against the odds of fate lest it may be checkmate!

The Jungle

The board of life is a maze of squares
Tropical grassland or Savanah bush, beckoningly it dares

The only difference in this game of life there no rules
No time and no holds barred with absolute no scruples

Life in constant battle with known and unknown
Foe you know but friend you certainly don't

Two foes your soul does know one your mind other your heart
In constant war agree to disagree they are but poles apart

Survival is an everyday battle in order to peck
For primal fear of being always in constant check

Predator and Prey territory, they share
Only one law prevailing for all to care

Live to die another day for all you dare
Entirely depends on how you really just fare

Fate unknown until mistaken move too late
If not careful, check, check and checkmate!

The journey of life you always walk alone
Along the way, in the wild jungle, you are thrown

Family, friends, companion, soulmate and kids too of your own
Crossroads, Forks, U-turn or No Entry decision to dwell all alone

Long before time in hope for you to come in your zone
Many moons pass before the sun on you finally has shone

The Game

Chess in political moves no holds barred contest
No pedigree, blood, friend, no boundary in test

A game of consequence but no sacrosanct agreement
Results stark, till final in dark to appease or impeachment

Magnitude harsh intent to crush beyond the will of a victim
The tenacity of a quarry to endure and combat its system

Nothing more consuming in a devious and conspiratorial plot
Family politics sinister, diabolical, high octane always on the dot
Even in family small, there are favorites and underdogs

Ruthlessly spinning a web of deceit in exploiting each other chink
Survive, consolidate and inherit to rule, how to? Constantly in think

Realty game played intensely inside family, friends and outsiders
Bloodbath will be in kind as fodder for fire plenty in providers

Fate unknown till mistaken move too late, with your back to the wall
Sadly, winners none to take it all but losers plenty in a feast for all

A reality in life a lesson plenty in history to peep, yet we repeatedly fall
Checkmate barrier of wall in all millenniums many still standing tall

Black and White Life is always majestic and bright
Between Truth and Lie in dilemma we all are tied

Life's stark naked, rude harsh reality to own
Death a great leveler, in it all share the same throne

1. My Final Days in High School

1.1. The Condescending Clergy

"Namaskaram, Namaskar, Namaste"
Sadhana in my Bharata since yore
The profound greeting comes to fore

Young or old palms in reverence fold
An obeisance from one to another soul

A resounding smack across my face
Riposte for Namaskar's humble grace

Rudely admonished by the priest of an abbey
Decree indignation in English only to Gabby

"Namaskar" antecedents so profound
Bharata's culture libeled in presence many around

Intimidated violence on a child under silly ground
Hidden memo bore in senseless abuse found

Holy Gracious School Bandra in erstwhile Bombay
Small made cheerful baby-faced kid was I

In sporadic aggression, I wouldn't shy
Against predators' big bullies I would let fly
But in tyrant Fr. Vijay simply couldn't get by

Unpredictable and temperamentally in mood
Fleeting display of calmness next 180 and crude

Bespectacled face with a moon reflecting balding hood
Priestly teacher a misplaced belonging from his brotherhood

1.2. My Alma Mater and Me

Holy Gracious School a co-ed convent
Run by priests of a holy diocese as God's servant

First principal an upright priest in Fr. Prakash
Emanuel in succession was gentle never brash
In the abbey but Fr. Vijay a demon very rash

To emulate a fine predecessor in Fr. Prakash
A disciplinarian righteous Principal he no hogwash

Abusive in his powers he never was
Respect from faculty and alumni as boss

Set morals of elevated self-control and learning
High percentage 100 in results kept churning

Alma mater revered first among equal in discerning
Passed the baton of flame to keep it burning

Me as student none so studious just an average
Scale but final summit without any leverage
For love of the sport on time I would pilferage

Sneak back into court after school
And play table tennis together in a pool

In Gracious High to pursue sport a taboo
Academics a focus, games a big hullabaloo

Many a jack no play became a dull boy to boo
Talent snubbed, competitive gust crushed too

1.3. Preliminary Practice Exams

The public board exams drew near
Our last schools' days became dear

In our class of 1977, few shed a tear
Whilst some grew anxious with fear

Preparatory trial exams called prelim
Like training mind in a mock gym
Practice to raise our adrenalin
In readiness, a public exam to win

An unfortunate incident so dampened
In a chemistry lab, so it happened

Practical mock run for an alkaline test
Using the litmus to do the rest

Pipette to pull in exact volume in precise
To calibration sucked in my mouth by devise

Ammonium Hydroxide a chemical aqueous solution
Kept in a flask on table for careful manipulation

1.4. An Accident and Barbaric Act

For reason beyond control in my critical execution
Fatefully I drew little more in alkaline solution

Agonizing fiery sting instant, my oral cavity totally was slain
My entire mouth now extremely sore in agonizing pain

On consent from teacher ran down one floor
Then along classrooms in tearing hurry through the corridor

Only to reach quickly to the washroom door
Needed water plenty in the mouth to rinse for

An inauspicious day for me to bore
Fr. Vijay to him I was an eye so sore

Path, perimeter secured by him and more
On that day sadistic cruelty came to fore

Halted in flight, burning sensation in mouth entirely
Could not speak lest even a word in pain so utterly

Reluctantly he let me continue
In harried stride rushed to the loo

He brooked intention evil on second thought
Rudely stopped me on the return walk

Despite many mouthfuls aqua I had in a rinse
Sizzling sensation still tangible like pokey pins

Obvious it was yet I could not talk

Without warning a huge searing wallop

Sadistically smashed his hand across my face
In distressful pain, I now was also in a daze

Seething pain engulfed my temple
The clergy had lost all his vital in mental

Searing pain through cells in my brain
The reason he vociferously demanded in his reign
My scurrying to the school washroom drains

Assaulted with sheer brute force in disdain
Across my ear in temple main

Lifted off ground and flung far like in theater entertain
Shuddering uncontrolled I was now in extreme dual pain

Small and no match for a full-grown man
His an act of raw cruelty of barbaric clan

Choking in humiliation with raining tears
Lifted self on my own finally conquering my fears

In bold confrontation close peering fiercely in his eye
In silent anger, trembling lips, I asked Why, Oh! Why?

Brazenly he just turned back and strode away
A triumphant marauding beast I dared his way

1.5. Priest Holy or Perjury

He a Priestly teacher out of his groove
What in hell was he trying to prove?

Discipline a mask in him was coldly sinister
Fulfill his sadistic fantasy as a holy minister

Hideously wicked a dark persona
Coward he to be summoned by right in a subpoena

But papal to his atrocities blind
Vandal in the destruction of innocent minds

For the blameless innocent far from few
Would just not care to have him removed

Physical ferocity on weak so vicious
Accepted unopposed intent violence so malicious

Tweaked in a shield of discipline dark he imposed
With spiteful brutality, he simply disposed

Predatory designs were his true intentions closed
Openly never in public in admittance disclosed

Diktat primitive a ruthless rule by fear exposed
His mantra was to control and so in it he reposed

Guinea pig definitely made to be I was
To simply instill fear in students a cause

Used for his demonic experimentation

An example of a live demonstration

He simply chose to purge the weak
To submit in surrender to him in meek

His fear of strong was similar in validation
Lest on him, it flops in angst of scandalous retribution

1.6. Helpless and Humiliated

A child I was enveloped in a stifled feeling
Wounds and scar so deep and un-healing

So desperate and completely helpless
Against me a heinous crime doubtless

Offender senior parishioner so senseless
Acted like mercenary extremely merciless

Had to be booked for offense headless
His act beyond inhumanly so pitiless

Teachers' reaction mute and speechless
From classroom adjacent absolutely clueless
Respite none from beast so heartless

Damage physical inflicted so severe
Eardrum in imminent damage a fear

Deadly was his assault so potent
Punishing in nature grossly violent

Buzzing sense in ear steadily so prominent
Fortunate in a week it became silent

Yet till date relive moment so vehement
Psychological mutilation till day is permanent

Complaint to my mother, but was to no avail
Made it out to reason, unfortunately, his act will pale

Huge Mountain for us, it would be to scale
Clergy up its sleeve, protect its flock in plenty a tale

Witnesses many, to come forward they will fail
For in vain but no justice, will ever prevail
Rascal would definitely, smoothly sail without bail

A reign of Fr. Vijay coming soon to be a reality
Inevitably he wrought abuse of power in cruelty

Psychosis, fear of coercion he built, case many of sheer brutality
In coed school girls too, not spared of his dastardly impunity

1.7. Coward Clergy Escapes Justice

A coward he so obvious in facing bigger boys
In pretense to mingle and jingle, act friendly and coy

Dubious in appeal they fully aware in prance and toy
Knock him around a bit, in banter was their ploy

In summer few rumors several, Fr. Vijay debarred from seminary
No surprise operated with indignity, his kitty in crimes so many

Far from true 3 decades later in our alma mater a reunion grand
Nemesis of many turned up, ironically for an honor in hand

Bodily big and strong now, confidently able to hold my own
Pastoral brute stole out at my glance, terrified now it was my turn

Haunting memories flooded back as my eyes intensely burn
Rogue amidst revelries, no regret nor remorse fills his unholy urn

Sham of night reigning principal Fr. Zachy, grants in his speech call
Fr. Vijay by name in mention to loud jeers and boos in the hall

A lively crowd of ex-students, at his expense having a hilarious ball
To boorish and cynical guffaws, a subdued wave his grace was mauled

Deep down known it was not enough an evil man is still on the prowl
Devious nature in priest garb he committed so many crimes in foul

Sanctity shred in every child mind, by this unholy devilish ghoul
The papal knew it all yet, shielded him a brotherhood coverall

Two summers later yet another hopeless saga of my life to unfold

Another missionary from the brotherhood, in his ego he was blindfold

Healing time they say, nothing since changed despite
Yet another cruel blow for me there was but no respite

Fast and furious was its flow helpless I felt as I was told
My fate he brazenly sold a nemesis of old yet again so prude and cold

In my resolve to fight any evil now ten-fold
Molded in me a person today steely strong and bold

2. Academic Dream Shattered

2.1. Debarred from Final Exams

The clergy bellowed, "You are rusticated!
On what grounds, have you deliberated?

Not much but, a small matter in class presence
Required were 75%, Failed by 2 in absence

Now wasn't this a huge coincidence of chance
The ministry to use his malicious power of lance

Throwing young aspirations down with a thud
Nefarious cruel way of nipping a blossoming bud

Bandra, Bombay, the summer of Seventy-Nine
St. Sebastian, a convent, ruled by none so pious man

2.2. Fr. Poe Domino Rias

Principal keeper of holy diocese, Fr. Poe Domino Rias
He was shrewd manipulating master of bias

Adorning a face, French beard to groom
With index and thumb he would casually broom

Ponder in absurd trouble thoughts that may loom
Precious minds on life's verge he'd one day send to doom

Gifted teacher his handwriting like calligraphy neat and pure
Master linguist and powerful preacher, crowds thronged to hear
God in him a complete aberration for in creator he not in fear

A lean, wiry, confused, I was a typical teen
Hormones' kicking in, like any other sixteen
Energy plenty, needed direction, nobody mean
Hand to hold, patient ear and shoulder to lean

But firm old-fashioned priest he an ultra-orthodox
Rigid values, dogmatic traditions, full in his box

Unbending approach was his tool to out fox
Never evolved with time, for troubled minds to cox

He abhorred modern fashion, resistant to changing trend
Regressive in words and action the young had to fend

St Friar College as principal, admonished students to mend
More than a decade since his act on me, yet not learnt to bend

Once I recall at St. Sebastian, classmates played a prank call

Wearing just shorts and T, to his complete dismay and appall

Only fault to being, a leggy hairy show for all
Parents issued summons, as he refused to play ball

Banished a week from class, his reprimand so grossly tall
Juvenile decision it was, priestly teacher an obstinate wall

The crime blown as capital, was insignificantly so small
Neither regret nor remorse, His autocratic immature gall

2.3. Typically, Energetic Tiny Teen

Summer of 79, diminutive lad I was barely at feet of 5
Math teacher master Sharma, banter me playfully by

Handsome you are son but, least you reach my Everest high
Lovely lasses are sure to sigh; Master Sharma was just over 5!

Classmates like colossus, over me towered
In protective shield, they around me hovered

Small and tiny I seemed, all but covered
Funny it was half pint, they all always hollered

Shortcomings and faults, like any at that age
Immature to the point, of being silly and in rage

More often tried by many to be made a bunny
But always was, alert, witty and funny

There were many a good day, with friends to dig
Friendly repartee aplenty, filled many a gig and jig

With Abba and Boney M our adrenalin would rustle
Living it up shaking our booties, with jive and a hustle

2.4. The Truth about Roll Call Musters

No telling if any truth at all, in roll call musters
Entry made by the teachers only in class roster

All but one in class of Biology for me it was a disaster
Missed by marginal percent of 2, was certainly a doubter

Fr. Poe Domino Rias had already firmed up cruelly his mind
Predetermined a fate signed my destiny horribly in kind

Rightful claim for exams he vetoed to put me in bind
Dastardly way to take one year out of young life to grind

Just like any ordinary kid, I was then all of sixteen
Naughty, immature but unruly and wayward never been

Respectful towards teachers and obedient in regulations
Never indulged or brooked in thought of any gross violations

No students briefed on any requirement in mandatory?
Besides academics, everything else was rudimentary

Rustication a plot, of clergy's only vindictive fallacy
In class of 60, me alone debarred by cleric's conspiracy

Disallowed for exams, had me disillusioned and sad
To mom an unpleasant task to break, the news shockingly bad

2.5. Mother of Mine A Fighter

Mother dear in shock, so many emotions overwhelming her
Tenacious she was but now her mind a mental block in blur

In disbelief so, crestfallen she was as she turned quietly sullen
For our financial state, Fr. Poe's act was like I committed a felon

Those were desperate times, for every dime to crave
One whole year's money on fee, wasted with clergy's wave
A costly year in my nascent life made me cringe and cave

Adamant ministry unilateral action willfully not be changed
His rule of ultimate one-sided authority was absolutely deranged

Him the final alpha in power altering destiny in thriving young
Influence to motivate in counsel never was his favorite song

So, I heard, spent years in seminary, trained to preach godliness
Meeting mom, Fr. Poe a demeanor was far from any graciousness

Reluctant in bilateral summit, he was personified impudence
Met us in school ground, not in office his discourteous insolence

Mother dear ever so hopeful, greeted Fr. Poe with reverence
Response apathetic, rude and passive in complete irrelevance
Bluntly said he, time waste a meet in listless indifference
Tenacious, unflinching she was posing queries to him of significance

Flummoxed he acknowledged my iron lady in nervous cognizance
Attendance if an issue why capital action without notification?

Incredulously whole year not one caution in loud proclamation

An insignificant margin of 2 condemned in unilateral declaration
Every parent's child in imminent had right to every information

Stupefied and stumped a rapid fire round he couldn't leave alone
Cornered further in all of 2 years nothing against my son shown

Preacher undone, dogged mother's intellect had him simply blown
Where from an instance of absence of meagre 2 suddenly grown?

Fr. Poe in corner, a certain goner tried to regain his shredded bit
Divine intervention forsaken him displaying a shifty nervous fit

A scenario completely unprepared he was now in depths of pit
Bereft of rational answers he was edgy in complete loss of wit

Index and thumb groomed busily his manicured French on chin
Thrust right on mat by my iron lady he was now on prickly pin

Bio teacher now his foil to deflect the veracity on his heinous sin
Oh, mother exclaimed a matter of 2 yet she did not raise the din?

Answers none now livid mother to contend with calling his bluff,
Fr. Poe met more than his match certainly had his neck by the scruff

Tensely frantic, bound, gagged and ragged he in all sorts of knot
He fast losing a bout from tight situation he wished to wriggle out
Mother's bout for her son's right to exams had Fr. Poe in full rout

A troubled mind Fr. Poe axed an aspiration with thoughtless hoe
Uncontrolled in his infantile needless act yet wanted me to toe

Too late now for my future tampered by a manipulative foe
In one shattering blow he now become cause of all my woe

Situation now out of hand for information deliberately held back
Deadline for application passed now my time a year on rack

Relenting he was not despite my mother's final soulful plea
Oh please, let my son free but he walked away in mighty glee

2.6. No Teacher, Nor Mentor but Sly Tormentor

Fr. Poe mindlessly ruthless in action autonomous he was
Unrelenting, condescending and caustic too in his disgusting bass

Retorted, young still your son is only a year goes for a toss
After all a year in my life was not for him to bear any loss

Stung and hurt by words so harsh from preacher and teacher
Could have chosen to be motivator or persuasive gentle mentor

Instead a 16-year-old so badly treated he became his tormentor
Defiantly I implored my mother grovel no more to my persecutor

Met Fr. Poe in the eye as I spoke killing any faintest of hope
Again, he spoke in mock disgust of my unbridled rebellious cope

Crime unknown, if done a paltry 2, in class absence was only one
But crime certainly committed by teacher in their atonement none

Worse! Faultless I was yet bond of trust in her son was gone
Sadly, relationship with my mother began slide vertically down

One more from the clergy guild committed shameful act of guilt
Life so young and budding, redemption long, long way to be built

Priestly teacher falsely indicting a kid so young for class absentia
Condemning him as lamb to slaughter an action in total dementia

Terminating hopes and dreams denying a teen his future
Untold grudge held against him for reasons only he did nurture

Compassionate he could have been for the young and restless
Clearing clutter and confusion in teenage minds in being selfless

But he became an alpha incapacitating a career and life so carelessly
A brazen radical clergy obliterated a young light to shine so mindlessly

2.7. Brutal World of Unethical Clergy Practice

Two years, two wicked clerics operated in gay abandon freedom
Took for granted authority a power to wield as their personal fiefdom

Noble work said they undertake for the real world they forsake
In their quest to liberate and educate to eradicate masses of illiterate

Two clerics one more to come 3 decades later in my lifetime
This time involved was my child's fate as alarms did loudly chime

To educate is power to light future generations shining bright
Unfortunate some clergy in standing their status not so upright
Total power unto themselves to snub and shut door downright

How can clergy be told? After all, preach word of God to a plan
Politics a power game Fr. Vijay and Fr. Poe to be shut in a can

A scapegoat just I was in being forsaken for nothing at all
No morals or ethics involved blatant abuse of power to stall

Kid someday a rising star but slayed aspiration whilst small
One stroke of insanity, held no accountability, none at all!

Lost my way completely mind went astray totally
No one to share feelings cocooned in my own misery

Resolute in self-healing but relation with mom crumbling
In hushed tones many times she would be heard grumbling
Words harshly piercing she felt judicious in my admonishing

Intriguing thoughts several and queries why? On Reflecting
Power game always very bizarre emotionless in compelling

Both brutal and subtle power complete in destroying
Lives of victims involved absolute with no direct dealing

Time and place inexplicable way strike hard on unknowing
An enigmatic entrapment innocent many in game claiming

Winners none losers many, redemptions too late in coming
And if at all any it hardly matters to crooks in conniving
A silent knuckle rap that's all in act of show in reprimanding

Politics vindictive game brutal of connivance and coercion
Subtly un-predictive enigmatic maze of deceit and extortion

Trail of fraud full of murky guile very damning and vile
Does not spare even a child an orchestra not at all docile

3. Aarvan

Aarvan Rayudu is my name
My life I spent in extricating self from people's games

Protagonist main in this story of mine
A saga of my life a road wound serpentine

Through shifting sands of eternal crossroads in time
Mesh many in alley, street, highway no caution in signs

U-turn's, no entry lane it was an awful bane
Future appeared bleak going south in wane

Yet continued to walk and run
Kept up a bravado sans any fun

Kept falling and often thrown mercilessly down
By people, many I thought were but my own

Picking myself up though hurt bad
Crushed, shred and mown sad

Never ever to look back at those immoral souls
To think once we shared fun and frolic from the same bowl

A fresh start all over again in an eventful journey no brain
And it will continue consistently till the day my life is fully drain
Dismissed always being an anti-establishment rebel
An underdog for every situation nothing but was hell

Survival became second nature so dear
Time and again for me to emerge from the gloom of fear

Blessed with personality smart, regal and kingly quality
In appearance very, wealthy I was but needy in stark reality

Odds against me always pitted
Yet nothing really ever fitted

Nuances tried every in circumstance beyond any control
Brought upon by dears in family and friends on a troll

Try to control me by jeers and sneers they were surely for real
Philosophy of life nothing but starkly raw and in fear so primal

Despite the evolution of a race of so-called human face
To outdo one another like animals we prowl and pace

In cunning and deceit with grace or in disgrace
Glory in wealth and in gory triumph brazenly we embrace

Without hesitation, we stab behind in back not in a face
A dread of victim's haunting curse not willing to brace

Humans, we are always in a state of war
From birth till dust like a bottled vacuum jar

See others from afar
Wishing to be on par

To finish line, we drive in envy of other success
Crawl, walk or climb faster and do nothing but a lot mess

Race against time not stopping even for breath in fresh
Masters all in aspiration in deadly rat race we onward press

4. Family

Family a kingdom of parents and children
Affectionate bonding of laughter and joy

Bottomless well will never run dry
Magical fountain of love abundantly flows by
The only one in folklore never to fall shy!

Dad and Mom their babies they nourish
Till they are all grown up ready to flourish

Yet worries them still until they eventually perish
Leaving their babies all grown without blemish
Bountiful memories they want to hold on to cherish

Brother and Sister bound by blood
Bonding in life through drought and flood

Caring, Sharing, Helping, Giving a shoulder
Weathering storm and an avalanche of boulders
Rejoice in the gladness of rainbow lo yonder

Outsider a 3rd no well-wisher gets in by guile into the hole
A wily scum only goal to fuel fire he's a nefarious mole
Schemes aplenty create ruckus is his prime aim sole

Cannibalize and scavenge and to leave only an empty bowl
Long and lonely road, uncertain future ahead to unfold!

Greed, Jealousy and Lust of selfish mind
Nurse ambitions and virtues of betrayal kind

Kith, kin, blood or genes no matter but blind
Usurp, overthrow in a coup so deceitfully coined

The right to honored life so brutally disjoined

Now only bound by blood bleeding bad
Accusations counter feelings desolate and sad

Only if patience and wisdom prevailed a bit tad
Fruit of bountiful harvest reap if only had
Tree healthier and stronger a sheltering pad

The colossal tree mauled by brethren all
Come summer and rain, fail to heel the call
Bark of protection torn a chink in winter to fall

Once strong, sturdy and proudly standing tall
A withered monument victim of the family brawl

Many history lessons so blatant and clear
Purge and plundered from near and dear

A capital crime so violent, leave mangled victims perilous and bare
Despite events, so gruesome bloodlines indulge blindly without a care
Beckon again to repeat destiny in history all so foolishly dare

If only each cocooned in a loving walk and talk
No second or third would folly a brook to stalk

Unity assured growth in strength like a rock
Rest will follow and sorrow too forever dock
Family joy and happiness is way high in stock

Born by chance, not by choice
Our parents too could not voice

The journey of life we walk alone
Fraught with risk and dangers we are prone
But to hone we cut bone, to get our throne

5. Mother Janvi

A close-knit family of 6 we lived in a house so small
Many seasons of closeness spent in peaceful bliss all

Suburban Khar East Bombay from 1960 to early 80
Family run and looked after by a matriarchal mighty

Humble and small yet an iron-willed mother
Despite pain and hardships, she never did bother

A charge of 4 children she bore
Single-handedly she brought up her 4

Took great care in their nurture and more
Braving rough weather to bring them ashore

To prepare them for their life in store
Mother, Teacher and Mentor, she was to fore

My mother Janvi A lady of immense beauty
An epitome of tremendous strength and dignity

A woman of courage fighting spirit so doughty
Never say die an attitude and spirit in humility

A legacy we 4 children inherited in fraternity
Gift I deeply cherish till date with pride and sanctity
Unconditionally we loved her simple purity

5.1. Mother's Daily Routine in Life

Humble and small was our dwelling
6 inhabitants in a room complete in filling

Water! Oh, water a whole day to cater
Urban nightmare always for Bombay Greater

Stored in Kitchen in a big drum
Rationing for us in daily routine humdrum

Thankfully our home was self-contained
Otherwise for many unfortunate in common pain

Neighbors' cacophony in common verandah long
Music blaring, others screaming hammer and tong

We managed school and college in all the din and song
And now I miss those times as in life we all moved on

My Mother's day every morn used to begin 4am at dawn
First burr of sound, air like a song with water gushing down

Rationed by municipality
Just 20 minutes of parity
Two drums she would fill enough for a day
Cook, wash and bath wish for more we did pray

Drinking water filled in a traditional earthen pot
A wet cloth over it to cool for in summers dry and hot

Kids at 5 every morn she'd call gently each of us awake
Readying for school we at night prepared our uniform make

Hot paratha bread on fire she would lovingly bake
With tea gleefully, we 4 kids relished and ate

It was our full meal until afternoon too late
Simple lunch delicacy of lentil and rice plate

Nothing could simply beat
Loving hand of mother's feat

In school sporty in winning many an athletic race
Coming home victorious with a trophy and beaming face

Mother too occupied worries plenty in her mind
To notice my small winning for her to rejoice in kind

2 sisters, a brother and I youngest of siblings
Last of 4 in descending order of nibbling

Mother toiled hard daily on her feet
To make all family ends in need to meet

Tuitions by day to primary kids
Till noon and again in evening in two bids

Tailoring classes for ladies in full
Mom a machine non-stop yet cool

Ready she'd for us simple yet tasty dinner
4 hungry bellies in eagerness to feed

Last to eat and go to bed
Not done until the day's final deed
A small prayer for her gods to heed

From the earnings within her means
Her 4 were fed, clothed and schooled

So, in life, they would hold their own
And try never by the cruel world to be fooled

6. Father Jaisimha

Father Jaisimha typical male chauvinist
For his role as a family man he totally misfit

Nomadic vagabond very cool
Spent his life as a gambling fool

Lived in glory for the day
Without any monthly pay

A job he had none to say
But always had his way

Family life, not his sort
Misadventure he would not abort

Selfish and self-centered he was
Never did stop for once and pause
His wife and children's needy cause

Months on end he'd disappear
Only as a glorious hero to reappear

No word, no letter otherwise
He never ever heard his kid's cries

No hand as help or support in any family affair
It would mean just simply tearing his hair

Not a hug or kiss to assuage our fear
Neither did he ever bother to wipe our any tear

He was but still our father
His favorite one I was clear
And I still loved him very dear

6.1. Purpose Paid in Huge Price

Heavy air with dad always in den
Chain smoke in an hour at least 10

In a deeply pensive mood
Seldom was the air good

Small packets of each in an eager appetizer
Satiating our bid for his attention in hunger

For moments of joy would not for long linger
The tension he wrought in him was a major harbinger
Like an alarm ringer, it was a constant reminder

The hands-on the clock seemed stuck at 12 noon
Against establishment, he flirted to the moon
A mean fate upon family certainly not in a boon

Ignoring his glorious feats
Manipulative management beasts

Desired he in respect a President medal
A national honor he dreamt like silly daredevil
Hired by country's national airline
Toiled hard in sweat and grime

Professionally just battery technician
The man had brains of an engineering magician

Perseverance and innovation
Triumphed in his invention

Rejuvenated and expensive
Many a battery of aviation

Despite many in a corridor of management's negative clattery
A plane with rejuvenated battery flew an important dignitary

Amidst inter-city glittery
To loud cheers and flattery

6.2. Fight for Right

Denied rights blatantly in full
Mutinied against order like raging bull

His claim to fame rightfully
For title was his dutifully

They would not relent but only made dad hell bent
And to the court of law he went, then it just a long lent

30 years for agony, torment and pain in us all had pent
There just wasn't any vent in a long struggle he was sent

But his spirit they couldn't dent
Lawyers' country's best in bench
Hired by the corporation's management

Raised a huge messy stench
In parliamentary well to quench
Politics was the backend Hench

3 decades of trial and tribulations
Hearing in vicelike grip of a wrench

A drama of unnecessary suspense
At the cost of taxpayers' expense

To cover a bloated ego of management
Not negligence but sheer nonsense

Gained they nothing, but dad lost a lot
On his appraisal, it was a big blot

His posture put, bosses in a spot
Lion he was direct in his shot

Insubordination was their plot
Show cause notice to tie him in a knot

Charades run by coterie in rot
Sacked him keeping the iron hot

6.3. End of Road for Family

Dousing the fire of our cooking pot
A family now of 6 very hungry dots

Speechless mom was too dazed
Reaction whose home was razed

Dad simply remained unfazed
Unruffled and calm his eyes blazed

In reckoning their script to be erased
With grit pursued his case he simply was crazed

An obsession in oblivion for hours he gazed
Unacceptance it was an oasis so hazed

Decoding the system in a corporate so intricate,
The devil too would have been amazed

Mom and Dad relation tethered on a line
Now at lunch and supper, he did not even dine

At home, things would never ever again be fine
Plan or strategy for fight none to define

Spent at court all his time, dawn to dusk daily till nine
Acclaimed lawyer none for him in B-line

Moolah not even in sparse for fees of liars' those swine
Fire in the dark now a long wait for intervention divine

Lady Justice just a curvaceous figurine

Blind and so justice always in brine

Evidence twisted in deceit of twine
Notaries bury it for their careers to shine

Verdict never swift against any crime
Manipulated by powerful high the law just lacks spine

Dates and Judges change on a lifeline
A lifetime has gone in pleas and whine

And for justice, you will merely pine
All was lost now dignity only on fine line

Memory dad's strong like elephantine
Never diminished a bit over time

The wait was very long and serpentine
A paltry sum in return not worth any dime
Worthless wait in 30 years of wasted lifetime

6.4. Once a Nomad Always a Nomad

Long since now, he left home
As nomad was free to roam

Supporting him monetarily
Monthly in dues, I was dutifully

Wily he no quitter once a freedom fighter
1942 quit India challenger now automatic state pensioner

Money not for subsistence
But comfort for lone sustenance

Since 11 Dad, nicotine his adrenalin fuel
A quick one-two inhale ready for his next duel

Now in his early seventy
Energy in him still aplenty

He went seeking
Wrongdoers in reeking

What he anyway did?
He privately hid

Where we went?
Definitely there a dent

Whom and where he met?
Was anybody's bet

How he passed his time?
7 decades of a story to share

With spice and lime
And a small token in government land

6.5. Freedom Fighter

Carefree Living in Abandon now

Grant of 2 free lands
Appreciation for being part of a fighting band
For India's freedom against Brits brutal wand

Lived in solitude in a village of Nelamangala
In carefree, happy go lucky Bohemian gala

A relationship clandestine it was too reserved
Suffered treatment he felt in the way it deserved

Share in property she sought
For that, she was thrown out

To me he said this his logical reason
Her demand was very high treason

After all, it was just full right
Obtained it with all his might
Always his favorite son in sight

For years he said was my fare
Reward just for dad's care

Solemn promise deed to transfer
Exclusive he said as your share

Wry in my smile equally dismissive I was bare
10 years later Dad then still under my care,

Matter of factly I quietly called his bluff in open dare
Dispassionately he fell in an obvious open snare

Without batting an eyelid
Right to transfer now in closed lid

Change in laws had it disabled
Till his demise he sweetly fabled

Dad true self-came to fore
And prodded him I a bit more
Settle forever final score

Bequeath me a will
With my name in the bill

In affirmative he nodded
A distant look of a bore

Intention of his word to be honored
Not anymore in his core

Real estate piece was not there
For his son in giving any more
For dad, this habitually was a routine chore

7. Matriarchal Run Family

Mother smart and savvy housekeeper
Shuffled duties as an efficient manager

Held her children together like a fastener
Dad, one could say always a traveling bachelor

In reality a lingering absconder
Mother like a tough and sturdy wagoner

Truly she only family's sole breadwinner
Took life head on like a possessed vanquisher

Foresight and will of our mother so strong
In time girls would be married and gone

Fixed deposits in bank small sums of money she collected
Devoted to jewelry precious for their marriage was credited

As years in her children's age got debited
All were emotionally and spiritually to her indebted

Soon there would be winds of change so radical
Entry in our lives a stranger slimy and impractical

Events unfolding annihilate the nucleus so critical
Once a close-knit family soon dysfunctional and paralytical

8. The Siblings

Abha docile and genial
Dark, beautiful and very shy
The eldest

Abishta followed next
Attractive Personality
Canny and sharp at her best

Arihant talent abundant but lacked killer zest
Squandered most of his time in preference to rest

And I Aarvan the youngest
In our family's nest

9. Abha

Abha, she was tall, dark and slim
Beautiful and graceful to prim

Simple and Idealistic to the brim
Homely and loving her needs trim

Education not her priority as a tool
Dropped out after high school

Helping hand in support to mom in life's duel
A huge impact to family's kitty pool in daily fuel

As a secretary in a gas station from 9 to 5
In Bandra West a place so always alive

Delicacies of junk food she would often bring
Variety for us to share we all equally in craving

Rarely affordable at one time now we thrive
Her happiness in our smiles of joy
A sense of fulfillment she would enjoy

Romantic always she at heart
Novels of Mills and Boon and
Barbara Cartland in solace she caught

Prince Charming of her dreams
In real she hoped and sought

True it would be but in reality
It would amount to naught

For life in pragmatism is fraught
Beyond your imagination and thought
Thrown at you like arrows in one shot

In time how Abha would evolve
Tells us just how in real lives revolve

Change over years was dramatic
Transformation of meek girl so frenetic

From one with a quiet demeanor
To a short-tempered and violent tenor

A change in an individual so drastic
Her caged reality stifled and traumatic

Distanced from her family she loved
Consciously by her wretched unholy beloved

10. Abishta

In every home in South Asia as it always happens
Second girl child and the mood invariably dampens
In rightful share denied, claws then she sharpens

Inborn since an infant her nature strong in instinct
For reckoning, she had to remain distinct

Striking and bright she was, repertoire needed more
Giving an edge to personality in obsession became her core

Didn't give a damn it made people sore
As long as her shot got her a high fore

Shrewd, canny, crafty, wily now in her pore
Never did I grudge her ambitions she wore

But not at cost of any lives she tore
Ruthlessly many emotions she had to gore

Dreamed of glamor and riches beyond her means
An attractive personality matched with very high self-esteem

A persona built on her physical attribute
Devious, fiendish drive, mania, added onto contribute

List long of unenviable virtues to her in tribute
A result of possible discrimination in her retribute

But in any final say too high a price to pay
Material wealth in full, peace of mind but nay

Of course, a good side in her plenteously to abide
Worked hard for the family in financial support to provide

Solid rock in care and fare to mother in crunch time to tide
Did all and more for in crisis time for the family to override

Family member any in distress, rush to aid in a long stride
Affectionately from her heart, she'd berate in gentle chide

Genuinely sensitive she would mist in teary eyed
Childlike innocence in affection she was long denied
And now she became an enigmatic lady personified

College for girls' life anew found freedom
Playground of minds clashed in varying wisdom

In there they found their very own kingdom
Held their own despite distractions random

Too much as children brunt to bear and cope
Mingling with a mix of middle and wealthy in scope

Their thoughts and action now their long rope
It gave them satisfaction in life there is hope

11. Arihant

An elder brother he was Arihant quintessential
Mother's favorite and always given preferential

Outlook in personality in a sequential order he 3 dimensional
Self before family, friends next, then his own family intentional

Diligently a pattern through his life in chronological
In a matter of family first his interest not influential
Tall blessed with immense talent and good looks
Languid and laid back, an ambition not much to brook

Meticulous, articulate, would often go by the book
Subtle one liner's framed innuendos he would often cook

An expressive eyebrow in variation crowds he shook
Have all us in laughter splits he was quite a crook

Although he was 4 years older
It was I who was bolder

11.1. Growing Years

During growing years by default in nature
An elder in Arihant to look up to in stature

But none of it he would ever have
A pest invaded his space I was never his fav

Rudely banish me away in a loud cry
Warm up to him consistent in my try

At supper finish first his plate of share
Tear into other's portion he would then dare

Tease in humorous banter without any care
No, bother if the other has had full fare

In thought and action principally this his flair
His share was not a fare for others to care

Whilst others share was his common fare
For his fare would then be a lion's share

In time to come his venal trait would hold good
For in siblings share truly he made his own food

Connived even with a friend so called to deny
Against his own blood, he played deaf and blind eye

At any cost a share in all for him, he was shrewd
They lived or perished selfish he was and rude

11.2. As Friend

A friend among friend he was true indeed
Every place popular he was for his wry feed

His own family priority none for friends high in creed
All indulged in unruly mockery as a normal routine deed

One day he ventured into a challenge of me too can!
Friends in loud chorus dared him to be a real man
Puff of cancer stick an offer to him to fan
Just a misfortune his luck for him just outran

Snitched by my classmate his eye wide in a scan
In turn, I snitched to mother in glee for his ban

Dad duly informed and roughed him up with a nice tan
Swore no cancer stick ever again dare I can
And vouch I will on this count he lived up to it as a man

Many years later ironical twist to a tale
On request cancer stick he got me in a bale

Morbid vice in moderation of 2 yet not hearty and hale
Nicotine targets the body and minds to fail tellingly pale
Long since now given up blowing those rings of gale

11.3. Dad's Plan to Fail

Whisked away hastily during growing years in his peak teen
A floundering business no plan to assist him in was dad too keen

An idyllic land of Goa with opportunities, far and few it had been
Just plucked from Bombay, dropped a kid in alien space too mean
A far cry from the hustle bustle of Bombay Goa was far too lean

Shuffling work and study involved distance and time
Sapping his energy leaving his spirit without sheen

Margao and Mapusa daily one-way distance of 2 hours to cream
Gifted sportsman natural he was for some a distant dream

Reigning no. 1 table tennis champ in college he walloped in best of 3
A win in Bombay his college cricket team he led their treat was for free

But relentless in his admonish dad was a constant nag
Son not enough for business growth was his daily line tag

More of dad having no clue of how to have business in the bag
The technician he was upright and direct just not fit to gab
The knack of astuteness in sales and marketing is only a wily brag

Dad was the boss with no clue neither a business plan
Direction or goals to achieve was not his savvy or élan

What then can you expect from the teenage clan?
After all a novice to be educated with guru's Gyan (knowledge)

In solitude mostly, no one to share his thoughts and to call his own
Dad unmindful would puff like a chimney ignore his son so grown

Only a helper for a company a stout and robust body and bone
Near a flowing river swim together sometimes but mostly alone

Arihant missed Bombay, Importantly missed his home true
Miserable in empty solitude was like shackle that in him grew

The long journey hours to and from college, friends far and few
To share camaraderie with teenage chatter so many to chew

Training and business in limbo he was just another idle crew
Manacles of emotion and guilt binding him to father in lieu

Eventually, in him, a rebel began to ponder of a plot to brew
Luckily Dad sent him home before in rebellion a fit if he threw
Regretfully his son held liable for business he himself blew

11.4. Back Home Finally

Happy to be back home noticeably in him a sensitive change
Try to engage me in small talk creating a bond within his range

Only too happy to oblige to being accepted though it felt strange
Finally, between us at least there was some little exchange

At Jai Bharat in Bombay rejoined college for Bachelor in art
Morning College and afternoon work in sales honing his craft

Skill and Experience that would eventually get him a draft
For a future in a distant Arabian land flying him out in an aircraft

12. Dad, Mom and Me

It was late in the summer of 1975
Recall it was those awful 6 months that changed our lives

Dad fledgling business in Goa he wished for it to thrive
Whisked mother and me in a land he wished his trade to ply

With no plan, he took upon the family a huge gamble
3 young kids left in Bombay alone, they could end up in shambles

Made mother work as a supervisor in a Garment factory
Whilst his own work was completely dissatisfactory

A school a mile away from rented home I was put
St. Barreto a school now but my foot in Bombay was my root

Early morn every day at 5:30 wind my way down and uphill
To fetch a bottle of milk for me became a routine drill

Alto Duller we lived at the edge of the forest a place so serene
Brazen Black Langurs swing by looking ferociously mean

On Mother's monthly earning of Rupees 300
Landlord fetched rent from us Rupees 200

Leftover was now only a hundred
Still, wonder how my siblings were funded
Mother could not take it anymore and she thundered
In six months, you have failed and only blundered

It was time to move back to Bombay again
Yet again dad had failed us in not using his brain

In different stages we 4 were in our growing years
Significantly each our priorities to change was clear

Wielded influence over mother the elder girls now shifting gear
Relieve pain and sorrow mother bore with father in a period of fear

Emotional, moral, or financial support from him none
Appreciation in return for her toil and hard work simply never done

4 kids nourished with love and dedication alone a battle she won
The girls vowed any partner like dad they would in life always shun

Bold decision but only time reveals what the future has to unfold
A path to riches is never a quick fix, not all that glitters is real gold

Unfortunately, in man's world morals often in an auction are sold
Society still primitive in many ways for a woman to her own in hold

13. Captain Alok Pethi

An ex-serviceman to proclaim his Punjabi ancestry he did not wince
Returned to civilian life had a lot to ponder how to milk and mince

Mother dear impressed on her like magic he worked his charm
Suspicious I was as Arihant perceived his intentions with alarm

Smooth, silky and sucking approach typical way for a boy to farm
In my gut, I felt this bloke was no good but only painful harm

14. Abha meeting Capt. Alok

An Indo British company in Mumbai of McNeal and McNeal
Abishta had a job of a secretary with a good package deal

The late Seventies for Arabian Gulf was a favored workplace to seal
A building firm in Saudi Arabia post of Supervisor locked in his zeal

Abishta helped influence his candidature shortlisted in a pile
In an otherwise stack full of biodata bunched in many a file

She helped push papers for Capt. Alok through congested mile
Succeeded in securing a job eventually he with an appealing guile

With a box of sweets landed at home an expression of gratitude
And that was my first brush with a man with a nefarious fortitude

Very soon I was to experience he had garnered a lot of latitudes
Politics in our family made its first foray in Capt. Alok's attitude

And it was then Abha and Capt. Alok for the first time they met
Rest as they say is history a cliché for couple scripted and set

Marriages are made in a heaven a platitude such a pet
An angel in compliance gateway a must to have this inanity whet
Because when it begins to fall apart there's no help even from a vet

In love, she was my dear sister Abha shy, simple and elegant one
She deserved a lot more for her family selflessly she had done

Expecting nothing in return at least an idealist in her having won
Dream fulfilled may her life be in shining sun having a lot of fun

15. Marriage Proposal
Our Home His Base

6 months into his contract in Saudi Arabia he did not last
Returned back disgruntled in haste time had moved on so fast

Abha too stunned to see her beloved though in delightful aghast
Wish I could tie him on a mast and blast him back into past

Capt. Alok proposed marriage, Abha in her approval was ecstatic
Looking forward to blissful marital life, reality dream so romantic

Mother was now well and truly his loyal fan so fanatic
The real test of times now in a meeting of 2 states will be traumatic

Capt. Alok's elders, their spouses in reaction expectedly dramatic
Rejoinder so spontaneous calling her Blacky Madrasi so emphatic

Remark racially discriminatory in an offensive verbose stigmatic
Old Parents compassionate Abha felt they were charismatic
Kind words too from Alok who was caring yet diplomatic

Then Alok self-invited himself making our small house his base
Saying no was taboo to future son in law, it was his strong case
Any family member in protest, mother dispelled without a trace

Typecast Indian for boy side demands met, as our humble grace
Rub into us as a favor by marrying our sister, his undoing in disgrace
Lucky father unaware and in Goa or resounding slap got on his face

16. Capt. Alok's Influence of Nefarious Intent

In the passing of time, our home for me was like an ordeal in hell
Alok intrusion into our daily lives his true colors began to tell

Worst, mother impressed, to her his transgressions he would sell
Instigating her to make me work and fetch as he rang the bell
Rebel in me rapidly rising an opportune moment on him I would fell
Many fabricated stories just to impress upon my mother
Succeed with her he did, I simply did not care or bother

My friends, boys and girls mostly Catholic
Roots from Goa a beautiful resort place so naturally idyllic

Taunt me caustic calling me a wild Goan bombastic
Livid and spontaneous in retort "Hey Punjabi" me very sarcastic

Arihant guffawed in approval for it was rustic and caustic
An unqualified tight blow below belt to his ego always so plastic

Shut him up for sure he whined to mother for a cure
Younger son so disrespectful, he an upstart so impure

In an admonish attempt; the rebel in me did not relent
Mother, I said, "respect is earned for keeps, not in rent!"

An elder he is bent on inciting, reprisal now only in dissent
The message was crisp, loudly clear and to him very brashly sent

Certainly not the one to be taken for granted, I am a gent
But trouble if I scent from you then I will be your torment

One occasion his influence in our home a culture he wished to wield
Like a termite, he tried to chip away wanting his power to build

Touch his feet and call him big brother a crafty design as a shield
Pay homage to rogue as an Alpha in our home his plot be fulfilled

Message cleverly in through Abha first sign of her identity killed
Backed by mother a tradition to adhere, in us she dutifully grilled

His sly act I shot down, his ego beaten vociferously I was thrilled
Forewarned mother ignore my words now and invite your own peril
With this two-faced man always on alert, you cannot be chilled!

In time his designs were to grow more sinister
Preparation in many motives he was a corrupt minister

Use his wife to mingle in the family to collect information as sister
Then devise a strategy and plot, use Abha for his ideas to administer

Eye on our small house, in crafty strategy was my sister and her mister
Nipped their plot in bud Arihant and I and blew it apart in a canister

Abha's docile demeanor desolately underwent a change so radical
Alok awashed her mind with cosmetic lies so devilishly mathematical

A veiled control freak in his ways he a slimy dirty crook tyrannical
Sadly, it led to a self-isolation for Abha from her loving matriarchal

17. Abha and Alok

In a simple Hindu ceremonial wedding at Arya Samaj
Abha and Alok eventually married in summer of 1978

The only time all were present with my dad as one family as in fate
His presence in token a role for a wedding otherwise zilch in any rate

Fortunately, the crook Alok secured a job in a good position
Senior Manager in reputed Kitchen appliances firm Cookins

Company accommodation was a major perk provided in
Glad to be rid finally of nosey, pokey, pesky, rapscallion vermin

But Abha's woes in marital life were to begin just
Family tree of Alok for us one of unknown first

Apparently, their siblings in total were five from the crust
Their pecking order for me now an irrelevant dust

Rude cultural shock their kin marrying a girl dark skin a must?
Abha my eldest sister was dark yet beautiful shiny color rust
Simply a lovely person whom you could humbly just trust!

To Delhi to meet Pethi's family the newlyweds went
Harass and mess they began with Abha's dignity to dent

Habitually teased blacky, soiled clothes to her for wash they sent
Dirty dinner plates and vessels to wash and dry her job their ill intent
Abha physically weak but her mental resilience would not be bent

18. Pethi's First Child
Not Without Drama

By 1981 Alok resigned from his job after benefits booking
In his mind, an idea for a business was surely cooking

Moved into a rented house on 11 months leasing
Apartment owner in his choice of Pethi's soon to be ruing

The Pethis in late March of 1981 blessed with their angel girl
But delivery with a lot of drama and tension had slowly unfurled

In 9th and due Abha slid and fell on bathroom floor lying curled
In pain she was, her maid of alert mind in action she swirled

In those days owning a phone an extreme luxury so dear
Posts relayed over friendly neighbors with one, in crisis was clear

SOS to Abishta in office, then to a neighbor and on to mom dear
Rushed to Abha's aid with our minds racing in anxiety and fear

Point in maid's call a little disconcerting made mother reflect
Abishta plea to get money, so to a bank first we went to collect

Something amiss for sure, instinct in me strong to detect
Incorrect moment to discuss, my mind in other I began to deflect

We three met at Mulund railway station a spot advance in select
In tuk-tuk, we traveled urging driver who then flew like a jet

Each fervently in silent prayer for our Abha and child to protect
Joy and happiness swelled grandmother, aunt and uncle now set

A little angel named Keisha now amongst our midst so perfect
Alok not around and at least in thought I rather have him forget

He ostensibly traveled to Delhi on business in an urgent gain
A tall claim his timing was lame, more he was hopelessly insane

Leaving his wife alone, no funds to tide over in event of any bane
Left to fend for her own care he merited many in his bottom a cane
One of many instances in proof this nerd in the rear an absolute pain

But so often a case Mother sealed our mouths in a promise to date
Traditional thinking as the girl's mother further sealed Abha's fate

Abha too no less to blame in silence suffered the agony of her mate
Shackled mind warped in cruel stern era unwilling to open the gate

A princely sum in bygone days in thousand all of three for free,
An equivalent in 3 salaries ask any lender without any collateral fee

Alok's audacity in masked words said money on homegrown tree
For daughter and grand in moral duty comes for absolutely free

Corrupt irrational full of him as a Punjabi he would sermon
More in rant and extra venom to come in time from this slimy con

An effort in every and none spared small games like these he won
Every prospect to belittle mom soon to become he an entity none

19. Ungrateful Capt Crook

Month-long in my mother's tender love in pampering and care
Entirely in attention unfailingly she would scamper to their lair

Abha's post-natal gain in forte was mom's fervent fare
Awaken to Keisha's midnight whimper without any fuss or tear

By day her home chores and tuitions a routine of eons in week
Our home to Abha's in 2 hours or more a distance in a time of peak

No time to rest children her priorities they after all her ilk
From Khar East via Sion to Mulund West time would fast leak

Changing 2 buses and a packed train by dusk, not for any meek
Many times, beyond 10pm she reached; Alok he a usual freak

Mom's wellbeing, not his concern home in time she better seek
His Highness in sleep disturbed and in energy then he so weak
Hurt and sad mother was shattered in utter disbelief

Veneration towards mom so plentiful in service only by lip
Livid I was but for his wife and child she used to make a long trip

Abha too tame in this senseless game of unwanted flop and flip
Did not prevail with her ungrateful half and yet again she did slip
Only this time with our mom Pethis cut an unnecessary sorry blip

20. Defrauding Captain Con

Ever since to Pethis, mom never paid a visit on her own
Time moved on Abha's nature then took a huge 360 turn

A girl once so shy, simple, humble and docile
Now in simplicity lurked a diabolical persona extremely hostile

Reference drawn towards Alok straight it was so obvious
Racist taunts to mom often in discrimination so unchivalrous

Madrasis you are do not know how to make any money?
Skill to defraud learn from us Punjabis, try and imbibe you looneys

One such case in those days came to light one of his many frauds
Pethis rented an apartment in Mulund intent over it was to lord

Law on leave and license grants licensee just to pay and stay
Licensor remains owner solely only the right of notice so to say

Owner sought reclaim on his flat by notice of time to vacate
Alok snubbed owner by slapping bill in court to falsely implicate

Terse in a message to the owner, aces with him so averse to negotiate
Given time in court rulings Alok confident owner would abdicate

Alok's plan to play patient vulture's game of wear and tear
Ironically owner a learned dogged Madrasi astute without fear

In court frayed his criminal mind costing him more than dear
Retrospect rent with interest also trauma in damages to bear

21. Ambitious Abishta

Abishta's plan was simple and straight to carve her life of own
In total control as an Alpha her skills, she would hone

Over-ambitious she turned, obstacle any would simply be blown
Her genesis on roadmap built shrewdly in her mind it had grown
Devious vain narcissist from cocoon she had long before flown

From onset in the first job cultivated relationships in goals beyond
With knack intact like a veteran pro in verticals, she forged a bond

Seeking high life, she swam in flow with them an able fish in a pond
Swanky lifestyles of celebrity in 5 stars were now her new life fond

An invite to some of the top 5-star hotels from hierarchy bosses
Indulged in newfound fine dine luxury of wine and salad tosses

A family affair nothing clandestine in reputation or dignity losses
All of 16, yet not so naïve my instinct marked all in bold crosses

Dismissive in arrogance on a blunt mention to our dear mother
Wrong in happening your business none, so don't even try to bother

But daily sponsored entertainment not for free in 5 stars
Not a word more in protest she chided lest be distanced afar

The girls were adults even in concern would heed no bar
Ever if life turned out to be cruel legally they were on par

22. Dad's and Arihant's Arabian Adventure

Finally, dad's persistence and resolve paid dividends at age of 58
The Middle East beckoned for the last hurrah, glory is never too late

Hired by the biggest gas companies in Qatar it was a kiss of fate
Battery technician and in salary a windfall after years of incessant wait
A thaw in hope now dad and mum to finally start on a clean slate

Arihant and me, a man to man we had a long talk
He was 23 and I at 19, had a long arduous road to walk

New pastures in the Middle East my gut feel life for him would rock
Luck favored Arihant a job in sales a sense of cheese and chalk
A stationery line in a top firm in Oman his key to future will unlock

Both left India within a month of each other late in 1981

Mother's favorite son for a better life traveled to a foreign land
Useless me for her I was busy wasting time with my merry band

A dig and jibe my mom threw at me always ready at hand
Hurt and sorrowful surely I was turning into a rebellious firebrand

23. My First Job

A large electronic showroom RFsons in South Bombay
Hired me to work from noon so I could study by day

Life bit easier not having to listen to mother's daily taunts play
Pop music at work gentle to ears than endless nag a loafer to say
In 1981 I too began my working career with 475 rupees as pay

24. Sivaraman

Sivaraman an archetypal South Indian Brahmin Iyer boy
From a deeply conservative family was naturally very shy

Strict patriarchal rearing even in reason could not question why?
Affection and interaction between siblings just a monosyllable cry

Nationally ranked chartered accountant no. 14 in exams at first try
Opening batsman as 1st div cricketer runs off his bat would fly
West Indies his favorite team Sir Garfield Sobers an idol to go by

Siva quiet by nature, instantly garrulous in just a feeder
Likable person humble simpleton more a follower than a leader

The essence of injustice to an intellectual ability naturally ingrained
Always on fringes of the corporate order, he felt so horribly maimed

Lacked skillful guile playing game of dirty corporate politic
In shades of father so strict a guru if only, but was his worst critic
Then his wife Abishta at a drop of hat was terrible in her vitriolic

25. Abishta and Sivaraman

Abishta and Sivaraman's was allegedly a marriage of love
Apparent it was from onset Abishta had him in her glove
Siva a clean soul, gentle genial giant fresh as a peaceful dove

Constant in our mother's pressure and rile of being ostracized
In an emotional guilt of blind belief, fear of society Abishta capsized
Finally walked Siva down the aisle a sensitive case to empathize

In 1983 Abishta the neglected avant-garde girl got married
Same Arya Samaj ritual where ceremonies are not so harried
To an unpretentious, simpleton Siva a human not so varied

This time Dad and Arihant were sadly in their presence not around
Leave an issue their jobs in Gulf they were contractually bound

A marriage certainly it was of the convenience of sorts
For Abishta a perfect fit her long-term goals in a plot
Siva smitten with Abishta's felt himself in luxury yacht

Seeking love and compassion for which she always felt forsaken
She wanted to be doted on, showered with pampering and affection
Love to hold, one who is bold a deeply understanding companion

Abishta a history of few liaisons boldly she nurtured in past
An Alpha in her invariably ensured relationship would not fly fast
And before long, few weeks maybe few months it would only last

For Siva who hailed from a deeply conservative Brahmin family
Perhaps glamour quotient in Abishta for him an attraction holistically
Awakened the rebel in him although passive but dramatically

Abishta an opportunity she grabbed in action thoughtfully

Would not discount mother's hand in joint decision deliberately
After all, we live in caste system order prevailing yet so blatantly

Siva in sense was from the highest order in the caste hierarchy
And subtle undercurrents in inter-caste union are often anarchy
No different in case of Abishta and Siva events were ugly and achy

Abishta met Siva at Rashtriya Insurance office a place of work
Love Romance of course never included in their employment perk
But Cupid is known to shoot from any corner he chooses to lurk

Rudely rebuked and snubbed by Mr. Thangrajan, Siva's father
Acceptance was far, Abishta's step in extreme also not his bother
Placating Thangarajan in his home for approval, mom was in disorder

A real instance in occurrence one week on Monday morn
Brother Ranga and sister Swetha accosted on a road turn
Whilst Abishta on her way to the office in confusion did frown

Stop seeing Siva in caution they forthright in high demand
Very nasty awkward position to be in like it was a legal remand
Amid onlookers of familiar office crowd, she choked to be calmed

On working tour was Siva in the unknown of the condition of his diva
Natural at my workplace I received a call from our very own dear Eva

Irate I was, called Siva's house to give a mouthful to bro Ranga
Mother and sis then in talks for appeasement with dear Thanga

Mother discussion of an alliance was more in despair to voice
Thanga clear stands on Abishta for Siva she never to be his choice
No regret if in attempt she jumps in front of a train or Rolls Royce

For mother, it was more in scaling up the society in the stratum
Siva a Brahmin after all value and status high like in sanctum
It did not matter to Abishta for her it was just to be her fulcrum

26. Abhikya

Sivaraman's were blessed with their only son Abhikya in 1985
Abishta and son Abhikya spurned by Thanga's for any house invite

A lineage of a superior race now his status had in bit nosedived
Such was his obstinacy being learned yet dreadful rigid drive

Moral of the story simply literacy is not an accomplishment in mind
But an enlightenment we human being are in DNA just one of in kind

Irrespective of caste, color, creed or race, erase all religion in a bind
Just transcend barriers heaped on us by the zealot of different kind

Reflection in time and turn of events disjointed so poignantly
If only courage in your belief spur your action in right deed bravely
Many a kingdom saved from decay and collapse so drastically

Opportunities in life plenty a matter simply on your call
Ponder in sense uncommon, weighing pros and cons to play ball

Ticking all the boxes in final decision whether to grab or stall
Brave in glory or to the grave in disgrace for you to stand tall or fall

A situation on hand back in our home we had all over again
Siva since his rebellion against tradition trouble began to rain
Daring his father, he was homeless, clueless and possibly in pain

27. Alok the Dubious Messiah

Not for long though our small dwelling now new couple's shelter
Decent in earning duo to build their nest in time to apply in a letter
Our home was leisure for both; Siva could never have felt better

Abishta in Kitchen for mother was never ever any help
Siva's new found freedom to down 2 pegs whiskey daily for self

Quietly in kitchen corner mom would wait in her quiet space
Be considerate and prudent I told them in etiquette and grace

Enter Capt. Alok once again troublemaker and freebooter
This time as pompous savior, he sold himself as a troubleshooter

Owned flat in a distant suburb of Virar he cited in passé in a footer
Defrauded some poor soul's money possibly he a habitual looter

Surprise, Surprise in generosity offered his habitat for free
It did not matter as long as the Sivaraman's pleased to be

A ploy in scoundrel's trap it was a cunning ruse only I could see
The reality of sympathy just an illusion stakes certainly in high fee

Virar is 60kms in distance to Bombay in straight rail route
Churchgate to travel one way 2 hours of daily grind so brute

Bitter to taste certainly not expecting in life this kind of sour fruit
At least no part in her life she so fastidiously had always in refute

Dual role of working woman and domesticated homemaker
Not her cup of tea and in this case, she could not be a faker

In compromise was willing to help to mom in the kitchen as a baker
Life values untold till you have much less when one forsakes her

Alok's villainous quirky dirty true self yet again raised his hood
From Sivaraman's demanded rental for 6 months made it really good

A handsome amount of 1000 rupees per month they should
When in the early 80s even 50 rupees value in rent was just too good

Extortion, robbery, a fleece expectedly from a man so greasy
Alok Pethi, a scalawag could sell his soul for anything meaty

In a matter of wealth, he would with Satan sign any treaty
Satan too had to tread with caution in deals with one so sleazy

Siva a harmless passive South Indian flagged instantly in white
Knew he was being conned sought a truce without an ounce in fight

Mom too in know of wrong, a side she could not take was her plight
How I wished it was me not Siva, the con would have a blurred sight

28. Return of the Nomad - My Dad

From my salary ample contribution provided towards home
From 475 rupees 275 to mother and rest for me to loaf and roam

Went back to college to graduate so in future not to bemoan
Used it at best to fund my studies and rest no support in any loan

Dad's first contract completed, at home, on leave, he was in top gear
Funds in flush so in recce his old haunts, back to his old ways so dear

Vanished for a couple of days worried I was for him in fear
Past midnight on 3rd stone drunk had one too many gin and beer

3 months into 2nd contract back in India from Qatar he was
Silliest of pretexts unsuitable place given his dumbest cause

And in short time all the assets he bought would trade in loss
An incorrigible conceited man to family so underserved he as boss

The revisited journey in academics lasted only a year
Mother's nagging continued despite stability in life so clear

It was time for me to take a call and move on
Opportunities I had to seek and create on my own

Naturally, Dubai for a job the seed of thought in mind now grown
Soon in an aircraft, I would be bundled in a group to be flown

Dear friend Manish's house evenings most time would be spent
Confer with friends a path in life to embark for each how it meant

29. Friend and Ship

In my life's journey, many friends came along in a time of course
Truly were they friends who cared, shared your good and worse?
Rejoiced in success stood by in failures and guide you to the shores?

Supported and helped in darkest moments with dos and don'ts?
Time would tell to share or be the cause of most of your woes!

True philosophy on any human relationship is always baffling
Unconditional and free it should be otherwise it is too stifling
And right on top of my list is Friend-Ship calming yet harming

Friend a buddy and ship a link to drive 2 individuals as mates fast
Indelible bond beyond race, religion, color, community and caste

Sex, social status, standing it is so humongous beyond and very vast
A bond that weathers vagaries of every season uncaring of any past

Of life's glorious uncertainties a pledge stitched staying steadfast
Vices of greed, lust, envy, jealousy and manipulation it will outlast

Delicate yet like a strong silken thread for winds of change a mast
Compassionate, caring, loyal grounded protective canopy to last

Torchbearers upholding the sanctity of virtue that travels in a ship
Enshrined unwritten unspoken oath of sacrosanctity never ever to flip
Unbridled joy in each other always in triumph a sun never to dip

Truly if friendship was anything so fructus
This world would never ever have any Brutus

30. Friend

Friend a soulmate to lean to drain
Sailing together in storm and rain

Comfort in sunshine and in pain
Laughter both for loss and in gain

Rewinding, reliving memories some coy
Nostalgic moments of happiness and joy

Sharing a shoulder in grief to cry
Lessen the burden of barren and dry

Times of famine and drought
Assured strong arms reach out

Gently but firmly are caught
Rest is all but sought out

Through life journey, we will walk the talk
No mountains or chasm will make us balk

No hurricane or terrain shall wither our will
In face of challenges calm and firm we hold still

Protect one another from life's travesty
Besides each other always in any adversity

Strength in moments of others weakness
Guiding light in the path of darkness

Wealth not measured or weighed in gold
The principle of faith, trust and value too bold

31. Friends Today in Real World

Sleaze, money and profits too slimy to hold
Friendship invaluable in percentage to be sold

Brutus too pleased to welcome into the fold
Present he will a septic serrated knife of old

And so, you will be the last one to stab the steely mold
In the back of trusted one, so gruesome and cowardly cold

Forsaken for the lure of lust, power money and glory
Sneak, honey trap, value threat and stolen story

Events etched in memory now so vulgar and gory
Dealings manipulated for gains a dear friend your quarry

Divesting of precious time invaluable for pinnacle to scale
Robbing of just share in equal wealth you've become stale

Mocked, gloated and laughed at the inability to be on par
He was not even an enemy friend oh, he was too far

Friend, Kith and Kin just in any bloody relation
Connived an equation in a providential amalgamation

Bridge of faith and trust built over time in unification
Smashed in a matter of aptness in circumstantial situation

A legacy beautiful and strong could've passed over many generations
But in usurping a right only causing many in irrevocable obliteration

32. Ramin Davle

Ramin Davle classmate, a friend of Arihant in Class of XI
Over time constant presence in our abode for him a haven
With Judson Oliveira, Ramin and Arihant a trio was interwoven

Bygone days Ramin too a short-statured but taller by just a wee bit
Probably common ground for us as a duo at start together we hit

Enjoyed cycling, owned an identical brand, color design to the hilt
Loved cricket and in banter always ready in repartee and wit

Girls like any other lads our age a natural hormonal inbuilt
Our likes in preference differed in each we harbored no guilt
Reveled in fantasy boy talk heady at times ultimate in pits

Another bond mutual love for music an X-factor
My favorite anytime past time was music in my genes a reactor

70's to 90's a golden era of music filled with iconic characters
Hindi Classics, English Pop, Jazz to Rock and Roll my benefactors

Jugal bandi or entwined twins a rendition so incredible
Musicians egging each other in a duet of vocal or instrumental

Brass and percussion rhythm in sync so delectable
Music is universal symphony so beautiful and divinely epochal

Movies too I loved an unaffordable luxury in our childhood
At neighbor's house on Sunday TV as kids, we would all make do

In time as I worked good English movies within budget to view
Fun it was, train fare of 1 rupee 10 paisa and Vada Pav to chew

Ramin and I bonded well, met at least once a week
A regular feature either his or my place like two crazy freaks

Sunday at mine Idly Sambhar a delicacy my mom a cook unique
Malvan kalvan curry I relished at his, a sumptuous meal so mystique
Ramin's mother simply sweet lady, culinary skills in her Magnifique

At our home, Ramin was vocal in his suggestions and expressions
He was liked and an acceptance in our family as an extension

Early days of building bridges a humility shyness in confession
Niche he carved for himself in each our hearts an impression

Whilst in our home involved in many a light-hearted repartee
Sometimes mother too would join in the laughter of youngster's party

At his place warmth plenty and food I would eat full and hearty
Respectful in all humbleness towards both Uncle and Aunty
Whilst his sister was simply her father's cynosure and earthy

He found a personality in my father a different cup of tea
A willing ear in Ramin my father found to buzz like a bee

Politics and religion in animated fervor and action live to see
The expressive outburst of invectives and expletives thrown for free

Exchange loud guffaws and high fives like in golf one to tee
And sometimes relaxed with chilled beer and cigar both in teen glee
With dad for others, he was always an entertainment full in melee

His rapport with mom and dad he established strong and well
Trusting Ramin they in blind faith, he had them fixed like a gel

33. The Dual Faced Ramin Davle

Moments on occasions I noticed he opted to have me to fell
There was something in him that was quite sadistic I couldn't quite tell

Yes, appeared it was my mother sought a rebel in me to quell
But my instinct kept tugging my inner being like an alarm bell

Few actions markedly unconvincing to fathom he tried to sell
Instances many, hard strike on the head I hated he'd often on me fell

But would cry foul in my revert with cold stare he would in then dwell
Callous glare back in monotone my response a taste of your own hell

Sometimes as a fashionista I would indulge in fine casual threads
As usual budget just enough to relish the common man's bread

Fashion Street of South Mumbai in 80's choice of clothes it fed
Export quality shirts at little as 15 rupees in chains across a spread
Lucky if a few looked a million bucks to wear it once overhead

Ramin's glance on my thread in a blink snatch it and will have fled
Seemingly, a culture among mates in his college so uncouthly bred

One more thing stood out over time I noticed in his action
Use your goodwill for his deed when in need and desperation

To repay in turn he would deadpan and be bland in reaction
At best extend his hand in sundry that's all his expression

The chivalrous benefactor in generosity he so genuine in distribution
But promptly take back in primary + interest in utmost discretion

These were early signs in growing years I just accepted to ignore
So often instinct is true friend helps your being to know your core

And it keeps flagging red maintaining a steady score
For your chi, it is but in constant a daily chore

Never does it abandon or for your indiscretions abhor
Lest you be treated otherwise like a helpless loathsome whore

Until realization upon you dawns and you swear enough and no more
To so-called friends with a roar, you show ultimately the outside door

34. Arihant's Golden Period in Oman

September 1st, 1981 a new beginning in Oman in life for Arihant
Making his mother and family proudly rejoice in his development

A young life that had seen many trial and tribulation so turbulent
His blend of hard and smart work very meaningful in achievement

From 1981 to 1987 his was Midas touch like a huge accomplishment
Against all odds, it was his golden period in being triumphant

For Gulf sales job spots I scanned in Sunday Daily's perfectly timed
Found one in particular for Arihant in the list for him I had primed

A company in Oman dealing in products of stationery and allied
Biodata sent in post with dreams to achieve in high excitement eyed

7 days later in telegraphic date came calling his fate to be grilled
On D-day outfitted all set for an opportunity he had in success sealed

Arihant worked from his heart in short span mastered the art
Nuances of showroom sales in a wide assortment of kits of craft

Used in art, education, healthcare, corporate, architecture draft
Extremely focused and determined to excel without any graft
A salesman to a showroom in charge he wafted in his own shaft

Arihant's meteoric rise on ground and site now in close monitors
Bosses, peers and competitors on him in covert reconnoiters
Poach, Pilfer, Steal but have him sealed at any cost for his caliber

In secret rendezvous, prospects offer from the rival finest canvasser
Accepted from a prestigious firm of repute in the business of copiers

In a short span of 2 years 125% jump in remuneration
Achievement incredible in surpassing seniors in his corporation

Many spent a decade to reach a milestone his reward in promotion
Happiness now doubled a favorite son coming home on vacation

Mother's joy abounds after 2-year hiatus a star arriving at the station
Abishta and Siva joined in to complete a family in revelry and elation

35. Arihant's Eventful Holiday

His first trip back for a well-deserved holiday from Oman
After 2 years in 1983 at home, Arihant like Roman felt a showman

An emperor after conquest having returned in triumph as chosen
In courtesy parcels carried for his friend's families to be given
Letters in fold unaware a high price to pay for his kind service of token

All parcels its contents unknown, to mother given for safety
Advised marked parcels to be handed to names only in their custody
And done as deemed in courtesy with parcels for everybody

Husband and Wife of friend's family landed back again the next day
Claimed their bro in Oman hemmed in US$700 notes in solemn pray

But when an envelope was given just a letter to the family to say
Friend's illegal act risked Arihant's life and betrayed his noble way

His deliberate criminal misdemeanor Arihant would have to pay
Unfortunate how dirty and cheap people stoop down dirty in their play
At stake don't bother it is not theirs but somebody's life in the fray

Arihant in shock recoiled completely at loss in any sort of react
Foreign currency to carry beyond sum an illegal gross in an act

Information shared in parcel only a letter for the family in seal intact
Then so-called friend claimed a certain amount no proof of actual fact

Binding Arihant to reimburse smartly in an emotional guilt pact
If it was me in his place my response he to go and counsel a quack

If at all there was a theft no indication of any foul play

Abishta had access to draw did she have any hand in slay?

Many moments, after all, she would be alone at home in a day
Straight away in denial with a straight face, she had her final say

Yet another friend in casual ask in Oman on Arihant's return back
Eko watch I had sent along did you give my father in a pack?

Your brother, Arihant replied claimed parcel from mother in the stack
The friend replied watch was missing maybe went in another rack

A year later spotted on Siva's hand Eko watch smartly strapped
No guesses on mystery of lost dollars and watch in reality who hacked

36. Judson Oliveira

Ramin at 23, late in 1983 was dating Mony his neighborhood girl
Their love blossomed and then came a small twist and a twirl

A hypotenuse triangle in a bizarre manner to slowly unfurl
Judson Oliveira and Ramin's fate to entangle and cruelly curl

Judson a simple and sometimes a hilarious personality
Somebody who can be called a homebody for his morality

Unflinching dedication towards his parents in domesticity
No offense to being riled by his friends his magnanimity

However, an issue he had in crisis with his own identity
Overwhelmed in face of his domineering father his paucity

Dignified in demeanor despite his father iron control atrocity
Fair to say Judson little short on confidence in face of adversity

In grappling with a situation, he could not make a decision
In case of personal or professional a case of severe erosion

Briefly worked in travel firm for a year was his only commission
Many offers from gulf he rejected on his father's whimsical cognition
Remuneration not good enough reason for any offer's rejection

Judson after the first year in college lost interest and dropped out
Made no logic in his refusal of a good offer even from word of mouth

And from reputed car agencies in Gulf so much to shout about
To work in Japanese auto showroom matter of prestige a lot

37. Jolene

At a party, one-day Judson met a lovely girl named Jolene
Instantly smitten she was for him full of caramel and praline

Coincidently through a common friend in prior I had known Jolene
Poised young lady charming, intelligent and an adorable darling

Judson now a regular every evening at Jolene's house
Carey his brother squealed his little secret and the real cause

Judson truly gushing radiating in love not wanting it to douse
Ramin and I engaged in light-hearted teasing without any pause
Glad he finally found someone and change a little in who he was

Judson for Jolene effusive he was in his likeness and praise
Only too eager for him we did everything for his moral to blaze

38. Meeting Jolene

Ramin and I finally met Jolene on a party invite at her place
And then noticed something unusual we could not quite trace

Guests whilst regaling in music and making merry in dance
Expected Judson to be mingling in small talk with a stance

Of course, Jolene in equal display a posture in refined advance
Bewildering there was nothing in the air so much as a chance

Judson busy with Jolene's mother running errands in a prance
Not for one moment did Jolene or Judson exchange any glance
For two people if in love the air was void of any spark in romance

Jolene joined us with a wave of her hand and smile so charming
The conversation flowed with her ready wit it was just warming

Judson strode in as a matter of fact in our wellbeing inquiring
Mingle; Jingle, loud you need to be in the groove and swaggering
With a half, you wish to be complete and need to be all-conquering

From Jolene, it was seen chemistry in her completely lacking
Turned her face without making much ado just about anything

Judson himself inconspicuous vanished among guests partying
Jolene offered drinks a dignified way out from the topic of courting

Jolene's elder sister Roselyn a girl she was a bit temperamental
Her boyfriend Ratish was full of fun always in jest, a party fundamental

Then an invite from Jolene to join in family picnic so cordial
To a hill station resort in Lonavala so beautiful and genial

Mostly couples on a picnic but Ramin and Mony sort of betrothed
Declined I did being busy but minus Mony, Ramin still accepted

39. Weekend Retreat

And so, the story told as bus over winding roads manipulated
Quiet but obvious move from Jolene in front of known she executed
Unseated from Judson, in next seat to Ramin she now populated

Ramin pondered it seems perhaps typically a lover's tiff
Maybe she wished Judson to cringe and feel limp over a steep cliff

After some bit of sedate silence, Ramin felt like a gossip aperitif
And bluntly inquired was she trying to give Judson an envious whiff
Surely, he wouldn't want to be in their midst lest he gets a tight biff

Without fuss she looked in Ramin's eye honestly and said with a shrug
Nothing fanciful at all between us with a disgusted look so smug

To sing in duet, chords to fine tune but in Judson's vocal there's a bug
Beyond a hello chat between us, the tongue's tied snug inside his mug

And rest of evening he on errands after my mother he will lug
Sad but true nothing common in us to draw us together or tug

She poured her heart with clarity so blatantly true
A person intelligently cool in saying did not feel any blue

For the next couple of days Jolene and Ramin a couple in glue
Probably beginning of something latent between them in the brew

40. Dreadful Triangle

Developments new for Ramin excitedly in me he confided
Childhood sweetheart Mony smart and pretty will be devastated

Mony a wound up femme, IQ not above group gossip so mitigated
Jolene an intellect in comparison her repertoire was vastly extended

Ramin's pull towards Jolene was extremely obvious
A big risk he was willing to a point of pulling it off so devious

Though closer to Ramin, as a friend I was common in bias
Foretell triangles of sort emerging in relations extremely impious

Jolene clear and candid, Ramin's life now a double-edged sword
Mony and Judson two innocent in one wrong choice to be floored

An unlikely situation for anyone, better it would be to be dead bored
Pragmatic and gentlemanly reasoning the best way to stay assured

Ramin kept Jolene in dark, a relationship of his with Mony in a wrap
Ill-conceived motive to deceive so obvious it was going to crap

His tango in the triangle would end in a tangle an embarrassing trap
Like a caged bird set free but for clipped wings he could never flap
Helpless and resigned he came to the ground with a resounding slap

Ramin never could walk the path with Jolene even the short run
In a committed relationship with Mony on his head already a gun

Ruin in deception both his would be half and bosom friend Judson
Doom many life's relationship in darkness leave no room for sun
Unheeded Ramin yet went on a movie date in known just for fun

41. Fissures in Friendship

Rathish a soft spot for Judson spilled beans on a newly found couple
No matter to Jolene, Judson it did for his close friend was a double

In angst, he asked to confront Ramin to clear dust of rubble
Foretelling rant Ramin sought my presence to sort out trouble

Distastefully an awkward moment it was to mend broken bubble
Empathy for Judson's broken heart in pain on one leg to hobble

In private told him to let go; on one wheel the bike does wobble
No future at all in one-sided relationship to squabble and cobble

Unfortunately, wisdom too in Ramin defeated for a path to dibble
A decision briefly he had chosen only ends in relations being gobbled

Jolene maybe in known on Mony by Ramin's own filtered version
Trusting him she would on their status have her own built illusion

Nothing wrong in her thinking she did advance not on an assumption
On basis of selective sharing only on Ramin's cautious misinformation
A logical view of Ramin encouraging her on his own selfish gumption

And then the unexpected and unthinkable had to happen
Jolene with Roselyn walked into Ramin's house had him totally flatten

Impromptu surprise visit on his Birthday just to have him gladden
A handwritten Birthday card enough to state an intention in a caption

But for Mony's presence naturally, it was a complete dampen
She threw a fit alright her sense to securely have her man fasten

What happened next was absurd and for me extremely offensive
Judson on Rathish and Roselyn's shoulder cried foul his defensive

Ridiculous tactic quoting me as a villainous piece he was so expansive
Recited Jolene interest is Ramin and him to quietly become elusive

The icing on cake Ramin calmly upheld his tirade as a unit so cohesive
A million pins felt stabbed in me like bulletin board so abrasive
Ramin had his cake, ate it too for him an experience inexpensive

My first brush with Brutus in reality in a friend called Ramin
Politics of lust in desire and control no-brainer an invite to famine

An opportunist in Ramin surfaced for the first time its ugly face
Hung my character and image in sacrifice for his hormonal craze

Two mature people shot my character and flung it into the ravine
The only intention was honor and grace for all without any damn

The finale in a plot so twisted the two protagonists came out clean
And in bargain plea, they totally had ripped out my spleen

Degraded, betrayed and mentally crushed bond for me in cause lost
It's true meaning in purity its sheen for me now completely a hogwash

Jolene a mature girl exited in self-esteem ever so gracefully
In self-respect, she exemplified strength in her character substantially
We met just once thereafter and greeted each other cheerfully

This incidence was in the summer of March 1984
Time to introspect on friendship and if it matters on the points score
Meeting Ramin or Judson for me it was from henceforth no more

42. Dubai Beckons

In the year 1984 late January cleared a job interview discreetly
Mother's constant daily tirades got to me eventually

A decision was made to get to the gulf on a job very quickly
Lucky break nailed a contract in Dubai at first try instantly

Kept it close to my heart till my employment visa came finally
Even my mother was not told till I got my ticket ultimately

My Salary in AED 1,100.00 in 1984 an equivalent Rs. 3,300.00
A princely sum for a start for many in thought they wondered

A mess so sordid at home and with friends who just blundered
Wished me away alone far away for my mental state cluttered

April/May passed received my visa papers for employment in June
2 months since the saga of Ramin or Judson an episode of doom

Fleeting thoughts quickly brushed away than rather have me in a fume
One day towards the end of June lo behold two jokers now in tune

Ramin and Judson, their presence betrayed my reaction of gloom
A shocker in seeing them together after a huge string of misfortune

In Ramin an ego no remorse, no apology, no guilt, no regret
Undone a friend in quest of a lady's conquest, he rather forget

Put up a charade nothing ever happened as though it was in jest
Confided broken ice with Judson and saga of Jolene put to rest

Reluctant I was as my chi kept on tugging strongly in my chest

Broken strings tied in a stricken knot they failed wretchedly in test

Tried hard to convince me an incident as a one-off thing
At back my instinct warned me this was dangerous ruinous fling

Manipulated emotion clouded my judgment in cutting off this string
A decision to rue 6 years later for in life I had nothing left to cling
In future Ramin with one Ajay Mehra to con in a team as yang and yin
And joining them in a game of deceit and purge my very own blood
Cruelly assaulting my faith and trust Arihant opened gates in flood

43. Mother's Dream House

Dreamt of an independent apartment of own always my dear mother
An ambition nursed since she married, dad did never ever bother

Urging in topic dismiss he would in a nonchalant wave of smother
An onus by default was on sons from funds they would gather

A thought never shared with anyone in my heart deep
Quiet wish to buy a house for my mother in constant beep

Her dream I gladly turned into reality her reward she had to reap
In her lifetime a dream come true in pure joy she wanted to leap

With my hard earned money in Gulf built a house in her name
In pride drummed to all and varied in praise she spread my fame

But a twist in life was to follow the same fame became my shame
Yet she dared to dream again 20 years in a schemed up game

My visa and ticket arrived six months since my interview
Long wait from Jan 1984 till June indeed a relief it was phew

Broke the news to my mother, it would matter to her but few
Finally rid of her useless son at least 2 years on leave not due
In reaction expectedly in relief finally a loafer change over new

Congratulations poured in for my achieving the unthinkable
A job hunts on my own and that too in Dubai I did the un-doable

An extended family arrived to wish me luck led by captain trouble
Ramin and Judson too came looking good together as a new couple

Siva and Abishta came along with certain plan so notable
Alok wouldn't have slept well without a passing shot so humble

Bet not more than 3 months in survival, run home on the double
Sniggered in revert not like you in 6 moons to fumble and stumble

My mother knew in her heart it was from the family jumble
I who wanted to get away especially from her daily grumble

44. Etron Enterprises Dubai

Etron in the UAE a leading and reputed trading company big
A salesman in their showroom Deira learned the ropes I had to dig

In my resourceful mind for their flagship brand Hitech to rig
Sell range in electronics and Appliances became a routine gig

A few months later moved to a bigger showroom in Bur Dubai
And in the beginning of 1985 to Abu Dhabi and life just passed by

Exposed to products absent in India learning was an exciting try
An occasional cricket in desert grounds was welcome passing shy

All through growing year to adulthood unaffordable were brands
The luxury of threads was but a distant dream always so grand

A Levi's Jean pair cost half my salary another half to mom in hand
Rest would be to survive the month out or seek a magic wand

Dubai from onset a world bazaar a land in plenty a wonder
From clothes, electronics, jewelry, music you stop to ponder

3 months walking down the bazaars in a daze I only grew fonder
All fanciful cassettes, jeans and jackets I indulged in squander

Food allowance of AED 225.00, a bit for toiletries and launder
Rest blew away my salary of AED 1100.00 in sheer hopeless blunder
Then struck by reality in purpose, not for willy-nilly meander

Etron a decent place to work in those days not much stress
Barring few cases of stray petty politics among colleagues no less

Working in break shift left you with no time in excess
How many bachelor parties can you enjoy? It was no bless

Loneliness and boredom two factors cause of depressed lowliness
By May 1985 inertia set in, I craved an outlet for my restlessness

Then a new position in local daily advertised in middle of May
Al Fateh the largest trading company in the region made my day

In sales of consumer electronics in Oman, I applied to pray
Fruitfully secured a contract besides perks a 70% increase in pay
Buoyant and felt great now I graduated to next level in the fray

45. My First Holiday From Gulf

In September 1985, to Bombay on a well-deserved break
Shopped for the family from savings of 10 months I had raked

Jewelry for my mom, saris for my mother and sisters to take
For dad, a set of trouser and shirt certainly happy him it will make

Oh yes for Ramin a pair of branded threads for old time sake
A washing machine for home completed the shopping shake

Finally to mother all money saved in full to her I gave
Lit up in smile her face glowed for her dream house I saved

On vacation, it was Arihant 2nd homecoming and mine first
Scaled up notch higher job wise his was an unquenchable thirst

An accent so quick for many only in dreams they are nursed
Now awaiting visa a governmental process we were well versed

46. Dad's Taste of Own Medicine

In both sons absence from home, dad was back in his groove
In sixties now back in his element as though a point to prove

For 6 months in Hyderabad, he was constantly on the move
Or so he told us justifying his action for us to approve

Leaving mum vulnerably alone a hopeless case we disapproved
Mom then left with Abishta to her new abode in a counter move
Completely justifiable move we brothers wholly did approve

In Jan Seva Nagar a distant suburb of North of Bombay on loan
Sivaraman's bought a 2 bedroom flat now finally could call their own

Seemingly a pending gift as the builder was very much known
Siva's father many such favors to builder he had shown
High ranking government officer in leniency their bond grown

Mom coaxed Arihant to invest to own in same vicinity a flat
Reluctant at first a blessing for future he would give himself a pat

Not surprisingly mother asked if I too would be keen to bat
In an investment, she said in defense if I would approve of that
Affirmative in vocal but then I said only if she wears the hat
With her name only registered in the registration of the flat

Ostensibly Arihant in clarity flat booked in name be surely his
In all realism, a decision correct for future holds nothing to miss

A decision was his to make and mine to my future a goodbye kiss
But for that moment the light on my mother's face a perfect bliss

47. My Arrival from Dubai

On my arrival from Dubai, Arihant and Ramin at the airport went wild
Breaking news on Sivaraman's firstborn son Abhikya their child

In January 1985 they were blessed now I was really riled
After almost 10 months and you drop the news just so mild
And then met the little fella looking right in my eye and I smiled

They drove me not to our family home in Khar but to Malad
To Sivaraman's new home and the story told was real bad

Abishta coaxed mother in leaving the Khar home our old pad
There was no telling what unexpected was coming next from dad

A room to herself with the security of Sivaraman's she had
And with little Abhikya to fill up her time she was indeed glad

They quietly left our Khar home in the silence of the night
Dad awoke next day to find mother and daughter nowhere in sight

Dad's version as told to Arihant and me relating his sad plight
Never talked on leaving mother alone to face many demons in a fight

He left his family vulnerable to the onslaught of those in might
He would vanish for months on end in thick of night
And yet today he was whining and complaining of his right

Patient ear to his side of the story with compassion
Swayed him to move on with wheels of life cycle in motion

From now on to relax and enjoy not anymore a notion
Let us sons provide your needs as much as in proportion

48. Scheming Capt. Alok Pethi

The situation of dad being alone was an opportunity
Not missed by scheming scavenging Capt. Alok Pethi

Drama scripted for Abha and him to visit Dad in regularity
Aware Dad despised his very sight ever so irrepressibly

His was a single-minded approach in pretense so convincingly
Have the house transferred in Abha's name dad to willingly

A small 180sqft studio in 1985 prime real estate after all
Converting into an office space in rent it would be a windfall

Dad was but too smart for Alok the fraudulent con
Caustic comments for South Indians always blaring on

This sudden show of affection was more repealing
His inventions made him only more unappealing

49. Sale of Our Khar Family Home

It was then we were made aware bank mortgage to be paid
From the money earned in Dubai, the money was squared

Our small home we finally sold with many memories of old
In mother's name money secure in the fixed deposit as told

Dad with us shifted to Malad at Sivaraman's home
An arrangement unanimous in the family soon to be blown

50. Ramin's Whine

Many scripts in 1985 too happened in the interim
Story unfolding as a Bollywood film live in streaming

Ramin in matrimony with his girlfriend Mony tied a knot
Marriage on rocks in his letter he made out as a plot

This time around did not want to be a part of a new round
Once already bitten the drama not worth even in a pound

Ignoring I stayed put my feet on the ground
And with them to I imagined things moved on

Since moving to Malad our visits to Bandra was less frequent
Whilst we awaited our visa Siva flew to Oman on a job assignment

51. Ramin Inheriting Family Business

Ramin inherited and settled well into family business
Rehabilitation of old building structures was their core process

Set up by his father with strong business acumen
In short span he was reputable professional gentleman

Ramin on a platter given a business running well
Davle's Concrete Facilities as a business entity to swell
But, the wisdom of senior Davle rubs on Ramin? time only to tell

52. Ajay Mehra

Ramin inherited an established running business
Hands-on he was but lacked skills intact and finesse

Competition in his field of building rehab many
On the last mile, the tender would go down to a penny

He lacked charisma and panache
To drive the business steadfast
His Achilles heel was lack of turbo blast

Wily but he was in a plan he eked out
Even willing to sign the Devil in a joint bout

Enter Ajay Mehra, Ramin's college friend from past
Simultaneously was honing his work skills very fast

In the construction field, he was under a mentor
Sharp eye of older brother Vijay 18 years his senior

3 seasons was enough to harden him like toughened glass
An industry with professionals who lacked ethics and class

Ajay Mehra a cookie molded from the same cast
I, Me and Myself about himself he would blast

Like Alok a windbag Punjabi with a bloated ego so vast
Abhorred his sight a forced association that was not to last

Tall and smart yet crooked and conceited braggart
Unwanted equation by default was added to my cart

He was indirect, cunning, smooth talking and ruthless
Ramin in him saw an opportunity for his growth in his business

Ajay Mehra eventually shunted out of the family business
His older brother Vijay felt threatened by his influence

Ajay on monthly retainer plus 10% profit for his business care
Well as an intern that was really huge like lion's share

Decided to claim once and for all the moolah in a lump sum
Accrued over 3 years deprived of his share now grown plum

Business like an adrenalin game of poker
He who owns an ace is the king the rest are jokers

Ajay Mehra with 3 jacks in a throw played show
But Vijay Mehra had 3 aces and refused to bow

Felt his money not meant just to throw
Ajay's right over it must negotiate and go

3 Million rupees in cash not for charity inflow
An unfortunate end for cash cow in sibling row

3 Million rupees in Nineteen eighty's
A lot one could do and still leave you in plenty

With the matriarchal unbiased intervention
Seemingly got his money in painful emotion

53. Ajay's Burning Ambition

Now to own his venture one big ambition
First, build his identity a platform set in motion

Timing so perfect Ramin was all ears in attention
Joint venture with Ajay in his works of civil rehabilitation

In firm handshake Ramin in his thought of big expansion
Whilst Ajay dreamt of an opportunity of his own corporation

Two parallel thoughts in a divergent sector
Destined never to meet were individuals of 2 vectors

Bill of quantities drawn up in any contracting
Template format must for supplies and ordering

Ramin complacent and laidback in list always floundering
A scribbled note his style more in professional functioning

Leave it to juniors for the cost of materials and estimate
The tally at month end for all accounts in accumulate
A disaster constantly would unfold in unwanted pilferage

Ramin a calamity in running admin of his company
Boon for errant employees in circumstances so many

Ajay an intern once now a professional so meticulous
Nuances of contracting now second nature in diligence

An equal JV partner in selective Davle's Building projects
Many on Ramin's plate but now glad he could all accept

In a matter of in 2 quarters ongoing projects complete
Mission accomplished Ajay grew in confidence for his feat

Saying so cliché "Once Bitten Twice Shy"
This time around nothing to marinate and then fry

Settlement of accounts on project handover
50% net at stake and now he no more a pushover

3 Hundred thousand in one quarter a lot
Now this game of poker for him a big jackpot

54. Oman 1986

Arihant and I left for Oman on February 5th, 1986
Both on a two-year respective contract earlier fixed

Al Fateh Electronics was the company of my call
Arihant joined Omaniya Stationers all set to roll the ball

Al Fateh Electronics was a mixed bag of affairs
Unlike Etron in Dubai, they were no clients at all to dare

Our division carried a brand called Zaper
In music systems quality it was certainly a dapper

A small yet cohesive team led ably by Mr. Pran Ramsani
Accomplished impossible and challenging feats so many

We were in market operation clean up collecting bad debt
Recovered 90% dues of former management's dumping fete

As a team we a group of 8 all had bonded well
Enjoyed our work, stood for each and celebrated like hell

In Oman travelling long distances by road on call for sale
An average of 400kms a day for orders without fail

From Capital Ruwi to Ibri or Sur and back
Constantly month on month we had to be on track

Besides challenges of targets other internal issues to tackle
Victim of immoral HR head Rudy Rebello tied me in a shackle

Human resources meant for the welfare of the staff

Ensure contractually maintenance and perk is up to mark

Mr. Rudy Rebello would deliberately withhold our right
From the management would quietly hide our plight

Play cheap politics in sucking up to MD Govind Narend
Show saving on budgets provided for HR to expend

Deliberately he withheld my right to a separate room
In sharing room for 4 months in a grind, he put me in a gloom

Holed me then in a single room infested with live maggot
Rudy such shoddy crass an individual just like dirty faggot

At 48 Rebello twice my age he was nothing but a lousy rascal
Staff life made miserable though they fought a frontline battle
And this vassal did suck up his boss big time to live happily in a castle

Not one to hold back I met him at an appointed time
Diplomatically let loose a barrage with salt, chilly and lime

In no uncertain terms, he was told a lousy leader he was
Failing his own people to only and only further his own cause

Pran Ramsani backed me to the hilt
The evidence I provided him of Rebello's filth

Despite resources huge in the budget at his disposal
Deprive us of our basic right and yet he did not wilt
Rebello, as I knew, had no conscience to harbor any guilt

Became self-reliant and learned to cook different food
Trying and treating an experience for me indeed very good

3 bedroom apartment in sharing with a couple of colleagues

Together in turns we would cook and share the cost in league

Arihant was quite contented with his job and lifestyle
But he literally parked himself at my quarters now for a while

Arihant a regular guest at our haunt for dinner for a year
Play every day a game of squash and relax at our pad with a beer

At Al Fateh enjoyed my tenure of 2 years from 1986 to 1988
Management had no policy of promotion or to negotiate on rate

Though happy with my work their act on my wait was rather late
Stagnation once again setting in I would soon be daring my fate

55. Winds of change in fate

In the winter of 1987, I arrived on my annual holiday
Arihant too applied but his management had a different say
In a month they said he could proceed for now he had to stay

Arihant wanted to sync his holiday with mine
But not everything may go your way in time

Many chances will beckon in life to enjoy together in wine and dine
Till then just relax and bask in your own little space of sunshine

My exact spoken words and he was in complete agreement
A fortnight later he was in Bombay to my utter bewilderment

Kicking a job just like that on a pretext of lack of fulfillment
No backup plan or failure to reason his naivety in amazement

New life in and the beginning of dark ages
Failing to plan equals planning to fail an old adage

If you do not have even a semblance to foresee or gauge
Eventually, you lead yourself as a victim in your own cage

Not much in savings to tide over in event of any crisis
So seek a new job opening from any newspaper it graces

Payments to the builder for a flat he had in his name book
Now had to think to obtain money by hook or by crook

56. Arihant with Ramin in Business Partnership

With the little bit in kitty Ramin came with a proposal
Trading in construction chemicals and sales at his disposal

Arihant accepted without any thought or due diligence
No self-analysis on industry his aptitude and its significance
Just plunged in on Ramin's words unknowing of its consequence

Comforting in thought keeping him engaged and busy
And in the process learn the ropes eventually making it easy

But life in the Middle East just spoils you rotten
Tough life in fast-paced Bombay completely forgotten

57. Back to Roots in 1988

In February of 1988 returned back to Bombay to roots
Ensured a dream house for mom a bill in full I did foot

Fully prepared in seeking first a job in hand
Turbulent times ahead in mind I had scanned
Separately saved a sum of forty thousand

Besides contributing to the family kitty in shared costs
Join Arihant in business in the event nothing working out
Naïve I was in thought, things now a different sort

58. Arihant of Old Back in his Mold

Shocks and aftershocks for me in wait
Never was looped in on happenings of late

Relaxed in Oman in mind all under control at home in Bombay
Reality starkly grim Arihant let complacency come in his way

From the 40K I saved in my account
Only 18K showed in balance amount

So what happened to the rest?
No answers forthcoming as Arihant grimaced at best
To him, I now was an avoidable pest

Point blank he refused to entertain any thought
Joining him in business along with Ramin a full stop

Plain and simple ways of saying just get lost!
He was now Arihant of our childhood past

One serious revelation came to fore
Arihant invested 30K in the business core

All money lost in business for him it became a bore
No guesses on account balance now matter was sore

Hopeful for joining him in business a platform for us to grow
A vision in larger interest is not necessarily in shared inflow

Many reasons behind the business debacle
A consistent work pattern of slapdash cycle

In a week just one day in attendance
Relax next 2 with work seemingly a nuisance

Venture again for half a day more in penance
Only return back in a pretext of back pain in abundance

Mother told me about this arrangement
And I witnessed his lazy disengagement

Construction chemical business in choice totally wrong
Technical in subject Arihant in aptitude did not belong

No help from Ramin or Sr. Davle who in knowledge strong
Lacked acumen and no clue in how they would get along

A complete year in precious time and investment wasted
Down the tube and poorer in work experience is all he tasted

59. My Own Debacle

My one year sabbatical in India was a real downer
Nothing much to shout about for the moment in crowner

Keen on joining an airline I was as a flight attendant
But the path to get there was not without being 3rd party dependent
Knowing someone important key to your application in ascendant

Jobs I applied for locally despite my experience and credential
Requirement graduate in qualification a minimum essential

Gulf experience was void and looked down upon
In late 1988 decided back to Dubai, I should be gone

A lucky break in a good job offer for me made in Fiji
A coup in the country brought me down from heights so dizzy

60. Ramin's Business Offer

Around this time Ramin threw me an offer in business
Join his firm Material for Construction Services (MCS)

Aware no money for investment for business in my kitty
All my apprehension Ramin dismissed as one man committee

An equal partner I would be with zero investment
50% in equal profit sharing on accounts assessment

In Gulf, you will make 20K but from home far away
At MCS you will make 20k and have fun all the way

An offer attractive yet simple
Left to ponder if any a pimple?

At the back of my mind fully aware of Arihant's showing
So what went wrong as a failure his complete undoing

61. History in Partnership with Arihant

In history, we have to dig a bit
To establish the sequences to fit

Senior Davle, Ramin's father an entrepreneur brilliant
Davle's Concrete Facilities brainchild his own in development

In civil repairs and rehabilitation of structures dilapidated and old
His expertise across India in many significant projects struck gold

Passing the baton to son Ramin an intern under his tutelage
Many a skill and craft he mentored him from his fuselage

Through senior Davle's network, MCS acquired an agency
Bauchemie Werkstoffe (B and W) offered a trading deal graciously

Bavarian company construction chemicals in India made locally
Range encompassed products in civil and concrete technology

Diverse applications in reinforcements of structures of multiplicity
Unfortunately, no standards and measures in training their laxity

No demo videos presentations available to train
The products required orientation to disseminate a cognitive brain

Essential to grasp product features and benefits
The path to target specific industry in reason scientific

Unavailable it was and sure did plenty in frustration to suck
Only technical manual to review mind now full in a nonsensical muck

Recognize the science of it if in your aptitude and then good luck!

Now here is a simple logical analytics
Arihant and I no science genius
Bauchemie Werkstoffe (B and W) products in all technical grimness
Technical products a new concept in the market in all meanness
No marketing support apparently their budget in leanness
No Training or hands-on orientation was ever provided in realness
Evaluation in comparison to conventional products in wellness
Only clue sale through Architects and Government in all keenness
Selling to bureaucracy required efficacy in greasiness

Price of course major issue in importance
Warranty of product of utmost significance

All key parameters essential to product sales seamless
And none ever was given a complete waste so needless

Arihant in misery disoriented, demotivated and directionless
The entire business concept lacked plot, was full of weakness

Ramin nor Sr. Davle were no natural mentors or motivators
Professionals in the ultra-conventional mold they no innovators
Straight-jacketed, out of the hat they were no idea detonators

Davle's understood stress in concrete and steel
Action to resolve and strengthen they knew its feel

Failed to understand Arihant under severe mental duress
His confidence eroded a quality crucial for his sales prowess

They really did not much care on trading firm then
It just fell by default into their lap their lucky gain

Knowledge of merchandise syncs with crafty skill of selling

Strategy a science of presentation to the client in doubts dispelling

On innumerable occasion in my sales career seen
Failure for a lack in perception of micro issues been
A major cause of problems in macro issues occurring
In Ramin's own proverbial words
If companies construct poor quality structures

In repairs, we will always be doing wonders
Rehabilitation work is all about original blunders

Projects on merit for Sr. Davle's knowledge, he was well connected
Professionally astute, sharp and skilled he was highly respected
Management, expertise and quality he delivered as expected

Ramin not at all in Sr. Davle's mold
Lacked mind, ambition and in spirit he was cold

Acumen and charisma in feat your own need to hold
Initiative so critical influence in a network has to be bold

Trading for Davle's meant B and W used in own projects
Margin surely a big bonus too went well in own pockets

An important matter my mom brought to my knowledge later
Mom was against the idea of Arihant joining Ramin as a partner

An investment risk she counseled for business, not in his genes
Certainly not in business unfamiliar for you know what it means?

Ramin dared Arihant's on being a real man on his business career call
Said he, a huge windfall in a unique business, Mother a woman after all

For Arihant friends were first and family was an in-between wall
His decision was made in an irrational call leading to his eventual fall

62. Negotiating My Terms

Finally met with Ramin with my conditions on partnership
But then chi in me reminded the duality of his friendship

A second chance I told my chi at friendship deserved my trust
Time would tell this phase in life was to be my perilous worst

Right to bring in any new agency for distribution and sale
Any investments, of course, Ramin would have to bail

- Profit percentage at 50% net apiece would sail
- A monthly retainer I need without fail
- Paltry Rs. 1000.00 for travel only agreed to avail

In principle a Partner in full faith
An agreement in gentleman's handshake

No MOU or deed though discussed was drawn and signed
Arihant and Ramin's failed attempt for him in grim remind

Ramin did not want another document to grind
No reason to suspect in foul he would rescind

In days of yore word of honor was in kind
But control still absolute only in his hand
Material of Construction Services (MCS) was his band

An outright amateur in business matters
Nuances of company formation, not my platter

63. Start of Career in Building Materials

A working-class executive in sales with knowledge and knack
Trading business unsustainable on one brand I knew for fact

Prior to joining Ramin evaluated B and W product range
Pruned list acceptable to general trade I would try arrange

Just two, from many too little in offer, nevertheless now in fray
1. Waterproofing membrane applied in brush or spray

2. An additive mixed with cement crystallizes inside cracks
Applied on vertical surfaces and it will penetrate sealing gaps

Genuinely I felt an opportunity with these products

Next task was to identify potential market
Obviously, players in the cement trade to demarcate
Product through their network to smaller shops could filter down
A market controlled by a cartel on one look only had to frown

Cement and steel trading humongous game in big bucks
Margin a pittance but volumes so huge to ply in a fleets of trucks

Construction chemicals to fetch an tiny insignificant fraction
For cement and steel sharks, in B and W, there was no traction

During this time met a businessman called Shekhawat
Centric power at one time in cement trade calling all shots

Changing times and change of guard now another in his spot

B and W he thought in his trade a fit but time to introspect a lot

Somewhere in future Shekhawat and I to be a team
Events would define how my path would wind up in extreme

Critically I came to a rude awakening of fact
Small time contractors used old conventional tact

In molten bitumen, lime terracing, Mud Fuska or brickbat
Waterproofing technique still prevalent and intact

Here I was who an absolute nobody in trying to be somebody
It mattered to me in creating awareness among everybody

They listened, technology sounded good
They ignored, the price was too much for food

Cost of conventional waterproofing was Rs 2/- per square foot
B and W waterproofing membrane was Rs. 20/- per square foot

At ten times the price obviously, no takers
For B and W principals' business only in large industrial makers

Comprehending B and W was neither bread nor butter
Put plan B and C in place or like Arihant, I would stutter
Alternative business options in my mind began to flutter

64. New Dynamic Agencies in MCS

Two major things happened just in the nick
Advertisements in daily were simply slick

Ceramic Tile Company Styles was one of my picks
Textrum a Textured paint company got my tick
The timing of such an opportunity I acted on quick

Drafted on the letterhead of MCS, Company's credential
A professional dossier of intent serious very prudential
Distributor for Bombay we are special full of potential

Soon a call from Vice President Mr. Tandon of Textrum
Invite for a meet in South Bombay Hotel Emissary in momentum

30 minutes in exchange in serious business thought
On Textrum and MCS in how we tie the knot

Textrum catalog showcased decorative designer paint
For sure a connoisseur delight who in joy would surely faint

Impressed I was on its form and shades
Also, waterproof paint guaranteed not to fade

Yes, in comparison to acrylic emulsion a premium price tag
A bet I was willing to gamble MCS needed Textrum in its bag

The final round of meeting in MCS office set
Tandon with Ramin and I expectedly met

Ramin as usual ultra conventional and always skeptical
The product is mystical and I added profits will be epical

Fifty Thousand rupees as security deposit refundable
An inventory of Fifty Thousand a deal was certainly doable

Getting Styles on board my next accomplishment
Not inventory only project based but surely a compliment

Ramin typically traditional in personality never bullish
Despite funds at his disposal on any take he always bearish

His roots of thought process so awfully unoriginal
Always a skeptic lacked imagination and in action very irrational

Adapted completely novel way in marketing Styles
Designs and shades simply beautiful even from miles

Showed Architect friend Diwakar Keni few colors in the tile
Immediately his face lit up in a huge broad smile

NGO, he worked for with social message in awareness
Restoration of human dignity in hygiene and cleanliness

Common toilets across cities and states
Local municipalities as the sponsor in land and stakes

65. Marketing Styles and Textrum (Tiles and Texture Paint)

Finally, in Business now and let's start earning a decent income
10 months in a struggle on a pittance of 1 thousand in sum

Diwakar elated on styles in price with tongue in groove
At his office, few designs pruned for final in quality to approve

Now meeting in earnest with the elite in design fraternity
Designs of Textrum paint a revolution in modernity

Traditionally design fraternity is always very cryptical
Tenacity and patience, of course, are so centrical

Queries posed by design professionals in experience so quirky
Aesthetics in texture and shades but inquiries rather murky

Any artist in the know of what exactly texture means
Feel and look of the surface be rough but not smooth or clean

Use of trowel, brush, even comb or spray gun
And create many a texture with plenty of fun

Dust naturally phenomenon in cosmic manifest
Yet a dumb question posed by every architect

Attracts Dust? Most cliché question of no essence
And they were some real celebrity big names
Amazing queries lacked in complete common sense

A product back in time a true statement in art

Redefine perspective in beauty from tradition apart

Expensive yes but for a must for connoisseurs of craft
Waterproof with 15-year warranty in ROI played its part
Adorn your walls but require balls from conventional depart

Sadly, in India, we still lack leaders to take one bold call
30 years ago, leaders short yet 3 decades later none standing tall
Industry leaders in a dynamic decision many a laggard
Live life in comfort whilst in toil makes others haggard

Still very colonial in thought
Process obsolete from British bought

Fear of Failure makes Indian Diaspora trend followers
Count it as experience and change to be trendsetters

4 decades ago patched jean wear to college I was called a tramp
Today slashed torn jeans have many celebrities walk the ramp

Confident I was anyways in Textrum's guaranteed success
Sadly, I not a part of history Ramin's backstabbed in unilateral excess

66. Arihant's Marriage Through Alliance

in the month of July 1988, awarded the possession of flat
Mother proud finally her own flat, she lauded me with a pat

Arihant her elder son next door neighbor
Glad a helping hand in event of any hard labor

Unfortunate both in India couldn't hit our bearings right
The Middle East was back at least right in my radar sight

To Arihant, I suggested its time we move on
A career in the Middle East is where we belong

Soon Arihant to make it to his 30th Birthday
Mother more concerned on his Wedding day

An arrangement in earnest for him through a mutual alliance
Unlike me, he was not the kind to indulge in a romantic dalliance

First, in arrangement get affianced mom clear in her intentions
Stable job in Oman in a year fetch your bride no interventions

Perfectly logical preparation under the circumstances
Except nobody considered taking life on with chances
Exactly what was in store with Arihant's changing stances?

67. Arihant And Rakshee

Arihant's marriage to a girl named Rakshee was arranged
From same community through daily advert it was managed

Purposes conveyed clear marriage to be solemnized in a year
Both families nodded in accord as were the near and dear

And Abishta's letter in post one tycoon friend in Oman she cited
Seeking manager for operations so keen on Arihant be expedited

The best news received in a long, long while
Stability in his life brought back happy smiles

But so often is the case life throws options in open gate
If careless on priorities end up daring wrongly your fate

In interim Rakshee's parents within them had unilaterally concurred
Induced on our boy's credentials now, for marriage date to be differed

Taking Arihant separately aside talked him into preponing the date
Arihant won over approved quickly in bringing home his mate

Both Arihant and Rakshee grown adults matured to decide
But in recent past, Arihant couldn't tell from high to low tide

Resigning from a well-paid job in Oman in 1987
Risked money minus plan into business with Ramin no heaven

Lost out on time in years and money so impulsive driven
Marriage without solid income like a pair of parallel lines in eleven

Arihant sought my opinion on topic now sensitive

First job security rest follows, in saying I was punitive

After 2 years in the wilderness, a new start all over again
One year to establish in time and money you regain

Your confidences to carve back demons in you have to tame
Self-esteem and image built back will be Arihant of old fame

Come home to fetch your bride all honor in your name
And move on with your lives it's all for you both to claim.

A bored look and deaf ear sincere advice in futility
On vagaries of life, I cautioned him in all humility

Disinterested he threw it to the winds dispassionately
Will face it he motioned with a snigger arrogantly

Advancing the event, a wild card mistake in call
Chain of events in life over time led them up the wall

68. Marriage Solemnized

Arihant and Rakshee were married in February 1989
With close knit family and friends an event went off just fine

Abhikya all of 4 years for him a carnival so was playing
Ramin and Judson too in festivity in mood and swaying

Abishta and Siva could not make it from Oman
Abha wanted to but for Alok in him she was just a pawn

69. Abha's Loan Plea

On account of Alok a situation, he snowballed
Whilst in Oman Abha once only made a plea call

A loan of 6000 rupees for her business not to stall
In 2 months, she promised to pay it all

Straight away knew Alok behind scene pulling string
After all sis in appeal never would hurt her feeling

Concurred with Arihant in brotherly conference
Knew we were dealing with a rogue in deliverance

Money in full immediately Arihant remitted
As expected the cad in giving bluntly retracted

For 2 years Alok made Arihant reach out for his right
In petty installments rub salt against sis for payment at sight

In hiding the rat, he was and put sister upfront in a sorry plight
Arihant couldn't hold back at final sum gave back mouthful tight

Alok's false pride his ego now had taken a massive beating
Taken offense at Arihant rap for his slimy intentional cheating
For 6 years next intentionally kept our sis out of our sighting

70. Sivaraman and Abishta in Oman

The Arabian dream ensnared Abishta in her ambition
Zeal on overdrive for Siva pursued a job with devotion

Contended person Siva constantly languid in his comfort zone
Even his CV typed by Abishta simple chore but he'd only moan

Siva gifted, brilliant in mathematics, an excellent cricketer
But in real life a quite unique, simple unassuming character

Happy in his space no complaint in life even in extreme strife
Any state of affair good or bad just accepted unlike his wife

Foolish with many names he was often called
Nobility in acceptance he was never appalled

Abishta an enterprising person but in extreme
In earnest sought jobs abroad for Siva in full steam

Phoned headhunters, networked to influence decisions
And she finally struck got Siva a job in an audit division

An insurance company in Oman of repute
As a senior audit manager, he was to depute

Siva traveled to Oman in late December 1985
A kind of job any aspirant would indeed strive

A cool 8am to 5pm job no stress no tax
End of day with a glass of scotch he would relax

Late in 1987 Abishta joined Siva permanently

In my final run with Al Fateh, I was to leave Oman shortly

I feared and anticipated many a trouble
Many relationships to be redefined or in the rubble

Life in Gulf different experiences of fast-paced Bombay
The day begins as soon as it ends in the quay
And ends as quickly as it has begun by the bay

Travel in Bombay takes your time of life in a quarter
Unfortunately, there is no way out even in barter

Oman as a place absolutely opposite diametrically
Beautiful idyllic in lush green scape symmetrically

Abishta as expected immediately in awe
She just did not want to be a homely cow

71. Abishta Working Woman in Oman

Abishta was a master of manipulation
Art in influencing and gradual domination

Proficient in her wish to achieve the final outcome
Her sweet-talking strategy like the beat of a drum

Waltzed into Siva's company with great dexterity
Jim Crown Head of Business impressed with her clarity

But of course, over time she proved her ability
Proficiency in Insurance she an asset as a reliable utility

72. Taking Mother and Abhikya to Oman

With Sivaraman's settled in Oman in respective careers
Time for Abhikya to join his parent's only son so dear

Abhikya closeness with grandmother and reason to cheer
She to go along on her first overseas trip to a new frontier

73. Redundancy in Complacency

Mother and Abhikya left for Oman in summer of May of 1989
Middle East a place in possibility of 365 days of sunshine

Living in Abishta's house in Bombay though Arihant had his own
Mother's house given on rent to a couple to the family well known

With all my savings dried out in house expenses
And Arihant still not coming to life's terms and senses
Rent from mother's house was taking care of our basic defenses

For 6 months next Arihant wasted time in idyllic family pursuits
Absolutely contented in married life and its sweet fruits

Did try many corporate jobs myself locally
Did not fit into my frame mentally
Qualifications in main essentially

Middle East Life certainly spoils you
The comfort of convenience a cue

Many suitable Gulf jobs in Sunday daily featured
Easily a break Arihant if only had pictured

From the ads I would shortlist employer's potential
Never bothered to even draft and type his CV credential

Abishta's Business Friend's visa drew a blank
Whole hype built around the opening was like a cruel prank

But life does teach you not be too dependent
Plan B, C, D ....to carve out independent

Arihant had already experienced 2 years in despondency
Yet he continued to live a calm life in complacency

Married you are now responsibility to show in urgency
Despite my many entreaties only displayed cool redundancy

How can one not see the mounting tension in adversity?
Respite far from coming unless your action now in diversity

74. An Injudicious Decision of Mine

This is when I took a decision one of the most injudicious
A grand idea in sending Arihant to Singapore became inauspicious

Abishta left behind Video Cassette Recorder imported
Demand for VCR from a neighbor for sale it was sorted

Lack of usage, dampness in walls no sunlight or cross ventilation
Electronics parts would soon start corroding without any aeration

Fetched a good price of fifteen thousand rupees
In her bank account, I was to deposit the fees

A unilateral decision I thought was noble
Incorrect but it was an act of mine so miserable

Misappropriation of funds in description would be apt
Although it would be returned any decision was her right

Huge risk in taking in those days the sum was steep
A gamble I kept contemplating a sin to sink in neck deep

Pros and cons to evaluate Arihant as the righteous person
Ability and potential huge but now he was a different version

Maybe Singapore would clear his mind of all and any distortion
A prosperous, progressive state cleanse him as a man in new evolution

Asia Pacific hub for many reputed multinationals corporation
His experience in sales of international brands his foundation

The downside was his history in the recent past was pure impulsive
Would he be prudent in being proactive or be self-destructive?

On personal guarantee of risk for once ready to be impulsive
My instinct nudging in me again but this time I was compulsive

75. Arihant's Singapore and Thailand Jaunt

Arrangements all done through a travel agent for 7 days
Covering Singapore and Thailand tour hoping in kind it pays

Drafted, prepared and typed his CV in several copies
He was still in his own world looking lost and sloppy

On dos and don'ts with him I ran over the drill
A wry smile on his face looked fed up with the grill

Organized separately 2500 Singapore Dollars in cash
An emergency backup in event of job ratification in flash

My heart said he would get a job
Arihant had to be focused right on top

Curious like a child I was awaiting his return
Gloom in I was for a job he had spurned

A job he had got he said but perks not with a family status
Almost 2 years in limbo nothing on hand he simply callous

Salary only 100 Singapore Dollar in saving
Impractical reasoning but not tenacious in braving

Young energetic you are testing times ahead
Opportunities many to come just think of today's bread

Singapore a destination for career and life so the allure
Progressive, democratic and in time you will grow for sure

Aghast, disappointed and despondent all emotions at once
Cried out why, oh why did you behave like an idiotic dunce?

Then I asked at least give back the balance amount
To deposit back tomorrow into Abishta's bank account

Sheepishly he turned to inform in a manner he was becalmed
At beachside night market from his pocket, 2500$ was farmed

Oh! What in hell has he gone and done?
Completely devastated I was now numb

How could a grown-up responsible married man
Mess silly around with time to be an absolute sham
Trust and faith unhesitatingly on my face he did slam

Regrets none expressed nor any remorse
Life for Arihant as usual back in a languid course

If Abishta to return now?
And mother to her explain and how?

Serene Matter of fact in a proclamation he elicited
No worries not anytime soon in response he limited

Money, he said I will return soon
When, in how many moons?

You don't have a job; you are not looking for one
And there are neither signs nor any source of income

A signature statement in rhetoric
From a person who blundered so historic

Betrayed my faith let me down badly
Made me feel even worse for his new family

76. Arihant's Flat Maintenance Charges

Abishta organized a visit visa and airfare for Arihant
Almost 3 years now, get a job the reading was blunt

Ominous words still not a care on whose tab was his fare
What has to happen will happen and still too foolish to dare

Not a bother of putting me on the line
That I was answerable he was fine

No small matter for I had committed a heinous crime
Tantamount to stealing, a stigma to haunt me till I call time

Just weeks before his departure
Arihant wished his flat to lease for starter

Got him a good deal on a rent of 1500 Rupees
And 20,000 rupees interest-free refundable deposit fees

Meantime an ad-hoc society for our apartment building formed
Each flat expected to pay in contribution funds all duly informed

One hundred rupees impact on the formation of society not very tall
Yet Arihant asked me to foot his flat bill not in plea but in call

Paid his dues too from rent collected from Mother's flat
For both Mother's and Arihant's whilst on his money he sat

Expected of course for him to pay his share
But free ride he desired no intention to pay his fare

Savings mine now completely gone
Survival on income from rental drawn

Expected share in part from his apartment rent
But said he his wife Rakhsee would just not relent

Principally fair and practical for your money to keep
But why from other's account do you then reap?

For better part since the time from Oman I returned
Resources mined from my reserved income

18 months in stretch expenses for the house I met
Dad, I and most of all Abishta's money for him no fret

Abishta's money he said not important with gall
Not running away, am I? Shall pay in time to fall

A look I shot in his eyes very stern
Fool do I look to you inquiringly in scorn

Plea in earnest he said just do it for now
Will make it up to you someday somehow

An altercation with Rakshee he in me confided
An ultimatum rent cheques in her name provided

Did ask Rakshee of development and in her tone so irate
Said to secure her and her kid her intention only to berate

Inquired then on money for Abishta to pay back
Her outburst "you sent Arihant, you pay from your stack!"

If only they had heeded mother's word in a pragmatic act
A year in time for Arihant to settle, today an altered fact

The decision of her parents in advancing the marriage act
Hasty one-sided plan now giving them a resounding slap

77. Notice of New Arrival

In October of 1989, eight months since getting married
Rakshee in breaking news to me was more than harried

Expecting their first child for me it was indeed glad tiding
Cheered her up saying life eventually in time enduring

Poorvi a beautiful girl child was born in 1990 late April
Adorable little bundle blessed their lives with joy to fill

78. Arihant's Disastrous 2nd Innings in Oman

Arihant arrived in Oman at Sivaraman's house to stay put
Gym to join at Sheraton Hotel start of struggle on wrong foot

Of course, no moolah in pocket Abishta a sponsor very reluctant
Keeping fit vital he enlightened pearls of wisdom so translucent

Lackadaisical attitude, irresponsible towards family and work
Not a care in the world, a misfit in practical duties he now a shirk

For him luckily job experience in previous
Good fortune favored in 2 offer he so fortuitous

One a 40-year-old Al Shaniya a reputable trading firm
MNC consumer brands in distribution ready to confirm

A decent start at RO 240.00 it was a relief so welcome
Perks in car + incentives like rain after drought in his income

But who can reason a mind displayed sense even in seldom
In 3 years now 3rd decision in a row only in doom and bedlam

With a fledgling company signed 2 years in contract
Airsmart selling air-conditioners in a trap he got wrapped

Technical product no idea he had or aptitude
Past mistakes an experience no change in attitude

In construction products technical he failed wretchedly
Yet his immaturity in a choice of job reflected woefully

As saying goes, common sense is not common
In Arihant's case, it was a blunder in full blossom

A reputed firm place to be for stability to display one's ability
Selling proven global brands adds value to one's credibility

At RO. 150 per month with a broken ramshackle car to drive
40% lower pay in acceptance his logic here only so naive
Despair in destruction merely an open invite for it to arrive

He pitched for family status for him issue always critical
Both companies offered him the same status in year physical

Singapore certainly a better deal for his career so typical

Arihant lacked the imaginative drive for thinking foresight
Trade Representative once an offer from US career diplomat

Proposed relocation to Bahrain on conflict interest in hindsight
Many dreams of this post and his truly declined this hat

He failed yet again at Airsmart and how very miserably
In 6 months, he was back home in India despondently

The self-inflicted goal only dented further his hard-earned name
He was his own nemesis in his unwise Russian roulette game

More reactive, impulsive he was no energy, drive or direction
Like sea tide dependent on pull and push on forces of gravitation

A pale shadow of himself he was now
Aged almost overnight, but ego refusing to bow

79. Arihant's Football Injury

Sometime in 1988 participated in local football tourney
A mixed bag of unknown faces together in a day's journey

Arihant played defense but football never his forte
With two left feet, the opponents had him in a sauté

In one rough tackle, he slipped and fell
In terrible pain, he let out a loud yell

Clinical diagnosis in his right knee confirmed a ligament torn
An orthoscopy procedure only option to sort what was worn

Gopal Gulwady dad's office colleague and friend
Wonderful human being, at all times a ready helping hand

Called him, knowing relatives of his many in the medical profession
Soon an appointment with a Dr. Nadkarni and fee in concession

Painless 15 minutes orthoscopy treatment and he was fine
Physiotherapy from home his leg to strengthen and align

Surgery bill of 3500 rupees footed by Uncle Gopal
He a retired person yet did not brook to take a call

Unfair a burden of an expense of magnitude on him
Survival on investment dividends his only prelim

Magnanimous he was in advance fee already paid
And didn't bother to even inform us of his kind aid

On my insistence only but hastened to add

He was not in a hurry to be repaid back

But repaid he was by me the amount in full
Arihant failed in an expression of gratitude so ungrateful

Last I met Uncle Gopal he was well in his nineties
Frail he was but warmth and spirit still high and mighty

May he remain blessed for his kindness and generosity
A truly humble wonderful human being shining knightly

80. Society Formation

The edifice housing mom's flat meanwhile was fully occupied
Few active members to form a society for all to abide

A natural progression in the real estate domain
Facility management its intention in the chain

Breakup for mother and Arihant's flat provided
Trouble comes in a bundle like ballistic missile guided

Total for both flats Fourteen Thousand in arrears each
An ache in doubleheader this was and now I was in a siege

Rakshee to her parent's house had gone
Arihant still to settle in his job in Oman

No phone, no way to contact Rakshee's parents' home
Calling Arihant waste of time and money hence left alone

Putting our family's interest first
An emotional fool I was at worst

Only to pay arrears for mom's flat in responsibility
Sold my motorbike paid Arihant's to maintain credibility

Blunder I made for in return instead of gratitude
Just add to tab cold in a comment he was skewed

An unbelievable response, I was too stupefied
Felt I was just put to the stake and crucified

81. Abhikya Taking Ill

Another development at the same time in Oman in making
Abikya our little nephew just blacked out whilst playing

On admission to hospital clinical diagnosis acute
Aortic stenosis of the heart prognosis was minute

Immediate surgery to undertake
Not another moment to waste

Just the fear for which I had in taste
Sivaraman's rushing to Bombay in haste

Premonition I shared with Arihant a few weeks ago
Dismissive he was and now a reality in full show

Cometh the hour Siva's father Thanga used his connections
Best doctors attending to a delicate case of his grandson

At prestigious Bay hospital, Abhikya was admitted
In an open heart surgery defect successfully corrected

Everyone in relief and delight
Abhikya recovery rapid and bright

Under his grandma's loving and doting care
Finally, home in a week time to prance like a hare

82. Drama At Home

Another twist in the dragon's tale
An absolute shocker there was no bail
Arihant Rayudu yet in another job was a fail

For me in life lot to change
Arihant a player in close range

Mother and Sivaraman's arrived at something amiss
Rakshee rushed home on being told on the crisis

Away at work, I was at the office in Parel of MCS
1st time in face to face sisters in-laws so ominous

Bracing for backlash from Abishta and Mother
The crux of an issue for me misuse of money main bother

Trouble erupted from least of all unexpected quarter
Upkeep of house Abishta's personal things a big matter

Unaware I was but for me matter too trivial
But surely had in Arihant's his stamp of approval

Unsparing Abishta tore to shreds in crude verbose
Mom instead of moderator in presenting a white rose
Made situation tenser with her own caustic dose

Rakshee more than up to the challenge for a duel
Volley so intense her batteries charged fully in fuel

Abishta's house certainly not her duty in upkeep
But in use her wardrobe and all benefits to reap

Had Arihant' approval in his choice to stay was cheap

Question your sons and brothers, please
Their character and integrity in a deep freeze

Rakshee was absolutely correct in her deposition
Abishta no right to take out fury on her in frustration

In a heated moment of exchange that was extremely virulent
Scathingly attacked my influence on Arihant she was insolent

Whiplash, as anticipated, came on me tearing down in a torrent
Expectedly joining in, sister in shaming me mom was abhorrent

Every salvo fired at me like a slash of a razor blade
Castigation so humiliating in time it will never fade

Yes, I had committed a huge crime
Retribution I received in worded slime

In silence, I hung my head in terrible shame
Till day in painful regret, I carry this negative fame

Sadly, even today for a person a step taken in extreme gamble
Has no qualm or remorse, nor apologized for his huge fumble

Rakshee took upon her in a situation to surmise
Decision rational to live independent was wise

As for me to manage subsistence on my own
No help will be asked nor any given a deep discord sown

In few days Arihant from Oman's arrival
A homecoming sans joy or sound of the bugle

This time a fallen warrior in a battle lost
Building liabilities in life at a huge cost

Abhikya in-hospital postoperative in recovery
Asked Arihant to visit he frowned in antipathy

Taking turns as a family to visit little fella in hospital
The family needs to be tight in tender moments not brittle

In visiting our five-year-old nephew his bland reluctance
His emotions in negative shades evident in abundance

Illogical behavior replayed in many family conversations
Unfeasible choices many self-destructed his strong foundations

My only bad decree of Abishta's money in helping hand
Became criminal tag attached to me forever like a brand

But in a matter of days, Abishta pulled off theft so heinous
Larceny if mine in a noble cause against me a felony ingenious

83. Ramin Davle's Indira Vikas Patra

Ramin for safekeeping given Arihant 3 funds in a bond
5000 Rupees each for a total of 15,000 Rupees strong

Ramin discreet in this investment so insignificantly small
Yet wished none of his family members to know at all

Bonds would double in value in 5 years
Fetch only 30,000 rupees for him a small mere
Hence custody in privy it seemed rather queer

Ramin passed on to me the custody baton
Just as well for when Arihant left for Oman
Never imagined one-day bonds would be gone

In my steel wardrobe enclosed in the folder of a personal dossier
Occasionally, I would pass my eye just to feel a good reassure

Only I as sole inhabitant living in Abishta's house
Wardrobe always unlocked no valuables to rouse

Now bond with one drawback
Blank cheque anyone could encash

Bond did not carry a name of the beneficiary
Or required proof of authorized signatory

In event of loss or theft no alarm or beepers
Saying inapt "finder keepers, loser weepers!"

Guaranteed windfall for the finder!

Abhikya in convalescence at home
Abishta had plenty of time alone in Rome

Without my knowledge or concurrence
She delved my wardrobe for any insurance

Always all my things clean and in order
Clearly a motive to create messy disorder

Disliked anyone touching my things without my approval
Fancied threads in feel, a zillion bucks like a lord feudal

As teen lovely pastel yellow royal blue striped shirt, I once bought
Prized possession I wore occasionally lit up like 1000 watt

An invite one day to a friend's birthday party
High and low I looked my shirt favorite to look smarty
But just couldn't find it, a prank I suspected of immorality

The wry smile on mom's face on inquiring
A small matter of fact now transpiring

Mom and Abishta together as duo my lovely shirt bartered
For a brand-new steel pot my favorite thread they martyred

Devastated my heart sank, in sadness, I raged
At my despondency they laughed I felt caged

Tears welled up flooding my eyes
Sheepishly promised to replace my prize

Choking in angry defiance furiously I snapped
How their wicked action just had me handicapped

Robbed once again of my dignity by people my very own
Abishta pilfered the bond cashed and to Oman, she had flown

Till the day Ramin asked I was completely in unknown
And he asked because he wanted me out of MCS blown

84. Abishta's Diamond Set

Siva left for Oman upon Abhikya's having come home
An invented wish Abishta confided Siva to fulfill on his own

Necklace set in diamonds for her she had since longed
A secret in making was meant only for my ears belonged

Strange under prevailing delicate settings wish to be met
Two scenarios in extreme son's health and diamond set

Never gave another thought on chances
After all, she was buying jewelry on her finances

Never fascinated anytime by precious gems or jewelry
An asset eats away your sleep and is more a Tomfoolery

She had twenty-five thousand Rupees on hand she claimed
Siva to send 15,000 more for a total in 40,000 she proclaimed

Her script was in bonds to put me off guard
For total value, the diamond set now on the card

Bonds for the sum of 25,000 prematurely withdrawn in year four
Abishta's story so authentic in the context in success she did score

Deftly made a killing at my expense
For bonds, she did with it in dispense

And Ramin to use against me this as a silent whip
In not paying my share in profits he would all clip

First Arihant spared no effort to royally carve me

In few months span, Abishta cut me like a queen bee

Two of my own ilk made me a sacrificial goat
Immoral needs to be met they were in the same boat
Do we really carry DNA in same to be dumped in the moat?

Check and Mate

2 years later in her Oman home, I confronted her
Aversely confessed stealing the bonds in recall now a blur
The damage however complete on me it was already a slur

85. Textrum Paints End of Road for Me in MCS

Arihant back in Bombay road ahead for him stark naked
No evidence yet in his productivity lest he gets outdated

Not wanting to talk, clueless on career move he looked jaded
Created opening for him in Textrum Paints a move I premeditated

Focus I would then on Styles tiles
Workload shared in steps of small piles

Textrum not technical a product more cosmetic
Great features apt for markets commercial and domestic

Discussed with Ramin over tea and walk
Invited Arihant over for a detailed talk

And then prior to the tripartite joint summit
Ramin threw the spanner in my work no limit

Asked my interest if Arihant too joins in the settlement?
Evident wanting to redraw our word in agreement

No change in my interest categorical in share not to be any trim
Willing to share with Arihant without undermining him

Ramin in offer 2500 rupees in salary to Arihant was generous
2-wheeler and an equal profit share of 33% looked humongous
Share equal for Arihant from us respectively in giving unanimous

A conspiratorial plot behind my back in parallel brewing

For reasons to become obvious I was not in any looping

Ajay Mehra a quiet backdoor entry he made
Ramin asked him his feel of Textrum shades

Ajay expressed his desire to be in the mainframe
Ramin over the moon to have him the game

Rehab and Construction Works, with Textrum Paint a bonus
Sweet Scent of Moolah, but small measure on him an onus

He had to handle this one issue tactfully, it was me!
One pebble at a time testing still waters was he

Knowing fully well I would have none of it
He played his card slowly steadily bit by bit

Standard dialog Ajay's construction experience to fore
Serves MCS purpose in Textrum operations to core

Your experience in construction too much already in store
Not in need added involvement to cut our share any more

Ajay and Textrum Paints Owner together in symbiosis
From same Punjabi culture for MCS, he said it is a bliss

An uncalled equation I in complete disagreement
He retorted only he possessed in complete armament

Ramin was hell-bent on having him on board
Got the first hint of him throwing me overboard

Unfortunate I was in Arihant no support
For him, I was fighting alone holding the fort

In his attitude and mind, he had become silly and fidgety
At Textrum factory in Gurgaon, he had a skirmish very petty

Situation by tuk-tuk driver blown out of proportion
Arihant in a rebuff to part Rupee 2 only in denomination

Embarrassing it was as the projected face of MCS he was
Jatinder Owner of Textrum paid a tip without a pause

Unnecessary a matter without any reason or rhyme created
In dealings with hierarchy an impression now totally dented

A matter of pride for the company I initiated
And one moment in immaturity became a time ill-fated

Sharks in business wait for such an opportune moment
Ajay waiting to grab certain now of his bestowment

Look in Ramin's eyes at such times all too sinister
Slowly building a situation for a swift kill to administer

He again directed his query on my share
Being curt told him he was getting under my hair

At the onset, all nitty-gritty sorted out with care
His word of honor was accepted in faith as my fare

Every initiative of mine into MCS an equal partner was I
My brainchild in getting agencies always well and high

Proprietary right in business evolution my share will not dive
Skeptical in nature in any venture now you are eyeing my pie
Ramin stuttered, guilt and nervousness in loss of words now a sigh

Together the conspirators plan carefully crafted

Ajay the master Ramin his slave willfully drafted

Said he in defense Ajay evinced high interest keen to invest
Experience of construction and in operations he had to stress
Pitching for his master and he was certainly doing his best

Both lines subtle affront to make me feel redundantly small
Professional trap in grace to fall their joint intention after all

Unequivocal in no uncertain terms on my protest
Towards Ajay, he was aware of my explicit disgust

For practical purpose avail his services as a contractor
3-way deal in an equal share to Arihant my only factor

Ace of cards he threw, asked me for investments in funds
Wickedly fired his intention clear, me in shock dearly stunned

In loud protest told him blunt now he was on a U-turn take
Renegading on his word of honor commitment he ready to break

Just so he could erase from his conscience his brutal guilt
In or out of MCS guaranteed 10% royalty for you I have inbuilt

Ramin said 40 for self, 30 each in percent for Ajay and Arihant
And munificently I share 10 from mine to you I am so benevolent

Final body blow to have me completely knocked out
No right in Textrum's business his final punch in a one-sided bout

Deceitful plan of duo Ramin and Ajay completed in action
Conspiracy executed to perfection blunt out any reaction

To have me out of the way an objective in purpose
Ajay the brain behind who schemed up plan in doses

Ramin a sadist anyways the one always played extremely filthy
Ajay his master, mind at whose behest also got his hands dirty

Dawned on me I was well and truly out for the count
Deviously used by a friend my life was sold at a 90% discount

No documentation in legal agreement to bind
Even if it was no more than toilet paper for any hind

Not once in thought did he even stop and spare
Staked my life in equal share just on his word I did dare

MCS was his company I truly worked sincerely and cared
My work in all genuine honesty always transparently I bared
He had nothing to lose but I would a lot if I had not fared

An out of box thinking got MCS back in business on the rail
B and W no breadwinner, Textrum and Styles did the bail

My brainchild in strategy a proprietary no patent
Ramin and Ajay just like that stole it in latent

Ramin's resolved in cahoots with Ajay was pure evil in stake
Below the belt, in calmness, they hit me in pleasure to forsake

Hand in glove for my nascent career and life that too in prime
Mercilessly in glee together they destroyed and buried it in time

Ramin the one who invited me in his business to join
In full knowledge of funds, I had nothing even in small coin

My intention at first to head back into a job in the Middle East
Ramin swayed me to join him with an intention of a beast

Only my knowledge and skill, an experience to share

In all probability could drive us together in the club of millionaire

No doubt he already was in the club of the elite by inheritance
Well to do he was yet in thought and action his deals in pittance

My belief in him unconditionally was my single biggest folly
Jolene's incidence came back to haunt me like a Grail so Holy

Deception of crime will surface often with different face
Chi in me rightfully prodded, darkness in readiness to brace

Two years in my prime lost I was staring in oblivion
No mentor nor godfather nothing else to fall back on

Second time cheated if life keeps throwing like Ramin a friend
Party like hell with the enemy at least known one can spend

Truly the life of others for this dastardly duo in a worthless while
Surreptitiously usurp others right in adding their wealthy pile
Imaginary belief justifying their dirty act in the professional style

Ramin was a fraud personified subtle yet a cold-blooded traitor
Corrupted deeply with a dark evil mind he was a vicious betrayer

Ajay a name in Bharat synonymously common a meaning of victory
His action in his deed for a win was manic, despicable and derogatory

Playing his role as a perpetrator in ensuring the noose would fasten
He triggered a death knell of 4 lives like a merciless hired assassin

Ajay and Ramin master and slave celebration high in rumba
In hilarity, they were slapping high fives in ritualistic Zumba

One down one more to go next target obviously Arihant
His complacency in long run made easy to have him out shunt

One vile repulsive look at Ramin I walked away for good
Knowing no intention of him in sharing the taste of any food

Modern-day Brutus in real life nipped a budding career alright
Ajay the duo in deceit an act in conceit for their future bright

Partners in crime for money and control fired by lust and greed
Heinous act bedeviled a young life for me an unforgivable deed

Ramin if a real friend could have been in his words true
But it turned he assassinated a faith for moolah in few

At least Ajay in person had his dark shades open and wide
But Ramin's character best described of Dr. Jekyll and Hyde

86. Many Grey Shades of Ramin Davle

Many more acts to follow too soon in near ensuing future
The malicious intent from Ramin and Ajay who else would nurture

No better instance of Ramin's many unknown shades in grey
Ajay too not spared as best friends though in dirty deeds they share

Time in early 80s Ajay with girl Komal in tender relation
A wonderful person she was valued for her special association

Like any relationship, there were ups and down
Hailed from a good family she from a different town

Komal in time to the US she had long migrated
Ajay immersed himself in work to be hands-on educated

Distance makes the heart go wonder and loved one fonder
Komal from the US to India to mend bridges traveled yonder

Only one cardinal mistake she did was to contact Ramin
Character assassination on Ajay he hurled like a vile vermin

Saddened poor Komal back to the US she was on next flight bound
Ajay did not even get a wind of it, kind of friend in Ramin found

For Ajay in me, no love found or ever lost
But to Ramin, I asked on what belief this rancid assault?

Among best friends, you'll always do each other count
Chuckled Ramin to what does your philosophies surmount?

With a wry apathetic smile, he said underserving of her he is

Saved her from callous hell without him she will be at peace

An afterthought to ease my doubts fueled he in speculation
He is in a clandestine affair now, really! He said just an intuition

Middle East rule of the land upright for all in an equal mold
A duty of every soul expat or local to respect and uphold

In a letter by post once Ramin of lady sent me a nude sleazy centerfold
Fully in know if censured trouble huge in major for me untold

Probed his dirty harmful juvenile act in extreme foolishly bold
Unrepentant in answer, candy only! The ghoul sniggered in cold

In those days a pretty girl named Selena I was dating
Accidently in happening with Ramin in upfront meeting

The formality of introductions I conducted in elegance
Ramin too engrossed in an appraisal of her eloquence

Selena very candid in her assessment said he so disgraceful
Not wanting to let go of her hand in a look he was so lustful

Observed his look in her with his usual wry smile
Pretty obvious in his mind he already had her defiled

A great weapon to adhere is a basic instinct
Selena a wise girl with meritorious distinct

Many instances in real Ramin played dirty trouble
Always directed his shenanigans at the lady in a couple

Intentionally he wished to create an air of controversy
Plant seed of suspicion to make their situation messy
And chortle in evil pleasure at couples without mercy

An elaborate laced fabrication of gent's bachelor escapades
In an unrelenting rant in tirades ruin instant mood in a rapid cascade
A sadist in true sense tension between couples his personal trade

Vishwabharam Ravid and Ricky Chavan two friends in the office
Chartered Accountant professional were both in practice

Vish not very social in nature but sincerely very nice guy
Again typical South Indian boy conformist, not excessive in buy

Ricky self-taught straight-talking fella extremely likable
From the same stratum as I his fortitude was unstoppable

Once Ramin sent them both at his home a dinner invites over
Drinks in hand his ramble once in full flow there no stopover
Carnal anecdotes of innuendos in full-blown vulgarity
Allusions of rawness all in double-edged impropriety

Vish called me by phone told me an event a complete disaster
Ramin loose cannon talked in erotic overtones as crude headmaster

Vish's better half Ruma a lady typical South in total simplicity
Scandalized and vandalized in mind in Ramin's verbal atrocity
Vish swore, with Ramin, it was the last of any social party

An incident so unconvincing indirect in time 7 years later
Despite cutting off full all ties with this terrible traitor

Of all places in Malad public bus he in transit
Mom in the same bus spotted the slimy bandit

Ramin in animated proximity with a girl familiar to our area
Mother in discretion moved on to avoid any attention or hysteria

She was girl known pretty, single and available

Coupled possibly through referral to be sociable

Ramin's past known antecedents
Clear this too was no coincidence

Travel by public-bus he who owned wheels in a fleet?
Inconspicuous he wants to be for any attention to meet

Caught in the act came up to mother in a conceal pact
Deflect attention from pretty girl played a line in old tact

How is Aarvan he inquired? And said, of course, he is still enjoying
Sarcasm in his tone nasty not lost in words he was totally annoying

In Textrum days Ajay's sister in rebel
Dating a consociate, he wanted to quell

Coincidently her alleged beau was with Styles
They were working together in marketing tiles

Ramin on behalf of Ajay asked me in confidence to investigate
Told him blunt on his face how much more depraved can he get

Slave and master act of amity Ramin to Ajay his vested interest
Unethical disgraceful means no reason in an alluding arrest

An adult she had the right to her own life to decide
Both Ramin and Ajay many dark acts had a lot to hide

On another occasion Rathod a humble being visually impaired
Asked help in building a low-cost housing colony if prepared

Ramin, I inquired, in turn, deputed Ajay Mehra of course
At site Ajay quietly hinted me at full MCS I have to divorce

He cited an instance of Sonam his wife's few family members
Having moved out of India since then doing well in numbers

The Middle East for me the place of sunshine
Forget business in India, I have to draw a line

Ramin and Ajay between them had this worked out truly
Ensuring to rid me of Textrum and MCS very, very coolly

Mind games! If Ramin vermin vile
Ajay complimented as fetid yellow bile

At MCS office during my tenure
Blank calls numerous without censure

On office line, it starts only on my arrival
My movements on tab there was no rival

An obvious fact a girl online could hear a giggle
At flirtatious best in adjectives, I would dibble

Ramin made this issue a mountain of a molehill
To Mom and Rakshee he snitched in a very canny drill

Out of blue inimitable style in pretense unoffensive
But cruel intent so subtle in damage so excessive

To blunt fact of actual effort, I put at work
Scheming ways to degrade, him a total jerk

Never one to admit his streaks of envious tinge as detractor
His persona amorphous next he playing a saving benefactor

87. Arihant Taking Ill

Abhikya now completely recovered
And back he was to his self-normal

Mother and Sivaraman's then to Oman flew back
Arihant and Rakshee, now settled in their very own shack

After the family skirmish with many truths unfolded in acrimony
Clear cracks in filial bond any greeting just be in a ceremony

Between Arihant and me wall drawn copiously invisible
Few buildings apart though practically not at all integral

Even under duress, she would never seek us out
Rakshee's sworn testament in arrogance she had tout

Their perilous situation reasoned was only my fault
Bad impact on her husband's life best to stay way out

Alone I was now living at Abishta's house independent
On rental income from mother's house solely I dependent

Arihant at MCS with Ramin for him a new beginning
The deal set up by me for him ironically for me an ending

Few weeks into work apparent he unchanged in attitude
Passing by my window on road his timing in huge latitude

His smugness was in signs ominous
Ramin and Ajay in quiet watchfulness

An opportunity to deliver its consequence

Started making noise for his incompetence

3 years a long time, not to have a paying job his inconsistence
Zest in him non-existent, in his perseverance no persistence

Averse he was to share his problems
False pride his wall to accept solutions

In MCS an opening for him was created by me, a truth
Did not cut any ice with him, was not his balm to soothe

And then he fell......................... sick, terribly sick!

88. Helping Hand

More than a month since going their separate way
Past 11pm one weekend night it was dark and gray

Standing by my building gate
With neighbor passing time in wait

Caught a movement in hazy light
Silhouette resemblance to Rakshee in sight

Entered building adjacent in the pretext
Certain in body language she seemed vexed

Nobody is known to us there that we socialize
Anyways thought in my mind capsized

But a few minutes later my name called out loud
Familiar voice indeed Rakshee it was in night shroud

Walked towards her acknowledging her cry in anguish
Politely in asking her presence in time so outlandish

In halting tone, she deliberately hushed
Arihant is unwell she said looking crushed

Burning high fever in action she was clueless
Summon a doctor home if he is feeling helpless

Said she unaware where to go and to whom
Pleaded with me to fetch the doctor home soon

Sure, I said plea not required it will be done

Go home attend to him and your little one

One more prayer before making her way home back
Secret pact not to disclose to Arihant her inane lack

To Arihant her request for help to me in tack
Forewarned her in contacting me for any act

Clear why she went to the building next
The intent was to seek me but on what pretext?

Composure she lost completely on seeing me
Her silly utterances in recent past weighed heavily maybe

Desperate, now she wanted to break the ice
In dark how would I react; will I hike my price?

Dr. Thambu a family physician to Arihant house I escorted
104 degree in high fever in pain he needed to be comforted

The doctor suspected Typhoid or Appendicitis as two possibilities
Troubles of every form and manner in life building only liabilities

Time in check till following morning for the fever to subside
Failing; in doctor's advice to admit him in the hospital to abide

Seeing my lovely little niece Poorvi the only bright side
Cuddling her in tender hug hoping morning would bring a glad tide

Hopes faded as fever began to rise high again
In hospice admitted diagnosis confirmed cause of pain

Acute appendicitis recommended immediate surgery
Called Ramin on his condition, his reaction in perjury

Voice was more out of exasperation than concern
Out for 2 weeks at least in a tone more in spurn

Moment of Truth who will take care of her husband
Little Poorvi not yet one, Rakshee at her wit's end

Both by day and night someone had to be by his side
The little child in daycare but at night mother must beside

No position to ask me after her crass remark
For some reason her parents not in her arc

None to fall back on she was in complete dark
Yours truly offered to stay by Arihant set a benchmark

The operation was done and over with within an hour
Under normal circumstances discharged in 2 days by far

Arihant's took six days to recover in deliberate procrastination
Blind in negative message conveying to partners his stagnation

This weak moment his own instead of being tough in mind
Inspire your wife together in strength we are one of a kind

His infant kid alone in a daycare
For her sake, he had to really fare

But for both Rakshee and I, it became worse
Cleaning his putrid mess by day and night as a nurse

On the 6th day, I told him enough is enough
Get up take hold of your life in words I was rough

Left with no choice I was now tired and sore
Funds to foot the bill there was no more

Both of us in getting you better trying our best to help
But you are in your own auto mode of only whine and yelp

Hospital bill could have been settled in five
But for Arihant's attitude, it was 3 times high

3 days after his operation a visit by Ramin
In restrained missive Arihant just another human

Typical of him a good side to show
Foot the bill for his trumpet to blow

Fifteen thousand in days of severe drought
Family's dignity for me is what it was all about
Paid from my earnings in tiles, I still held clout

Now that it was done and dusted
Four weeks later a scam was busted
And me the victim was completely devastated

89. Biting the Helping Hand

Poorvi little bundle of joy I went to see in 4 weeks
Open sesame! Lo, what do I see, too stunned to speak?

Astounded! Brand new dining table, chairs, diwan in adorning
Windfalls for sure natural in asking in skies you are now soaring

Arihant and Rakshee in exchanged glances disinclined to confess
The situation as foreseen for them complicated in a real game of chess

Finally, breaking news from profit share he declared
MCS partners concluded a large job spoils equally shared

When did you hear of it? I was now raging within
A month now he replied but did not bother to fill me in

Were you going to inform me at all? I shot back
In a fleeting glance, Ramin didn't inform you? He cracked

Avoiding any eye contact no feeling of guilt
My brother for you this partnership I built

Please don't give me any senseless sincerity
Brother dear our relation is a one-sided barbarity

Once again very badly you really let me down
Rightful share in my lifeline, yet you let me drown

Ramin my 10% kept for himself no intention to share
For you, I ensured a good deal whilst you pushed me in the snare

A few weeks ago, nursed him back to strength

Returned in huge favor by dumping me in the trench

Oh, so much for the family bond by blood
Sharp steel in my back to flow and flood

Helping perpetrators deprive me of my rightful gain
For short-term profit, he was their pipe to have me in the drain

No emotion in care nor did my brother spare any thought
Just discarded to write me off for small riches he was bought

7500 rupees in bundles of hundred flashed tersely
Rakshee said this first installment adding insult on injury

The final half will be cleared soon said she crisply
In a couple, she returned all squared up said curtly

How good is that?
A few weeks ago, at night for help in a plea to me, she came seeking
U-turn in total condescending and raw in attitude almost shrieking

Not a word of gratitude for helping hand
Job done, you are now once again banned

On Ramin's behalf she to me in a very hectic canvass
Let go of Textrum, intrusion hers in absolute madness

One more salvo she did fire for all help in monetary I did on loan
She refused in acknowledgment outright as a burden not her own

Never did I involve her in any such petty matters
Always between my brother and self that he shreds it to tatters
But willingly she would own Ramin's offer on a platter

He in deliberate fanned even more sleaze to her in family politics

Profit for Aarvan from Textrum? He now not even in partners mix

Only this fiend Ramin would stoop to a disgraceful depth
Inducing woman of the house any length to go he out of step

He a doubled faced notorious villain in this game
Bizarre dark side hidden in his medium sub-frame

All pent up me a volcano ready to explode
Made my way to MCS office at Parel to unload

Least expected in me as a guest of the afternoon
Crowded office as expected for me in a boon

Ravid Vishwabharam and Ricky Chavan
Financial experts waiting for their big time

Ramin, Ajay and Arihant partners in crime
Support Staff back at work after halftime
Stage set for me at MCS with Ramin for the last showtime

Your invite for me to join as partner make business agile
Equal share in profits your money, my mind for business fertile

Your word of honor is all I accepted in handshake and smile
Profitable ventures initiated despite your tack not so versatile

Despite my reservation roped a rogue in that was your ugly guile
Rogue was your interest asked if I could invest you are so senile

Hateful intent minus dime to oust me for profit and to control turnstile
Honorable you are not, weak in greed and lust, an unholy friend hostile

Sincerity, honesty and hard work, in transparency I filed
Initiative in hope building company together you deviled

Sanctity of blind trust and faith between friends you defiled
Two in a conspiracy behind my back despicable plan you riled

Robbed precious time in my prime, sins you have compiled
In deceit hoarded stolen wealth in abuse of my brainchild

All my efforts and time spent in 2 years you now enjoyed
For misery you on me piled in time for a crime you will be trialed

History this moment on permanently from my life you are in exile
Never let you anywhere close in proximity even by a distant mile

Friend you never were an enemy you are not even worthwhile

Feebly in reply money, he whined you owe me lot in credit
A pittance in 1K in time, I snarled what else will you now debit

In support of nothing and I never ever asked for more
For free availed my time you stole share from my store

An emotional fool I was in business class
Cheating is but your way for wealth to amass

IVP Cash bonds Abishta pilfered was lot Ramin hinted its cause
Deft he in collecting his loss though responsible only he was

Arihant unseated himself as I was about to leave
What he said next only got me more peeved

A clear indication he on their side fully
Sold his bloodline for a song so cruelly
And I their sacrificial lamb well and truly

Apologize I do for Ramin on his behalf
Forgot maybe to tell he sounded like his better half

So obvious now in Arihant shades of past
Do we really share DNA of the same cast?

90. Pedophile Victim

A hideous event of past in childhood, when we were hardly pally
I was 12 and Arihant 16 with other boys play cricket in the alley

A grassy area with an almond tree served as a pavilion
Buildings in garden cover alive in plants and reptilian

A crowd of boys sometimes in number more than 20
In small patch filled in raucous noise, the number seemed 40

Most lads were of 16+ plus in age
Two of us at 12 were on the same page

Small built I was with a baby face
A vulnerable child typically like any case

On that day human predator in secret stalking
Much older boy in 20's I his victim was in sighting

Short and stocky he lived in society as another boy of 12 close by
Ironically very pious his father sings godly hymns in season dry

Hanging next to almond tree waiting for my turn to bat
The evil sneaked in behind held my arm to drag me out of sight

I kept calling out loudly to Arihant a part of the same batting team
One glance he gave, no thought to it, stimulated in evil more steam

Dark stairway in his building he moved me quickly despite a slip
I continued to resist but his brute force had me in his vice grip

On building terrace just above his flat he began in a slow brain washing

Sleazy dirty talk about girls he tried to indoctrinate my mind in bashing

Then he tried to kiss me as I kept warding him off
Strong he was but my instinct kept me alert and tough

Let me go, hoping someone would show I kept on pleading
Maybe he feared the same in letting me go my plea in heeding

Not looking behind quickly I ran down fast flight of 5 floors
Thinking on my trail still was stalker a demented demonic boar

Too ashamed to share a horrid experience I just had
Felt let down by Arhant situation in early clearly looked bad

If my bro had even taken one step forward towards me
The evil stalker would have let go off and set me free

Mentally and emotionally violated though
Thankfully nothing predacious I had to forego

91. Friend in (Deed) And My Brother And His Wife

Their Corrupt Seed

Another day, another time and another place
In pack of 3 predators violate my right, emotion and space

On face bluntly Arihant was told he is one of their kinds
Cannibalize you too they will I said, hence stop playing blind

Within the family there were hidden daggers drawn
Ready to plunge deep in your back to kill their very own

My brother, I nursed him back to health a few weeks ago
Joined a pack of wolves and my fate he shreds it to the core

His wife who pleaded help too drew dagger in a bloody encore
Together they played as merry band my death knell they ensured

Ramin many times came home in an effort to mend the bridge
Unbelievably opening a new door for business, he tried to pitch

From reputed diversified group TRF in paint
Moisture pure it was he said, an act trying to be quaint
What a character he was already deep in a taint

But this was exactly him in two sides
Player and referee Dr. Jekyll and Mr. Hyde

Never since in almost 3 decades did I ever initiate contact
But a tab on me he always tried somehow maintain track

Ricky Chavan always used to be the common source
For Ramin, any information on me he was his glucose

Ramin, in a garb of a friend, destroyed careers and family
He a fiend indulged only in destruction an unwelcome calamity

Ramin and Ajay duo in crime a life they cheated
Money a worth only in while it would have them feted

But the time they robbed me in my prime had me gutted
Their wealth built at cost of a friend with their hands it was blooded

For me, Ramin was now nobody to history forever confined
A friend he never ever was; Brutus surely redefined

An old phrase "Friends in need are friends indeed"
The phrase in irony for me as a friend in you they only feed

As friends they only make you bleed indeed
Seek you out when only they are in your need
Their breed has only one creed in one-way need

For in need emotionally plead to fulfill their greed
And times, in turn, you are just a needless weed
Will vanish from your face they in lighting speed

92. Shekhawat in 1992

In next one-year big blunder again I made
Another partnership deal in it I did wade

In my time with MCS, promoting B and W chemicals
Vinay Shekhawat 20 years my senior I met, felt he was ethical

King of trade in cement apparently at one time called shots
Family feud eroded power and status now lean times of all sorts

Touched base with me with his business proposition
Money abundant for decent investment was his mission

Persistent in his follow up for me to join on an equal share
More on emotional rebound this was also one-way fare

Venture to set his son up primarily
So, in time takes over reins eventually

So, began my tryst in trust again
Shekhawat was the man now in main

In the sale of white cement he was in retail
Influence his trade contacts for wholesale
Existing network of dealers just cannot fail

Agencies in building supplies my role to acquire for distribution
Trade terms and market support to negotiate in business evolution

Shekhawat invested 100K rupees in deposit and stock
Sania Styles our company now ready for serious work

Agglomerated marbles and ceramic tiles agencies to gain
Luck unkind as ceramic tiles supplier failed due to labor pain

Ceramic tiles failed to take off in the desired time
Shekhawat then cannily asked me 50K in a loan in prime

Falling short he said in inventory need funds for stock purchases
A quizzical look of mine changed tact to liquidity in credit services

Vowed in a month he would recompense
Gullible fool I was it was in huge pretense

Money safe he said in my care do not tense
30days in lapse no intention at all to ever dispense

Considered covert but normal business practice
Buy stocks on credit holding payment in tactic
Hoping supplier write off as chronic diabetic

Father-son duo in big purchase of cluster marble made
75 grand in credit in various sizes and colors shade

Kept in a private garage far from the main store
I not taken in the loop they maintained the usual chore

Payment due date to the company in honor they failed
Sales Manager implored me in disbursement be bailed

Situation completely took me by shock
Now the boat indeed hit the rock

Shekhawat I queried need for materials without order?
Pre-emptive in expectation as instant sales converter

Concurrence in duty in the least kept me informed

Purchase since 30 days minus any orders armed?

Defaulted payment reflects on our repute and a strong ethics
Returned all materials to the supplier I was humbly apologetic

In a disclosure of accounts expenses debited too high, I found
On probe; expenses of his proprietary deep in Saina Styles pond

Business no way forward in myopic vision
No more in sync, I felt like a captive in prison

Ravid and Ricky helped to negotiate situation tricky
Clearly, at my cost, he out to make a big buck in a quickie

Exiting and forgetting money lent to Shekhawat now the only option
MCS a Fry Pan into Saina Styles a fire was regressive evolution

Piling pressure on ceramic tiles suppliers in the interim
Refund deposit amount or send tiles hopes in dim

Relentless perseverance paid off in a stroke of luck
Supplier instead one sent three loaded truck

Shekhawat's investment of 100K instantly soared
From breakeven, a bonus of 200K in a year profits roared

Excess stocks an equal amount of fifty thousand for me in kind
Sold it in open market at cost money owed to me self-assigned

Surplus stock for Shekhawat in excess of 200 percent
Profit for him, he at cost or added yield could augment
At peace with myself I exited and to Oman, I went

93. Arihant Booted Out of MCS

Shekhawat's mental games as deceitful if not more
In backdrop met Ramin who once said he was a bore

Not without reason for Ramin interest in meeting
Secret service on Arihant he was studiously inquiring

Selling products for Sania Styles? To Shekhawat, he posed
Nothing to deny here but Ramin's low mentality showed

Not bound by any contract Arihant an equal partner
Ramin's Textrum agenda of hastening his departure

Textrum awarded an International tender
MCS appointed their valued vendor

Painting works as a contractor in a turnkey blender
Healthcare facility in the Maldives a place of splendor

Contract value of 30 million rupees for turnkey project humongous
Profit @ 35% netting 10.5 million rupees simply enormous
5.25 Million Apiece in Textrum they'd have minted was monstrous

Ramin and Ajay coupled to hit the final nail in the coffin
Brusquely dumped Arihant to eat his share of muffin

In Business Parlance it's called Pie Chart
Partners in MCS followed a chartered Path

Ramin + Aaravan in 50/50 for a start
Ramin + Aaravan added Arihant 25 in a share of mine in part
Ramin + Arihant + Ajay 40+30+30 and Aarvan was torn apart

Ramin + Ajay together in 50/50 Arihant they shunted out

3.5 Million of Arihant between them walloped
10% Royalty due to me Ramin coolly scalloped

Mind I applied in strategy but proprietary no patent
Ramin and Ajay just coolly stole every bit in latent

Arihant in business never did he anyways assert
Lacked leadership, drive, prospectively never alert

And then he was one amongst two major wily perverts
Teamed with them in know against me in he did in covert

Saw it coming I warned they finally just ground him to dirt
Served out his utility for them in having me to subvert

94. Partners in Crime

Two partners in crime to destination holiday they flew
Thailand and Singapore with family for fun and yahoo

4 years in precious time lost from 1989 to 1993
2 business ventures in faith I brewed in profits for free

Trust! My folly in naivety
Business! Nobody's paternity

Shark infested waters ready to kill all
Inexperience my nemesis in my own downfall

Ramin and Ajay every sense slimy Machiavellians
Amoral, devious, covert accomplices' just ugly villains

No thought about the future of friend and their family
Yet calmly called themselves friends very cannily

They too had girls in kindergarten still small
Yet cut off Arihant heartlessly they had a gall

Odious deed theirs never will come to justice in any daylight
Robbery and Murder in 3rd degree without sound or fight

Theft of right fatal assault on two careers bright
Evil reprehensible exploit 4 lives they silenced out of sight

My dignity to earn and live in self-respect they stole
My right deprived to honorable life in meanness their goal

An accomplice bought in 3rd member and sold his soul

Profits in gain shared in conspiracy with another fiendish ghoul

His initiative it was an invite to join the business, he'd remember
Word of honor in vow only grail between 2 partner members
A petty miserly gain in murder premediated few lives he dismembered

Much later in time Arihant on a survey in Mumbai exhibition
Bumped into Ramin who greeted in him in subdued elation

Snitched on Ajay's doing a double on him in high extreme
Dumped Ramin to set up his enterprise on own without him

It should not actually matter at all to Ramin
To each other had exhausted their utility value as scum and vermin

95. Stock Market - Ravid and Ricky

Through dark clouds, a small ray of hope shone
Asked Ravid and Ricky for investment tip on phone

A small sum of 50K rupees in selling tiles made
They through sub-broker 2 scrips for me purchased in aid

Bombay Stock Exchange in heady Bull Run
My 2 scrips 30% in appreciation it was fun

Mandate if returns fetch in @20% for me so dear
Sell it off was my instructions my words very clear

They declined in saying scrips to raise more in price
Replied I am happy with profit on hand forget the rise

Sub-broker unwilling they said to sell
But ownership is mine he can go to hell

And then a scam happened in a massive eruption
Stocks in free fall for one man's heavy corruption

Bear with its fangs and claws just ran amok
Losses were in millions and many went bankrupt

Paper and Garment shares of mine crumbled in set
Now in dimes worthless even as a paper roll for toilet

Cannot figure out despite plea why till date
Ravid or Ricky sale of shares did not initiate?

Both in real a bunch of nice guys meant no harm

Help in times of need they were always around

Reciprocal I too with them at the slightest sound
Never would they make their hay on other's pound

My plight they in awareness they were duty bound
But this lapse in judgment still has me dumbfound

96. Abha's call in 1992

One weekend noon in May received Abha's call so stirring
Alok critical in the hospital she said condition extremely worrying
For me 6 years her first call; we put behind the conflict of sibling

On 2-wheeler Arihant and I rushed to her distress calling
At the hospital in Mulund, this bloke simply in comfort relaxing

A case of vertigo apparent his grey cells in disorientating
Yet in all in this so-called crisis alive in his usual boasting
Arihant and I in exasperated glances time to go lunching

Abha was delighted on seeing her 2 siblings
Now we aware 2 more additions to her elder Sasha

Last in naughty Rochelle and in 2nd Pretty Divyanka
Angels 3 in all her lovely sweet little darlings

6-year hiatus it had now been
Radical change obvious in her seen
Just became aware of offenses on her by her ogre shady
On my sis once simple, slim and just such a beautiful lady

Cruelly made to abort her babies
Just because they were all lassies

Now she was just big and rotund
For all in her had being expunged

Physically she was now obese
Mentally appeared not at peace

Her lovely long tresses once she proudly would wear
Were all but blunt in short boy cut crop completely bare

Abha in short time in plenty had weathered
Betrayal on a face of crimes he on her had battered

Rifled on her minutely for old charming grace
Not once did she emote all lost without trace

Tears in her eyes in moistness welled
First time in 6 years me her sight held

Enveloped me in a big sisterly tight hug
How I wished to rid her of Alok the bug

Mother and Sivaram's up-to-date on developments recent
Informed very soon Abishta in Bombay will personally descent

97. Abishta's Short Holiday and Visit to Pethi's

Abishta's solo 15-day trip to Bombay in 1992
On vital mission only, week in couple few

Buy property an investment for posterity
And meet Pethis in a review of their polarity

Basically, trouble real in calling them out of the blue
There was no love lost between these siblings two

Alok on his feet appeared completely normal
Abishta and I on reaching the Pethis's were formal

Post Cookins stint Alok after years in a couple
Service center of Car Company set up very supple

Huge land in Industrial center Mulund without any trouble
Never figured out how he managed realty many times double

25K square feet of land with enclosed structure in quintuple
Within the enclosure, he constructed rooms in a maze of tunnel

No windows, no sunlight, no cross ventilation so nocturnal
The strange setting at night it seemed eerily paranormal

Garage in 25K square feet altered as home abnormal
Abha memories in flood of our childhood so normal

Girls with no friends or neighbors in growing years
The locale was just an area industrial of tools and gears

An adapted environment in a closet of loneliness filled with fears
Camaraderie in each other with mother Abha to wipe their tears

Awkward moments many at Pethi's in silence
Each appraising other discreetly in compliance

Abha - Abishta exactly were not at all in balance
Abishta in reality check on Pethi's value in license

Statement strong wanted to make in dominance
Her intention clears she was solely in prominence

A few days earlier at home in the living room lounging lazily
Abishta's engrossed in her palm very intensely

Asked me to put out my palm very expressively
In humor, I did more than in reaction so spontaneously

In wealth, I will be more my deep lines show said she crazily
Where did that come from all of suddenly? And I smiled wryly

The competitor she obviously perceived in me expressly
It was like a sibling predator stalking me stealthily

Replenishing milk a pretext Abha's nifty eye to Alok
To a nearby store, no choice went along with this bloke

20 minutes upon our return
The mood in somber looked well done

Forensic sense evidence in grim deposition
Storm of ruin in super cyclonic proportions

Kids in a huddle around their mother
Abishta glumly seated in shifty bother

Tea just a mere formality
Ecology was beyond normality

To Malad on way back Abishta dear
Began trembling in a torrent of tears

In asking what transpired in my absence?
Abha's outburst in slander without substance
Lady immoral in abuse hurled in her children's presence

In askance at her a reason in Abha's eruption
Abishta's view sought on her unique abode creation

Never to miss a chance, opportunity in occasion
Anything but the house she said her caustic opinion

Rude insensitive remark ample for mental disruption
In presence of her children Abha in her character disintegration

She asked for it, she got it was my simple explanation
Abishta awkwardly said it was an honest confession

Smilingly looked her in eye I said it was in deliberate intention
She shut her mouth and there was no further conversation

Abha I did call her and disagreed with her action
In mollifying she only tried to justify her reaction

Both were in wrong my unbiased verdict in an estimation
Host and Guest were in reality siblings in competition

Abha Abishta last ever saw of each other in time's condemnation

98. Alok's Serial Wicked Ways

Duleep Sakrekar older than me by good generation and half
We got along like a house on fire our topics hot full of laugh

Partner he in Garment Company of repute in export
"Thread Company" flourishing brand in a foreign port
Human being very kind, helpful and wonderful man
Dog lover a pet named Rambo in breed a Doberman

On a visit, I once to Abha at her home just in routine
Inquired she in my help for garments in shirts and jean

For export, her African contacts were inquiring
The price fit 120 rupees apiece she ready in acquiring

Duleep in my request friendly and spontaneous
Anytime Aarvan for you in a gesture he was courteous

Stock lots in exports surplus normally auctioned
Garments mix in good and defective no precaution
In favor, he gave me leverage in quality an option

200 Shirts for 60 rupees to buy a good bargain in my view
Carried from stocks bought few samples for Abha's review

Eyes lit up amazed, Alok Pethi in overdrive for a coup
Supplier source, location, contact desired he was a shrew
A sixth sense in me now strong, his bait I unwilling to chew

Seventy-Five Rupees my quote in a door to door delivery
Discuss with the client for more orders to consolidate in merry

But Abha I said last week you were clearly in a hurry
Give me a week to confirm to notify a date for you to ferry

All info but the industrial area I held from them to find the star
Anticipated move from Pethi's in their conscience held no bar

Saturday in the same week, Abha and Alok then drove distance afar
From Mulund to Dadar an expanse covered in under an hour

Every industrial area in Dadar since 9am they inquired
Duleep of Thread Company in an audience simply desired

5pm in the evening a call from Duleep at home I received
In usual style played along for awhile in banter of jovial speech

Reciprocated in equal zest burst in laughter loud in amusement
Your sister and brother in law my guest he said till a few moments

Duleep aware of Abishta but ignorant of Abha or Alok's existence
Meeting in person at loss frowned at Pethi's unknown presence
Abha in friendly overtone stretched her hand out in elegance

Duleep regretted in apology inability for his poor recollection
Hints dropped from Malad to naming his wife Abha's dereliction

I am Aarvan's sister she said finally in defeated admittance
Duleep ushered them in his office offering them refreshments
He then asked a reason for their unexpected appearance

Alok aware of him as a supplier in garments now in lead talk
Evinced purchase interest directly from him on a stock lot
Duleep smelt rat, of course, he replied through Aarvan we walk

Abha's cut off @120 my offer@ 75 still 40% margin very pretty

Willing in blood a brother to sacrifice for all to fall into their kitty
Pethi's in their character so cheaply petty for a family such a pity

3 Siblings in a row all older to me one after other in tow
Prepared to let my blood flow for them to flourish and grow

99. Another Ploy from Slimy Bloke Alok

Instance once Alok asked me to join his enterprise
Working Director in his company without any price

Move to Indore a place far from my shore he did emphasize
Bungalow and car with servants on the call how he did glamorize

In my mind, I scorned at his blatant white lies
As partner a scum unworthy ally he I so despise
Two partners in a row bad experience ample and now wise

Leaving mother alone for me certainly never a choice
In parting he said old she is now time for this relation to amortize
Lest your career prospect, in my offer may just fully capsize

Filth in disguise his words no surprise a demon to catalyze
From then on, our relation I completely neutralized

100. Shom Chapra - Forgettable Character in Oman

Still, in Bombay, I was ensnared in a labyrinth of problems of own
Abishta suggested trying my luck in Oman in the market known

February 1993 Oman was a different feel
Missing from 1986 was my drive and zeal

Carrying burden of Abishta's accumulated debt
My own brother's selfish act my blood in loss he bled

Arihant's salsa with scumbag partners his epithet
Failures, two-faced friend and kin, time lost many regrets

1993 came along another relationship in compromise
Shady looking character Shom entered Sivaraman's lives

Façade he put up 2 faced and weighed his Punjabi drive
Confession own, his family disowned, a story I did not buy

Shady and diabolical a permanent glum smirk in his look
Barely acknowledged any person felt undeserving in his book

A sense of humor zero more devious scheming bureau
Face to face in clear discomfort he a monstrous Nero
No different from Alok in his haughty dictating term
Intrusive, serpentine he a despicable virus germ

Obviously, latitude in plenty in Abishta's household
Definite sway over her his suggestions was bold
Siva indulged him in scotch pegs many yet would not fold

Staying at Sivaraman's I felt queasy and obligated
Add to it I was compelled to feel it and often reminded

5 years ago, nail a job at the first instance in confidence
Now a month into visit no job offerings sign in consequence

The rudderless boat I was with no direction
Felt alone in vast ocean in total abjection

Shom factor fueled an immense frustration
Home atmosphere one of sheer desperation

The way events in my life in sequence did unfold
It was like a free fall in a dark bottomless hole

Abishta only would care always in her interest to maximize
Felt she couldn't care less even if the family in compromise

Instances many this Shom enter home minus any etiquette
On opening main door just rush in with nobody being relevant

In hushed tones with Abishta few words in exchange
And in a huff again walk away he seemed totally deranged

Her encouragement alone for a scenario of this kind
With exception of her, we all did terribly mind

Even with mother, I did speak out on this daily grind
Asked her this charade how long since been in a bind?

She shrugged in defeat said Siva her man is abject
Then who am I to object on a very delicate subject

Asked Abishta what hominid kind is this species line?
An offense meant and taken she was simply not fine

In revert, she implied I was averse to her kind of mankind
In him being freely assigned I said she was ridiculously blind
Outsiders, in a family diktat free invite for our name, be maligned

Deceitful ploy then devised by 2 to have me on their side
Buy my silence in continuing at home his autonomy wide

2 options have me in control or just do me away
Latter a better option I could never be in his sway

101. Ruwad Zaffar the Kindly Omani Businessman

Ruwad Zaffar upright Omani businessman
Looking for bright prospective venture plan

Minimum basic of R.O. 150.00 on offer
But bereft of business ideas he was improper
Not job but for me to build an enterprise proper

5 long years in Oman since I had been
Begin all over again I was not at all keen
After 2 bad experiences not, another scene

Alien country Oman felt now lot since had changed
Business Development and networking seemed estranged
Remotely no contacts in any field within my range

A few months earlier in a land of my birth
Familiar place, people have known no dearth
Yet everything in trust simply was not its worth

And now in a foreign land I had to unearth
Find myself to regain my identity in rebirth
A job at first would help settle my feet on earth

Felt hungry wolves in shadows lurking
Fangs bared ready for me in short working
Ensnared in intrigue indeed very disconcerting

Shom the menace it was time to get rid of
Crisply clear message to Abishta, enough is enough

Nerdy geek his presence like weed its time to rebuff

Abishta in defense said he was only helpful
And how I retorted his influence is harmful
You an exception for rest he is only spiteful

No issue with Siva who are you to chatter
Siva out of sorts no says in any family matter
At stake many lives he is like stale batter

102. Ruwad Calling it Quits

An overhead he could not afford next day I was informed
Ruwad Jaffar in gentle conduct last rites on me he performed
Theatre lasted but 3 months from the onset was deformed

Expected trouble coming suspecting foul in connivance
Naively in revelation hinted Shom's role in contrivance
Not surprised at all in their collusion of a joint alliance

Ruwad integrity and polite etiquette set him apart
3 months too early to wind and he was too smart
Accepted his decision gracefully nothing in my heart

In instant, he calmed down felt he was doing me wrong
On surrendering car keys my shoulder, he tapped strong
Keep the car he said till another job comes along

Try to set me up in a firm through a friend
A joinery workshop where my skills could blend

A complete shift in mood within a moment
Set me thinking this was an instant atonement

Seemed more an instigated orchestrated event
Original script by directors for them in lament

103. Operation Clean Up

Unexpected for duo so in a tactic they changed
Mother now in focus script they rearranged

Mother leaning on me for moral and emotional gain
Siva as non-state actor enlisted to cause pain
Abhikya still too small to be in the reckoning as main

On Friday morning in Oman a weekend
Family conference for a decision to expend

Siva who could never swat a fly
A statement he made in proxy to lie
Effective instant mother to pack her bag back to India
Conditions within his means critical she was now a trivia

Script cunningly penned by Abishta's with inputs from wry weed
Abhikya's lovingness for grandmother devious duo did not read

Siva the reluctant guinea pig for execution of a shameful deed
Mother probed on Abikhya's continued dutiful care and feed

Responded no worry in little fella's upkeep he'd do every need
Hurtful words to matriarch since birth tended him without greed
In a couple of days to be repatriated decision she had to accede

Abhikya completely heartbroken incessantly he sobbed
In his shell receded in shock his rock just been robbed

The quagmire of family politics dirty in a covert confluence
The protagonist in script her cradled own wielded corrupt influence

Cometh Sunday mother all packed and ready

Not a tear she shed she was tenacious and steady

Instructed Abishta only I should drive her to airport
Escorted by Abhikya advised him to be strong and hold the fort

Little fella resilient too did not cry till we reached the airport
40 minutes in drive cheering mother he a good sport

At gates of immigration for one final goodbye
Grandmother and grandson a sight for the teary eye

She gently enveloped him tenderly in a long affectionate hug
As she disappeared over immigration with both our hearts in a sad tug

Little fella fell behind me in our long walk to our car
Quietly sat on his seat behind for drive back home so far

Veered my car onto highway back to Sivaraman's house
Tears freely flowed utterly helpless feeling could not douse

As son felt incomplete to see my mother terribly hurt
Powerless, hopeless and miserable felt I was not worth

Peering in the rearview mirror to the core I was shattered
Little fella curled up in frenzied tears his mind all battered

Daughter and sister, she but humiliated her own for her cause
Her intentions clear barrier none in her life's progress to pause
Little did she see sense for a petty gain long run will be a huge loss

On reaching home Abhikya came up to me and sweetly said
Chide his mom, bring grandma back, to her tied he in loving thread
Smiled at him at his naïve innocence his apt words he sweetly fed

Doorbell in summons presence at the main door
Abhikya in pursuit ready for his mom to pour

In loud voice, he yelled and then silent he fell
Cried in delight in joy instant he did not quell

Grandma and grandson wrapped embrace in reunite
Melt even hardest heart to behold a heartwarming sight

Emotions clear in her eyes defining and palpable
Rest of her life vivid it would be this gross betrayal

Fear and guilt written all over her but no remorse
Not an apology but a confession of sordid source

Siva, she hailed it was in form of the devil's incarnation
Oh! Give me a break, nerve you have for dubious incarceration

Yarn over yarn she went on to spin
Siva's job shaky resources are thin

Unilateral decision to save our skin
Without informing cutting mom thin

Committed totally unforgivable sin
She added much to her tricky chagrin

Let slimy geek like flea stick in
In all drama made him a kingpin

For their sin put Siva on guillotine!
Her audacity just beyond my imagine

Mother with my concurrence a decision made
With Abhikya head back to Bombay we weighed

For his future not in any way should be jaded
Her decision in acceptance Sivaraman's swayed

104. Rental and Sundry Charges

There more was in store an aftermath in a new saga
In pursuit of money, she invoked the power of bhagya (fate)

But first, put many issues in perspective
Control of home affairs on mom effective

No outside interference in family irrespective
Slimy Shom disconnect was my objective
His dwindling presence became reflective

Ruwad Jaffar to me kept up his commitment
Jamal Furqan, he referred me in his fulfillment

Jamal owned a small joinery workshop
Relief eventually life @ 31 for me will even out

Monthly RO 250.00 in remuneration
Company car in perks a welcome salvation

Turbulent times of 5 years flashed in passing
Now below the belt blow from Abishta in bashing

Siva man Friday to do honors again dirty
Scheming in conceit my sister just haughty

50% in rental contribution for my stay
Electricity, Telephone and Food also to pay

Practically to share I thought was deal fair
Amount RO 80 too steep I was stripped bare

My input an average of R.O. 125
@ 50% of my gross was a big nosedive

An investigation I launched in financial
The mathematics was grossly illogical

From the landlord's rep, I inquired cost to rent
2 bed @ RO 80 per month from pocket to vent

Clear now Sivaraman's additional income in their sight
Their full rental money was at cost of my sorry plight

Nagged deliberate then on wastage on Air Conditioning
During peak summer that too so necessary in cooling
Bloodline your own entire ilk
For extra money extort to milk

105. Abishta Bickering on Kin to Colleagues

On request one day I went to fetch her from office
Office coworker Rahul I met, seasoned he no novice

Many good things about his work and nature I heard
From Abishta complement rare otherwise unheard

Rahul and I in deep discussion and animated talk
Business to politics, sports and music we walked

Time almost an hour now goodbye in a firm handshake
Manner unassuming Rahul said there's some mistake

Bloke, you are one fine take but your sister did forsake
Said you a lame duck good for nothing useless behind an ache

She the only achiever I am no believer just be awake
My smile said it all sister, now uncomfortable in a quake

In school historical and mythological epics many interesting reads
Gods brawled amid themselves too we but mere mortals as said

106. Mother and Grandson Relocate to India

Often, we in a situation due to circumstances forced
Helpless like a caged animal life takes a new course

Another round of family conference calling
Mom and Abhikya to relocate to India without stalling

Abishta's plea to Mom and me in appealing
Mom in affirmative instantly in healing

At 60 mom not exactly young and sprightly
But for grandson willing in responsibility brightly

She doted on him like one possessed
Little fella responded back in equal zest

The cynosure of his grandmother's eyes
She ignored his misdemeanor highs

If he feared anyone for his transgressions
Yours truly called in for his act indiscretion

Again, sis haggled on price for monthly upkeep
After talking tough agreed in the reason for price leap

In the month of May 1993, Mom and Abhikya flew back to India

107. A Job with a Stop Gap Arrangement

Finally, a job I had, lasted 11 months money in earn
Remitted in part to mom minus share to sis in her urn

The company shut in a span of a year for reason just one
Slack managing skills of persons assigned duty they shun

Entrusted reins of power to take decisions in firm's benefit
Abused by unworthy verticals they just were totally unfit

Salesman elevated as DGM, not at the helm of affair
Napping at home till noon he was only full of air

Draughtsman now a Jt. DGM with no experience in prior
Schedule of works, managing skill left much to be desired

Under instruction to zip my lips to let things be
End of month collect my salary to enjoy for free

Diploma in Business Management completed in distance
U.K. Qualifications in future, added boost to my subsistence

108. Conditions in India

In February 1993 for Oman totally in zero, I left on a job hunt
Arihant now defused by Ramin and Ajay after being their front

No means of livelihood 2 partners in crime had him dumped
Entire loot among them in share Arihant in barren life to confront

Knowing impossible for the family without funds to survive
Rs. 10K on eve of my departure I gave my bro in a lifeline

2 postdated checks for same from last in savings of mine
Total in 30K enough in sustenance for 6months in life to align

New advances happening at home in India with Arihant
In an update, he provided none, unaware of news on his front

Part earning in first 3 months with Ruwad also sent to Arihant
3K every month with a drill in share with Dad 1K he had to shunt

2K for his family in more funds provided prior to my Oman exit
More than enough for one's small family needs on daily merit

A top up to stretch him for a few months to get a job
Rakshee as a teacher too began working she was no slob

In diligence money, I sent for him to focus on new jobs to court
With Poorvi still little, to augment income for his child's comfort
@4K a month job signed but tell me he did not in wary, a bad sport

The unfortunate part in his deliberate glitch also he hindered
And dad's rightful share of money intentionally he pilfered

Dad since age 11 compulsive chain smoker
Blow money away in ciggies he a serial puffer

Money rightfully his no business for bro to be tougher
At 71 my dad was strong and fitter than any other joker

Without an ounce of guilt, he walloped dad's share
Nothing to subsitence on for his food and care
Irrational in reasoning he left him in cold and bare

Dad and Brother few buildings apart as neighbors
Save high cost on bank charges no sense in separate labor
Yet again in deception Arihant with own father gross in misbehavior

But he expected special treatment from dad, not a favor
But summon in duty on demand to cook food at home in labor

Rakshee sick with gastric upset expected dad as cook and baker
Whilst he in leisure relax in waiting for delicious food to savor

Dad in kind his time in a waiver for his son's family like the mayor
Taken now for granted 3 days in row dad felt this was a big caper

Upset and angry he told Arihant their charade was a faker
Father and son heated argument in frenzy turned out very major

The same outlook for mom and Abhikya in bro's selfish behavior
Lines his patent my family first his consistent nature in flavor
Never hesitate to take but never share in anything his as given
His right on share only his whilst rest to share firm in policy driven

109. End of Road for Shom Chapra

Shom Chapra eventually without trace vanished discreetly
Evil monster in the house of Sivaraman's wiped out completely

His exit was not without major incidence of purgery
Slighted in being ousted in the sphere of household judiciary
His importance completely waned he acted as a mercenary

Gold and jewelry in a daring heist at Siva's house in Burglary
Spotted design collection on his new wife in full armory

Dr. Evil Brain had performed his craft with arterial surgery
Outsider entry in our homes will only destroy everything in Barbary

110. Arihant's 3rd Stint in Oman

Mother left Oman for Mumbai in summer of 1993
15 months later I followed in August of 1994
Career-wise seemed stuck I was unable to score

But season's surprise was the return of the prodigal man
Arihant was in form and back again in Oman
This time on his own merit the talented showman
Post-Textrum fiasco new job he acquired month in a couple
To inform me he felt unnecessary as for him it was trouble

Four months he settled in his new job in Geco-India
Oman position in reckoning through print media

Oman job on merit not only commendable
Proved beyond doubt his effort laudable

Only if reasoning prevailed few years before in him
Stable strong in Oman his joy would reflect in a wide grin

Leisurely talking in candid admittance, completely relaxed he felt
Best family moments in weekends together they would melt

In thought, however, I could never put away till this day
Ignore our 70-year-old dad dependent on my monthly pay

Supported by me for entire length his job secured in the fray
Yet cold and insensitive he was towards dad in a cruel way

Arihant now with large consumer electronics firm
Marketing Services Oman (MSO) on good perks and term

111. Twist in Tale

Settling in well he was looking after resellers market
Preparing myself to exit, hunt for my new job still beyond target

And 2 weeks before my scheduled departure
Ad in Omani Daily sales opening for me to nurture

Large European company of repute Pantone Paints
Break finally! In Textrum already I was in acquaint
Instinctively felt this job's mine without any constraint

Excitedly ad clip with bro I did share
Opportunity is mine for taking I blared

He listened then read and re-read the ad again and again
A stunning statement made he couldn't miss this job in a bargain

He too in applying for same in being so foolish to dare
Too stupefied to react I went cold in a oblivion stare

Regaining my composure, I asked him how he could
In reply experience of Textrum in him for sure, he should

Job his for taking he told me in confidence
Are you for real I asked firmly on his impudence?

6 weeks in Oman in a new job you hardly've complete
The company's very good why now go in no entry street?

Huge break after a struggle of 7 years in wild
Don't throw it away for management may be riled

Incorrect to seek new pastures in an alien land
Invested in trust this company for you may have planned

In event of you jumping boats within no time
Ramifications I warned him measured for this crime

Typically, consistent as always he maintained blank composure
Practical advice, not an option his mind now in an enclosure

Then in point blank address, I said
Secure job, good pay and stability; instead

Danger it is for you into unknown road to tread
Reason immature he said 6 days in work I dread
In Pantone, I get 2 days to relax in my legs to lazily spread

Aware you are I have no job in secure
Need this badly, enough till now I endure

For my daily bread urgently, a job to procure
Aware in India no immediate job to lure

Still, he contrived to tell
Let's both apply to sell

Only one position to fill
2 siblings but one to kill

Knowing I would back out
He just did much care not
Illogical hence I opted out

Many an applicant for the post
The best would be the toast

112. Hired by Pantone - Trouble at MSO

Arihant successful in getting Pantone job plum
But costly gamble played soon make him glum

Present employer Marketing Services Oman furious
Instilling a sense of raw fear in brew something ominous

Arrived home one afternoon flustered and anxious
Trouble at MSO, on tendering his notice presumptuous

Not amusing for an employer to be ticked off
A covert coup in scoff asking for mean layoff

An investment made in trust in the market he'd blastoff
Bonanza in deliverance he in time for company will pay off

In grave situation now brought upon on his own folly
Obstinate and eccentric attitude huge error in his volley

Frustration for me no rationality of the risks in his thought
Prospects long term his impetuous choice in serious doubt

Life just began for a young family so happy in time been so long
Patience in maturity given chance makes them stable and strong

His passport stamped at immigration in red
Exit with return banned for a couple of years it said

Abishta and Siva too felt it was a foolish risk to undertake
Twenty-Five Riyals extra in earning certainly no big take

Already secure job in hand mistake to forsake
The job I was to apply in need I had a lot at stake

Threw a spanner in my wheel for me to apply the brake
Proverb and Fable for this story so apt in make

Kill two birds with one stone in this case a tragedy
Kill the Goose that Laid the Golden Eggs a parody

Tensed if sent back to India he in total disintegration
Back to a situation in obscurity an unwanted damnation

Seven long years to come out from a self-inflicted mess
Undoing stability of good times needless by calling upon stress

Factually he his own nemesis but victims along with him took
The genesis of his action absurd, call to reflect in him a deep look

In reassurance, I could now only try in consoling
For his action wait for a positive reaction in unfolding

Rakshee not to be looped he pleaded on developments
I no fool experiences of past on me an embellishment

GM of Pantone paints Bjorne Anters a hero
Keen on Arihant in the team on him he zeroed

Moved to resolve issues with diplomatic grace
Had Arihant's released from MSO contractual face
Storm clouds quickly then passed at a rapid pace

His dream realized with Multinational Pantone Paints
Close shave it was but for Bjorn Anters his patron saint

In departure prior man to man talk with elder bro

Emphatic in words first pay off sister's debt you owe

Affirmed his intentions in honor were same
Money, he owes me, he to return in bit frame

Bring his family to Oman once free from all claims
Time for him to return to roots and earn a good name
Now he reiterated to inform Rakshee on new MNC fame

113. Rakshee's Rant and Arihant's U Turn

No red carpet welcomes to look forward to
On returning to Bombay life to begin anew

Enough funds to keep mother and me going
Job in Bombay the top priority in doing

Rakshee informed on Arihant's new employment status
Slighted at me for this news as he just got out of long hiatus

Felt, surely it was my doing; unaware it was actually my undoing
Conveyed to mother in anger keep this man (me) away in pursuing

My husband and our family life his value useless in interfering
I am bad for their lives and the single worst impact in influencing

10 days later Arihant sent her message in a letter
Along with little Poorvi join him in Oman for better
U-turns complete on his commitment, his honor now in tatter

An elder bro in age but an attitude of an underage
Moral never learned from mistakes past simply not on the same page
Cardinal not small mistakes but he never ever reflected to gauge

Backtracking on his word now seasoned second nature
Extremely upset I was, dealt unilaterally by his legislature

Stood by him always morally, emotionally and financially
In arrogance then dump and ignore you his need done fully

In a week after all travel documents Rakshee received
Clueless she was as usual in course of action and aggrieved

Through message in mom, she asked me for help in needful
Chivalrous I was not this time but counseled in her being purposeful

She was right non-interfering I will be for then their lives be hopeful
Time for her initiative for future life would be a lot more insightful

Carped to bro she on my attitude being extremely distasteful
Event in couple he raked as an issue, humble pie in taste for him awful

Pantone in 2 years he spent, call none in courteous to inquire
True to his words his family first and the rest may burn in a fire

An incident in early years little Poorvi to turn 2
Dad in fondness arrived from Bangalore true

Brought with him many goody bags for little one
To surprise her, grandad waited till early next morn

It was we both who really were the surprised one
For those two with their little had us both shunned

Informed bro in prior, dad's presence on Poorvi's Birthday
Yet he felt it unholy to inform us their plan for her day

On inquiry why? He replied, do I really have to say?
That's my bro Arihant for all our grace in return he does pay

114. Mother's Woeful Tales in my Absence

Shabby conduct meted out by bro an elder he was
Our pact good as toilet paper his belief only in his cause
Expect me to close in ranks in his need without pause

Interaction thereafter if any in thrifty
Real live talk if at all measured almost in pity

Mom choked with huge pent-up emotion
In my absence spewed his sense of devotion

Barely visited mother in her illness his desertion
Callous in attitude her favorite son's dedication
An advice on passing, visit a doctor for medication
Rakshee visits to mother late every night
The same tale played on for mom now in frostbite

Abhikya center of attention root of all problems
Common for Arihant and Abha too they ran it to bottom
Grudge against little kid, not in any small quantum

He oblivious to this very caustic envy
Aunt and uncle unusual in their frenzy

Chuckle every time I heard this line
Question their silly intention in mind

Mom's closeness towards Abhikya
Why do always to ground this silly act they grind?

But mom's next disclosure had me seething
A term used for Abhikya in contempt reeking

Mother too stunned in shock to react
It was uncalled for a vitriolic vile attack

Failed to understand her disdainful dislike
Gross cruel and inhumane way to act

Herself a mother of a small girl child
Like any he a normal naughty child

More in envy for him a blessed child
Comparing him to your little child
Herself gregarious and happy child

Incident to me disturbing no end
A hateful act of lady bent in her mind

A foul word so nasty used in obnoxious bind
Defiled child's identity of our own bloodline

Just like that a testimony in gross dislike
Mother herself felt bitter in her blind strike

In perspective her maligning act I condoned
Letter to her father in strong words adorned

Queried in the same context to his daughter in an address
Vile word unflattering wouldn't he as father distress?

The letter reached the shores of Oman in the final destination
Arihant called me from Oman in 6 months his first in hesitation

6 months since I left Oman his first and last call

I let it rip not holding back years of abuse like a ball

Many times, over years twisted contents to suit their defense
Against me both alleged derogatory word in their offense

From this action two positives did work
Bro settled sister's debts after 6 years in shirk

Returned my money he owed too in full
But not a word in ask how in life I am able to pull

115. Marriage Proposal

Diploma in Business Management Qualification in rope
Decent job in prospect in Mumbai a measure of hope

Mother broached topic of marriage for me to settle down
Time though running out was not yet ready to wear the crown

Yet to settle down in a stable job for a career in the long-term
6 years now surviving on short stretch yet to stand firm

Mother changed tact get engaged first she said
A year in the job to settle down then tie the thread

Rational thought but alliance in arranged she sought
Against such tradition her reasoning in reluctance I brought

Her younger sister and brother in law lived in Bangalore
Arrangement she made for alliances meet on common floor

Mom in brief to my aunt informed my aversion to tradition
Discreet in their measure in how they present this fusion

Uncle typical male chauvinist huge in bloated ego
Matched his pot belly that looked perfect like a filled burrito

Counseling he on traditions and culture many in alliances
Girls in numbers like appliances selection based on finances

Uncle, Aunt and Mom all 3 in hard sell of arranged conception
Tossing me a line in bait unwilling to take realized it a deception

Though an inkling already never in this shoe before

Now neck deep in water how do I get safely ashore?

10am next day contingent comprising all of 5
With nephew in tow went to see prospective brides

The first halt in a decent little villa welcomed in warmly
Girl's parents courteously greeted us all very fondly

Family well to do strappings of modern home
An uncomfortable feel of predicament in my bone

Motivational therapy from Uncle now loud
A boy's in right to demand and feel proud
Material things all in wealth under the cloud

TV, Video and car is only a start
Big Plot of land we will together chart

No worry if in this girl you don't see your half
Many more in waiting for your stylish autograph

I felt like one commodity in the mobile store
In an auction to the highest bidder offering more

Girl an item presented as exhibit prize
Tradition and culture, I so utterly despise

In modern times until this day
This charade continues to play

Where the girl has entirely no say
And the boy can demand his pay

Can imagine roles reversal in play
Surely that will be the day

Every girl will have her say

The moment arrived as curtain of drama slid open
The girl emerged carrying in hand a tray of water in token

The drama unfolded, her edgy elan noticeable and obvious
Water glass on me splayed she was so damn nervous

Melodramatic uncle let out a cry so horrendous
Waved my hand firmly signifying he was opprobrious

For her, it was awkward at that moment
Retreated to remerge a bit more confident

The moment she withdrew to her room in seclusion
Uncle blunt on my face asked for my decision

Thoughtless insensitive he was for his stature
Father of a young girl he in action too immature

Mother instantly realized his blunder
Covered up only to worsen his lines of wonder
Said Uncle asked if you really liked this number

Eye to eye with mother in a very disgusting look
Calmly told her time and place to discuss any book

Heightened drama further as the girl again in catwalk special
Summoned by my uncle in loud he incarnates devil superficial

Ill-fated, humiliating for any girl go through such dreadful motions
Swore never again I to put anymore girls in the ordeal of traditions

Uncle every trick in the book in convincing me to say aye
The lure of house, money, jewelry and land just to get me high

Add more in demand as wish it shall be granted in thy
Like bonds in markets an agent setting my price till the sky

Suitable boy for purchase but bride like onions to sauté' and fry
I didn't see myself in this light politely a firm nay I said in wry

Significant it was the girl a PG in science certainly brilliant
Triumph in years of conscientious hard work being resilient

Due diligence checks on me or my family none
Uncle's word for it for them in conclusion done

Worthy credentials to speak on my CV zero
Just my persona and swagger I was a hero

In the current, I did not have a job to sing for
Future based on my past nothing to cling for

Comparative form for a girl all windows ticked in
In all fairness for me, all windows crossed out

Charades of humiliation in the grind for girls a routine affair
Medieval society tradition in bind spineless and bare
Voices in protest still muted of patriarchal hierarchy in scare

A trio of elders disappointed in my attitude complete
Goody bags in refusal a decision mom in a direct tweet

Girl in kind never to find for all privileges willing to meet
An unexpected statement from her left me red in utter disbelief

Own daughters in nuptial had nothing even in small for a treat
Let us be happy girl's family considered me worthy to greet
But she deserves better and I am certainly no cheat

Mother unhappy at the sudden turn of events
For her this now a big deal in dollar cents

Her way of getting back at Rakshee
Bringing home in plenty a fat queen bee
And yours truly to be her pig guinea

Sons in India mothers mostly don't let go
Possessiveness in bane for marriages to blow

Mother apparently seemed from that day on
On marriage subject with me never squared on

116. Daimex A Huge Export Opportunity

I began to gather threads of hope
To stitch them into a strong rope

As a partner, in Saina Styles plan B in parallel drafted alone
An export firm in proprietary I did set up my own

Snail mailers I sent to Europe and US to many potential buyers
In hundreds, I sent paid off it did, 2 years in time since in expire

Saturday noon at home I was when our phone rang
Kamlesh at the grocery store a fax for you in a roll he sang

A small business center with fax machines he ran
Adrenalin pumping hurried to his store fast as I can

Danish Company Daimex for me sent an inquiry in business
To Aarvan Exports my firm volumes for range all in bigness

Rummaging slowly through each fax sheet
Dawned on me inquiry very huge to meet
Life changing opportunity I only eager to greet

Scarves, Sarong and Stoles all in lady's accessory
Quantity in multiples of 20K each enough in a call for revelry

Sample called in for the specification of material and size
Silk in cloth to be machined and hand embroidered in precise
45x45cms, 64x64cms and 0.1x0.1m all cut to cut in size

Each in 6 design rough sides finishes in beading
Instruction simply clear assigned in each heading

A new company in test mine chosen in good fortune
Prospect handsome, strategy now in planned caution

Experience, resource or infrastructure I had none
Challenge embraced in confidence huge in proportion

An ace in back up support I had or so I thought
Veteran seamstress in skill 40 years tightly in a knot

Quality control chief in an export firm 20 years before
My mother a mentor for production for her this a routine chore

But count I did not on mom's attitude in salinity
A failed attempt in locking my marriage alliance in a holy trinity

No inkling of vicious backlash she would at me throw
Same afternoon called her for talks bursting with gusto

Develop a plan of action, a timeline for accessory sampling
Listened in focus first only to set off a storm in trampling

Budget! Who will provide funds? Asked she in rancor
In the look of perplexity reason for her angst in her manner
Funds there is none to spare you in the bank I shall not tamper

16 months in Oman every cent to her I saved
300K in excess savings in her name I spared
By now in interest alone appreciated in 30K raised

A mere 1% in 3K from it in asks to be shaved
Deal finitely small in risk for profits to be blazed

In my eye, she did not really bother much to care a look
Drawing money from saving even in mind does not brook

In a split I from Himalayan heights
Plummeted in a crash to dark depths

Feebly her help sought on sampling process in a plea
Cut my words incomplete she has pain in her knee

Like a fly, common swatted in discard me as a pest
Visions of business success now in part under arrest

Hopes dashed in flash by my dear own mother
No to alliance heavy in price my dreams just smothered

Took a while to gather myself decided I had to go alone
Now issues plenty for me to handle without time to postpone

Outsourcing vendors reliable biggest challenge in the project
Duleep my old friend in garments I thought he just perfect

Vendors for hand embroidery artisans in a couple to check
Beading vendor's couple in the area in a network I did connect

2K from little savings left in my account in the bank
Purchased silk material in 4 different hues by rank

Next to an acquaintance who owned a cycle shop
Dustom a kind man, name in a couple he did pop

Spot on embroidery artisans he then referred me
Experts crafting the finest works in swanky shops to see

Adorning mannequins of finest designer boutiques
Dress up in their couture the rich, famous and elite

Designer wear would be sold in price so handsome
But for their skill artisans paid in pittance from ransom

Rustom welcomed me in his dusty dinghy home workshop
Over a cup of tea finalized designs on sarong, stoles and scarf

Unwilling to charge me a dime in his opinion it was fine
Job work too small in volume for any value in his time

Appreciated his magnanimity but politely refused in kind
Effort and time same in crafting a single design to wind

Fixed on conciliation my dilemma in principle he guessed
Charge me by an hour completed all 6 in his skill he blessed

A small token of 3 hundred rupees for regal in workmanship
Grateful in appreciation, he was equal in sportsmanship

Final call machine embroidery proceeded to Duleep's referral
Person named Vijay but on meeting felt I should be in deferral

Much delay already in making the call I had no time forsaking
Machine embroidery with pruning a completion by beading

Eagerly for finish samples now I look forward to receiving
Baited breath in hope much needed a break in life now in coming

My heart sank in total at samples in hand when I looked
Machine embroidery in ruinous work completely badly cooked

Beading of edges shoddy and ragged like a tattered book
The royal workmanship of Rustom a tragedy he completely crooked
And the princely sum of 2K in a premium he actually overbooked

With time running out fast on sample deliverance

Only one choice left, send it in hope of divine reverence
Jobwise I had failed on all boxes in adherence

Expectedly samples were totally rejected
In finishing Daimex was absolutely dejected

One player could have made a difference
Mother a catalyst for success in my endurance?

But not meant to be more on way in a test of patience
Employment now only a resort for my sustenance!

NEW PHASE IN LIFE

117. Rebecca (Becky)

And time finally had arrived, an event in sensing
There she was a person in joyous blessing

Her smile beautiful and wonderfully influencing
Defining and very, very galvanizing
Contended and happy in her job no tensing

Laughter childlike so rapturously pure
She's my lady in simplicity so demure

Mellifluous voice and invite attention to allure
In quiet admiration eyes, all round galore
Bundle of innocence she a heavenly cure

When we first met like an engine jet
Our hearts did not whirr or fret

In chemistry, an ionic bond over time our souls met
The Lion and Ram, each other had in net
A friend for life cemented and forever set

Not love at first sight but slowly on me
She grew, roots embedded in me in all might
Not seeing her a day uneasy I was in strife
She's my light shining bright, a companion to seek as a wife
Her being lingers in lushness a sweet rose-like fragrance for life

Despite nails and daggers in words harsh from people my own
Behind my back at you violently sometimes subtly thrown

In their suspicion and fear of their inheritance, you will usurp

Their ire at you without reason always full-blown

With dignity and self-respect in silence and hidden tears
You spoke and all of them were simply outshone

Grateful eternally for faith in me you always have shown
My love and trust in you in infinite fold its roots strongly have grown
My companion soulmate in you into heavenly paradise I have flown

118. Expo Bharat - Mumbai

It was the time in the monsoon of 1995
As deputy project manager a job finally again got me to fly
Expo-Bharat a part of Vasu Vakharia Group gave me a try

Background of mine in construction products was a huge cry
Exhibition division to shore construction industry still shy
Aptly titled "Bharat Build" it was an invite for clients to go by

Reporting to Managing Director me in lead for business vantage
Brij Sohan in Expo-Bharat a smart and savvy MD to overall manage
Though perpetually tardy even stitch on time useless an adage

Huge force to reckon with carried plenty a company's baggage
Kept even the dynamic Vasubhai too waiting in his carriage
Years of loyalty to Vasubhai in shoulder was his eternal salvage

119. Meeting Rebecca (Becky)

Among many group companies in collaboration in class
An American Multinational Dyna Mount in a field of Oil and Gas

Stepped into office first day greeted in melodious voice by a lass
Beaming smile, bubbly, exuberant was all tacks and brass

Ably manning reception in many calls cheerful, none at all in sass
Her laughter contagious as was her smile you just couldn't pass
Rebecca a lady blessed in nature as clean as sheer float glass

In an instant, we both just hit it off

In my mind take stock of my work to get quickly organized
Got busy by the day as workload grew professionally and tied

Our fondness for each other grew as time moved on a steady ride
Rebecca would play little pranks on me like seek and hide
An otherwise day at work a dull and drab she would light up wide

Our mutual fondness for each other had office tongues wagging
Something definite brewing between us two so went the saying

We both brushed it off not each other's type even in praying
Rebecca simple and humble me a flamboyant guy in showing

Rebecca the person innocence exemplary personified
In blind belief accept a story as true spun in the yarn so glorified

Hilarity all around in expense she would as a good sport be dignified
At the same time an innate quality in reading people she well classified

Yet always tried her best in projecting their good side
Her senses of humor ready wit have me in splits wide

In disagreement, no conflict over rival or be sore with a grudge
Not the kind to even throw a battery of caustic verbal sludge

An opinion, of course, she had in that there would be no budge
Respect to your opinion and in reciprocal expect you not to judge
Put issue behind her and move on like having a sweet strawberry fudge

120. Falling in Love

Winds of change began to blow my way
Time in travels took me to distant places far away

Bangalore, Chennai, Ahmedabad, Delhi and back in Bombay
Time spent in travel, meetings would be a long winding day.

A tiring mind of mine refresh on constant attentions of Rebecca
Missed her, in my every thought she was very sweet angelica

Realization on me dawned she my companion lifelong
Person to share with time, growing old together steadily along

I had well and truly fallen in love with her so very headstrong
As so often is the case always twist of fate
Each belonged to two different states

Catholic she was Roman and I from Hindu faith
Our families did not want to look beyond their comfort in our space

A mindset of both families obdurate in rigidity
Non-believer I in religion any but only in life and mortality

Religion always an invisible wall for every human in adversity
Only divide along its contradictory fundamentals, the entire humanity

My heart and mind in clear sync Becky my soul mate in best
A long journey in existence make it together in our own nest

121. 1996 New Year's Bash

1995 New Year's Eve at an event at Parsi Gym for posterity
At dawn, I was to propose the 1st day of New Year in all sincerity

The evening passed beautifully with equals in fusion frenzy dance
Sparkling wine flavor for young and old in the waltz of romance

After dawn on the first train back home as we traveled
To surf and sand on the beach I asked, would Becky like to unravel?

In affirmative she nodded to the beach we then headed
Old-fashioned horse carriage ride in the countryside it blended

Picture perfect romantic setting and I popped the question
Spend rest of my life growing old loving you avowal in fashion

How sweet, a girl of dreams you finally met she asked?
Tell me the lucky name of the one you would like to bask

It's you I love Becky! I said, marry me please without any hesitation
Look writ large on her face she was quizzical in expression

And she asked in all goodness when did this happen?
Your magic grew on me unrealized in a natural progression
In silence, we looked at each other and smiled
Challenges many in our minds already filed

Our families, frailties in thought, in objections fragile
2 cultures in unholy alliance an act elders will consider wild

Gently in persuasion gather thoughts and clear all doubts
Only when sure give me an answer if ready for a long bout

Rest assured burden of duty on my shoulder I shall lead the rout

Morning @ 1030hours rewinding my mind in her thought
Becky reciprocated in yes to my ecstatic joy, now for next shot

Our families together in confidence had to be brought
This a mean task to be accomplished without getting caught

2 adults discreet in courtship a must choose wisely every spot
More out of concern for Becky in fear of brothers tying her knot
Or squeal to her mother to bring everything simply to naught

And so, began our courtship in days only grew stronger
Before and after office hours and on phone talks were longer

122. Breaking News to My Mother

Our conversation on our families to convince them a huge formality
But inform them was a must marriage now a big responsibility
A small part of me felt mother come around her religious bias
Sadly, wrong I was in my rational the alliance for her an abject virus

In a huge fit of fury pin pricking insults, she randomly threw
Unleashed wrath in fiery words she not my mother I knew

Like one possessed, expressed herself with demonic vigor
Unbridled in her venomous content her sting in hostile rigor

She linked Power of Attorney of her flat to Becky in worse
A thought my ladylove colluded, towards Becky she now averse

Unworthy son you are, your dismal life you to live in a curse
Perished you should have in my womb she said in manic terse

In shame your life to lead for all society to mock
Histrionics nonstop every night now in her unbridled stock

Upheaval mental, emotional destruction in me left its trail
Impacts followed next day cruelly jolting Becky in its scale

Mother called Becky next morning on the office board line
Blasted her with violent invectives desecrating her bloodline

Never in her life had anyone vandalized her space so cruelly
Unmitigated volley effusive in verbal diarrhea hatefully

Unprovoked, uncalled assault profuse on her so personal
Becky ached in migraine instant so severe mom's strike was surgical

Apparently, tirade lasting for minutes in a couple
In parting told her to leave me quick on the double

Becky was given no semblance of a chance to speak
Even if she had to she was too numb to squeak

Sobbing Becky called me in breaking news
Horrified at mom's irrational blowing her fuse

An extremist reaction she was so skewed in her thinking
Sequel to Abishta's experience 15 years ago gross in humiliating
Ranga and Lata protagonist in main were actually Siva's siblings

Mother met fiery Thangarajan in a humble gesture to relent
Accept her daughter for his boy in an alliance without a dent

And today a fiery Thangarajan of herself she was a superstar
Déjà vu! More caustic and nasty a sequel script fierce in her avatar

Not for one instance, she brooked a second thought
Once she a daughter was given into marriage in a knot

Man, not of her choice though both from the same lot
Then as a mother she fought for daughter in thought

Though the boy was not in any way from the same lot
In society norms he in fact from a superior pack of pot
Association under any circumstances never comes to naught

Finally, she a woman, daughter, sister and mother
Who better recognize the want of woman in other?

The woman dared to love her son though in the lot she from another
And unwisely chose to classify and disgrace her intent to smother

Rushed then I urgently to Becky's office to console
Experienced nothing like this before she in a dark hole

Could well imagine her thoughts
Mind in full confusion and doubts

Told me with no malice to forget her timidly
Moving on best for all she in distress bitterly

In life nothing comes easy for me I said jovially
Fight this together in time we will laugh vividly

The literate society we live in it is but a huge complete sham
Dogmatic diktat so conditioned their corrupt mind to wham

Together fighting these despots, we are strong
In time we shall certainly prove them all wrong

The problem was despots were from our own families to fan
Fighting I was on both fronts similar in personalities to damn

A long haul it was going to be with a huge price to pay
Willing to transgress paths our fickle society spiked to sway

123. Flashback on Power of Attorney

Minor issue in mom's apartment building
As a rep for mom attended annual society meeting

A selective coterie of 5 in admin affairs misconstruing
Funds in contribution members were quietly pillaging

On bringing to notice in presence of all
Embarrassment for them to avoid at all

Conflict of interest now they asked for a legal notary
To avoid mortification, produce a power of attorney

Appraised mom on the irrelevance of my presence
The rulebook was thrown on me to prove my significance

Asked her to provide me the power of attorney
To my disbelief, she reacted negative and smarmy

Instantly invasive her tirade alleging my dishonorable intentions
My nefarious effort in usurping her flat POA in discreet coercion

Asserting in her rage my intention in true to sell the apartment
Embezzle funds and put her out on streets was my real intent

Matter in entirety assumed a ridiculously tangential proportion
My earnings, after all, I bought in her name a house in devotion

Of course, I was the sole nominee on society document in registration
Strike me out at any time she wished entirely on her discretion

Eventually, she made it true for going against her in rebellion

In this context, she conveniently linked Becky in an unwise assumption

Hullabaloo unfolding at home I in complete discomfort
Siblings none even made a call-in token as any good sport

3 older siblings did not dare oppose me directly
Times many each one I helped socially, morally and monetarily
Help, I did never in expectation but with love unconditionally

124. Becky's Family

Similar in Rebecca's case too family entirely in opposition
An unholy alliance of different faiths mainly in deposition

Breakthrough of sorts in some good tidings to say the least
A formal request to mother in respect called for a small treat

Scribbled on plain paper plea sincere for Becky's hand in grace
Human messenger in transit with a letter for her mother's praise

Becky's mother in a foreign land on a work assignment
Common family friend en route to deliver the letter in consignment

My miseries rising by the day in meanwhile
Mother's tantrums melodrama at home getting hostile

Abhikya was now 11 years in a couple he in teens
Spoilt crazy by his grandma he was still but green

Mom now playing blame game card her act full in guile
Abhikya in my influence will turn corrupt in mind to act in my style

Her comments harshly acerbic intention to hurt in core
Hated going home from work I was sore from every pore

Family elders, siblings, prospect in controlling your life; why?
Exhort you for worldly virtues themselves have been so sly
Threat emotional marketed in family grid raising stress very high
Wisdom lost, your life scripted, now alone in despair only to sigh

A hypocritical system built on a guise of tradition very immoral
No business to dictate right over other life so delicate as coral

Reason for your life on earth an entity each we are by birth
Right to live on our terms no harm but a relief to mother earth

Put religion tradition out of equation harmony of new order
Stronger, healthier gene pool without inhibitions and border

125. Mother's Change of Tact

Battle had just begun firmly I stood my ground
A new day, time for another silly acrimonious round

Mom and Abhikya on holiday trip to Oman in annual
April to June schools shut for summertime carnival

Mother and Abishta relations by then normal
A couple of years in ice then it thawed in thermal

Now softened in truce the symbiotic two now formal
Both in need of each other obvious, it was just floral

Personality touch both at best very, very casual
Next in daggers drawn they are seriously infernal

Timeline Jan to April 1996 both our homes in a virtual mayhem
Intensity far more forceful in mom's onslaught in my condemn

Becky my choice in life partner mother conditioned 2 in tact
Leave the house and be my own way just as a matter of fact

The wedding she not a part of, neither she would attend
Ousted from home fine but dismayed in 2nd I cannot pretend

Best you leave the house before I return back her final say
Well not for the first time did she in this way make my day

Ironically now dumped from my own house technically not mine
All in power she had wielded to break Becky and my spine
Only fortified my resolve to fight to grind every hateful design

126. Buying a New House

Taking stock of condition in reviewing my options
With Becky had a talk on same of the grim situation

A house of own an immediate need
A priority now first before we get married

Pull out all stops to check best available
The issue in main within budget reasonable

Just 8 months into a new job
Savings comparatively a blob

Spent in a couple of hundred thousand in recent
Renovating mother's house money in every cent

Checked balance in the account and found
4 short of hundred thousand in round

Far too little even for payment down
A million for 1 bed flat in our side of town

Pragmatic to seek an abode in Mumbai outskirts
Place where Becky stayed my attention to divert

Two most critical missions in a plan to weave
60 days in perspective for them to achieve

A part in saving with mother locked in
Futile in asking she refuse to give in

Funds in loan an option to make do
House within the budget main key issue

127. Office Politics

During same days in Expo India a small storm in a brew
Interim General Manager Marketing among the senior crew

P. R. Naresh complete textbook character a nerdy shrew
No background in marketing only operational he knew

Import manager he from Dyna mount had absolutely no clue
Played politics to fore, the hierarchy in time decision to rue

Lewis Romello a hired head given the same position now we were 2
Logical in reason as industry-wide in the category to cover not few
Product, services and trade segment industry many in the queue

Instant block I felt P.R. Naresh put on our very first meeting
An initiative I took on his arrival self-introduction in greeting

P.R., as he was called bespectacled, looked studious in fleeting
Uptight in all, even an ad grammatically corrects in reading

Contrary to my thinking ad to be in words customer appealing
Acumen short in marketing to prove, him not worthy in managing

Coin a new slogan focusing on Strong Bharat in theme
Strong Bharat the New Paradigm! I felt had plenty in steam

Unbelievably he said next, paradigm too sophisticated in sheen
The industry still immature to grasp my slogan in a marketing scheme

Reply so ludicrous provoking in the thought of intellects to demean
Basically, he only indirectly rebuffing my work, how he was unclean

Many an occasion I was met with his snub
But getting paid in his own coin from an elite club

Senior Vice President of German Multinational on my request
Granted me audience on a condition in time 5 minutes at best
The meeting lasted an hour and as they say history in rest

P.R. sought through a colleague's father for a meeting in influence
An arrangement with the same person for a prospect in a confluence

SVP candidly told P.R., Aarvan he met already in a conference
Of course, he was taken aback by his rebuff and indifference

Statement P.R. in a gesture to me said did not mean any offense
Quality in me of a statesman in personality, he in surprise acceptance

Yet in another instance in meeting our chairman Vasubhai
Attended always as duo, P.R. and Lewis in an act as an ally
Ensured I was left out in the shared information they 2 were quietly sly

Camaraderie as partners beyond office hours a stage
Lewis Romello's lucid words said he making sure he was on P.R's page
In time Lewis Romello was made CEO of the magazine on space age
Another storm in a teacup for me to ingest
Too much already on my plate to digest

Accepted an offer from export trading firm Rustom Engineering
Owner Rusi Sethna a dynamic man and wonderful human being

128. Another Turn of Events for Arihant

2 years of progress in the winter of December 1995
Change of guard at the helm of affairs at Pantone to drive

An Indian production head now in position haloed high
Charismatic Bjorne Anters task in new markets to fly

Viju Kair intended to mesh with his people who snitch
A simple principle of divide and rule his policy in a switch

Create a trend in nepotism by fear and pressure his pitch
Breaking news up to the minute he asked Arihant to stitch

Lacked diplomatic tact in handling a controversial situation
Indeed, aggravating it was filled with tricky complication

Expert, I was not but if only played along minus divulging in caution
In guile, he could have been part of a future squadron in formation

Job hunted for an alternative with experience on hand
Now well known in a market he could've landed in any band

Always warmly appreciated for his consistent work by Bjorn
Confidence in good work sometimes in politics a vicious thorn

You don't fall in line you fall out of favor and completely torn
Favorites no matter how good you are the first one to be thrown

Arihant in refusing point blank made a single cardinal mistake
Justifying his stand further he morally questioned Kair's stake

No reason to ask Arihant to leave on principle of work ethics
Discipline and business targets, he was extremely athletic

But sack he wanted at any cost for his refusal in being his medic
Ploy on sly he re-invented his nemesis of MSO as his prosthetic

MSO immigration block on him since 2years now redundant
Kair called him in sullen to his cabin on reissue of judgement

Drama enacted surely Arihant not refer to authority incumbent
But he did only to be informed of dirty joke played in fraudulent

In a confrontation, Kair caught off guard now in his form was very bad
Off the cuff, for insubordination, Arihant was fired and he was glad
Order implemented in immediate effect said Kair was a mad cad

Shocked in disbelief Arihant in his mind went impromptu numb
What now? Kair's vindictively gone crazy in extreme and dumb

What does the future hold for him, his family? Oh, this dirty scum
How will he tell his wife? Poorvi's 2 terms in school looked glum

Egotistical senile leader wanting his ego to be sucked
Used his personal fiefdom to subjugate and to get others bucked
3 lives in one stroke into an oblivion of wilderness he chucked

Arihant tried his efforts to reach company chairman
Response none in despondence knew he was canned

Managed in saving his daughter precious year in academics
Allowed 6-month term in grace to earn her final credits

An impulsive act in flashback with MSO had he still stayed
Silver Jubilee completion his accomplishment till date

129. Rebecca's Mother Coming Home

Becky's mother comes back home in plot another twist
For good in May of 1996, this definite destiny in a tryst

Sadly, the news was not good already many crises in the midst
Melanoma of uterus detected all her kids down in a teary mist

Actions in urgency to be taken in fear of impending adversity
Recalled Uncle Gulwady his contacts in the medical fraternity
Called to request him for help in a humble plea of humanity

Immediate swung in action contact of oncologist of repute
Through reference, he provided assured of success in fruit

In a reputed South Mumbai hospital we visited the respected surgeon
For detailed clinical diagnosis and tests, she was finally taken

Advised immediate surgery and it was a successful operation
Followed up in routine checkup with few chemotherapy session

Declared completely cancer free amidst relief in jubilation
22 years on annually for Christmas we all gather in celebration

130. Housing Loan

Challenges still in plenty remained, housing in utmost
An apartment we quite liked price value high in cost

3 continuous weekends covered entire city of Mira Road
Time fast running out settled for decent 1bhk in future our abode

Lone building ready for occupation in 2 months it showed
The best option to close, for in mind I carried an immense load
Work, Loan, House, Marriage and more in gravity had me slowed
Friends remotely known but one of them Julie, Becky's best
Ready in help monetarily to my surprise without terms addressed

Train friends they were, for many 2-month salaries in equal
Did not even bother in a time frame for money back in retrieval

Becky's mother and my dad too pooled in separately in dual
Employer Rusi Sethna also added to a much-needed fuel

Old childhood mate Manish Mehra also contributed to the pool
Ironically one big-hearted noble Punjabi he from a different school
Bit by Bit in cash factor my kitty now was in cash amount full

Housing Loan from Bank approved for me in life first
20 years repayment in EMI I swore will be my last

Monies received with last of my saving added to final contributions
Paid up cash factor full to the builder for agreement and registration

Debts to my well-wishers over time paid back first in priority
Ever so grateful they were my saviors in extreme conditionality

131. Arihant's Permanent Return to India

Arihant back in Bombay, Poorvi's academic term completed
In May 1996 few days in prior before mom's return, I exited

A sullen look of exhaustion stress on his face telling a tale
Just a year ago on leave, spring on his feet, he couldn't fail

Radiantly beaming in confidence full of only him and his family
Even boasted of settling down in Europe in time said he calmly

My state of mind if I was fine asked not even in a mere formality
Becky, just drop her said he, in depraved emotion of absurdity

In reasoning he so senselessly, hopelessly completely bizarre
In duty, he married in mother's choice in her eyes he a rock star

Wry in my address, crisp in my word I am not you, you not me
Right to life in choices just mine not open to diktat for free
Live always on my terms harbor any force in peril to disagree

Sibling all 3 elder to me but none ever in any manner did support
Emotional Moral, Financial always was me at your side in comfort

Work in full accomplished in a selfish manner you'll then just rebuff
Cycle regular all over again when going for you all get very tough

Inquired what his plans in routine were for now in long-term
The standard answer in a record "we'll see" never had anything firm
Looked disinterested anyway quietly retiring for the night in turn

Rakshee spoke long that night on their journey and ordeal
How Arihant's equals cheated on him for his fate rudely sealed

Touched upon mother bonding with them in Oman gently
Equal share theirs in mother's house she declared very intently

Few moments in current a tale of many duplicity was in analytical
Talk about duality in character what could be more palpable
Husband, wife their own deeds in history themselves were culpable

132. Biz Tour of Sri Lanka

Mom and Abhikya expected on 2nd of June
On May 31st bags packed I left home by noon
Home just mine to say I felt like a big buffoon

To Sri Lanka, Rusi and I left in immediate next day
15-day business tour on my initiative in the expectation it pays
Relaxed I felt in long time clutter to clear my mind to say

In Colombo pleasing person in Suresh, I met on the first day
Ranjan an ex-equal from Al Fahteh, Oman his link in a way
Brother in law in relation humble and terrific guys every way

Returning back to Mumbai, no idea for me what's in store?
Lulled my troubled mind with thoughts of Becky in my core

Went straight to Becky's house collected my new house keys
It was already late evening riding in tuk-tuk I was all at sea

Force of lashing rains against windows sounded very eerie
Howling winds added to the choir in background music in melee
Just crashed in deep slumber alone in my own new abbey

Housewarming celebration an event had with just Becky and Me
A festivity of hope united we will one day be in holy matrimony

133. Judgement Day for Dad in 3 Decades

During all these years only, person dad in connect was me
In my care plus his pension fare he was just carefree

Months on end he in Bangalore a bachelor life he to revel
Pragmatic reasoning, friendly persuasion would be of no avail

Free bird from Bangalore to Mumbai he was juggling his time
Living life king size his way without a care for him was just fine

Around the same time, he landed in Mumbai for his court hearing
3 decades and now in the tribunal for all it was too much in bearing

Many ex-colleagues, management guys had all but passed away
For this tenacious little man going to court just a business day

Fighting Rashtriya Vayuviman in its defense flush with funds
Country's tax payer's money after all in kitty had in abundance

Every hearing hired paid in hefty fee, in panel country's best lawyer
Belittle hardworking employee in ordinary, they played dirty destroyer

May of 1996 a 2-bench judge passed an order of compensation
A paltry sum of One Hundred Thousand Rupees in duty to the nation

Payment from taxpayer money a huge crime in making
Denial by the management of employee right three decades in faking

Justice being denied to hide the managements own shortcoming
Case closure option in verdict a token of 100,000 rupees taking

Rashtriya Vayuviman in budget spend in same for one hearing
Dad's fight in 3 decades in prize value just so awfully tearing

Top echelons in politics and power hierarchy unmoved in bearing
No wonder P/L of public firms always in bold red in showing

Appeal for more in benefit to Supreme Court of land an option
Another decade in a journey to forsake only add to more frustration

Dad in glance an eye towards me for any advice in a suggestion
First time in any court for me I blinked my eyes in affirmation

Take it dad let us move on issue lingered on far too long
Took away everything from us peace of mind in main along

Judges in empathy prodded my father aware far too little to go
Mr. Rayudu verdict in your favor compensation nothing to show

No reward can reverse 30 years balanced on hope and despair flow
Moral win over rival in size to outlive your tenacity deliberately slow

Dad in his gesture of gratitude folded his hands and took a bow!

Paid his friends for money he owed them over time
Generously he loaned me ten for my apartment
Rest I guess he just went and had a great time.

134. Mother Calling Back Home

A couple of months later a call from mother at my new office
Abhikya in limelight, an issue in school played a prank of a novice

Locked a girl out in a classroom for his errant now he to pay a price
Mom asked me to meet his teacher and to gently break the ice

In more than 3 months since now, we were actually not in sight
A rap on knuckle in expectation he greeted me more out of fright

Mother doted on her grandson with her he had wide latitude
The only reason to send me to instill fear in him to change his attitude

Love in her for him blind, many offences of his not capital in nature
Growing years in need of being tempered or definite his fall in stature

Taking things for granted eventually will lead him to be immature
Just to tackle him in tricky situation shrewdly used me as a baiter

Mother asked me if I could come back home
Felt insecure with a boy growing up he trouble prone

Finding it difficult to manage Abhikya alone
Difficult decision for me just settling in my new zone

Concurred with Becky on this issue a big thorny bone
Temporary truce it was an agreement in silence known
Neither spoke about Becky, glass so clear why throw a stone

In my heart, I knew to stay in India our bond remains on the equator
The pressure of both family's huge stress on rapport of our barometer

Demand from my mother 60% of my salary to her I contribute
Insurance for her in any event but in a way against me in retribute

40% left to fend for me managing loan and self-expenses difficult
Resources thin made me reflect in next league I should self-catapult

135. Finding New Pastures

Firmly in the belief, I talked with Becky in job prospecting abroad
Averse initially, her mother still recovering I had to gently prod

Reasoned in rationality she came around to think plan not all flawed
Irony she the first one to be offered a job abroad and sign the accord

The only time to tell decision in consensus will be in rue or reward
Families ours thought we'd break but we both were bent on record

A dream sequence in the tale we both shared
Fusion of cultures at the wedding we dared

Hindu by day and Christian by evening
A celebration of a kind I always did imagine

Nagaswaram, Mridangam and Ghatam played in abandon
A south Indian ritual of nuptials soothing at first dawn
Typically, meals on banana leaf served in decorated tents on the lawn

Afternoon nuptial ritual at the altar in the church congregation
An evening reception in the hall for Bridal Couple in celebration

But then at least I dared to dream of the kind of carnival
Making it happen in reality looked very, very marginal

Both families opposed the other kind ridiculously as terminal
Reason in futility stupid it was against holy tenets in principle

136. Rebecca's Tryst with Dubai

Luck did smile on us finally
The break came in rather strangely
Becky got first opening incidentally

An acquaintance in known to Becky
Referral for a job in Dubai was so lucky

Interviews in nearby hotel 5 star
The call came in 10 minutes from a place not far

Interview at 5pm candidate she kept for last
Sharing the news asked me to make her CV fast

Nothing to lose made her way for an interview
30 minutes later called to give me the good news

In Dubai upcoming hospital facility UR Healthcare
Decent package to start good perks including in decent fare

As usual in the evening at the same restaurant, we met
Over hot tea and samosas talked priorities to set

Defining for us both that moment in time we felt
Becky looked lost, leap too big, good job though in net

In a big bad world, her first time alone she to set
Dubai distant land new people new job a big bet

Comfort in a secure environment of Dyna mount loyalty
10 years of career she rose to be Vasubhai's secretary

Like his own nurtured her a confident lady in her own right
Colleagues all-around adored and protected her alright

Leaving her family behind was tearing her inside
Her mother she felt recovering needed her more besides

137. Leaving the Nest

Contract signed Becky on September 1ˢᵗ, 1997
From Dyna mount, she resigned 10 years in time she had given

30-day notice flew so fast and how
In few, days we to distance apart for now

Dinner in quiet we had at a restaurant in silence sublime
Many things to say many miles to go our union in distant time

Becky vivacious and effusive girl that evening was quietly sullen
Butterflies in her stomach, not a clue she looked so very crestfallen

Comforted her things will be just fine, she would then just smile
Please, she'd say join me soon I am going to miss you by miles
Held her hand and said surely love by your side in short while

Tears welling up in her eyes as we hugged in parting goodbyes
Next morning on a flight she was on her maiden trip to Dubai

138. Goodbye Wonderful Rusi Sethna

Rusi Sethna prior to joining him in a year he said would wind up
Join son in the US to retire to a quiet life with family now full his cup

Before parting, Rusi hosted me out for lunch
The final time we would meet for me it a certain hunch

Not as employer/employee, we were more like friends
Wonderful one year with him this is how it had to end

Helped me monetarily when I needed funds most
An elder statesman he was but jovial Parsee dost (friend)

139. New Job in Architect's Firm

Background in building industry favored me yet again in luck
A job with Zatin Parlekar Architects in marketing I got stuck

Zatin Parlekar an Architect by profession
Crafty businessman more at his occupation
Charming but eccentric he in his own bastion

Excellent team of professionals flock
Design Heads in 2 Directors of stock

Assistant and juniors all rock and rolled
Turnkey projects in execution always in control

One in whom an instant rapport I struck
Faruk Himatpure as friends like water to duck

Zatin ascent in the ladder of success phenomenal
Professional charges in fee he was very nominal

Sometimes no charge practice in market acceptable
Unethical outlook in business trend so susceptible
Survival primal business grabbed by another in immoral

Brilliance in design outdid his faulty decision
Contracts for firms awarded in turnkey execution

Never an eye on them or any senior engineer in supervision
Naturally corners always cut for petty profit in negation

Sometimes felt he is aware of this indiscretion
Maybe spoils in petty shared after evaluation

140. Trouble Shooting Project

Along then came a major setback
One contractor big time messed up

Project major in Bangalore US$ 5 million in value in 2 phase
Software Firm Angfin in finance to house its staff as R&D base

Zatin was concerned extremely and very naturally so
Success of phase 1 to certify in 2 to him will also go

Factor disconcerting as Zatin was an automatic choice
But for contractor's faux paux 2nd phase now in jeopardize

Competitor's design firm in a strong pitch, for us now a real threat
Their Chennai associate and Angfin's CFO, for presentation they met

CFO of Angfin with his presentation indeed too very impressed
Simultaneously our contractor goofed up had us all depressed

Time to trouble shoot in brain storm deep get to matter of crux
Zatin, Faruk and Me in joint summit who will now grip this ruckus

Joined by Atul a civil engineer now meeting taken to next level
Person with responsible integrity to handle this project now bedeviled

Faruk with 2 major projects had too much already on his plate
One more design head Vikas Lad not exactly people's mate

Zatin certainly not primed for role to be spent out in entire month
Left with Atul and me, duo to solve an issue now at our forefront

Qualms none, willingly volunteered to take the problem head on
Atul's experience in tough contractual site issues in 10 years hands on

Us 2 now a team resolved to get derailed project back on track
To Bangalore we flew set base camp near site in villa we shacked

At project site, trouble shooting we in earnest began our review
List in detail pending contractual obligation of works in lieu
Messed jobs in simultaneous schedule for completion in our purview

Instructions to set up operations to work in tandem as team of 2
Ultimatum of 3 weeks, contractor to complete so to delegate more crew

Concurrently me now as PR in building relations with Angfin Director
Chepauk Patll person dynamic a key leader and strategic selector

A natural progression in creating rapport within their edifice
Blend seamlessly with Angfin staff routinely in day at office

Grilled the skilled work force Atul a duteous tough task master
Match or exceeded expectations in getting task done faster

Complimented each other we became a formidable team
Our bond grew with each passing day results there to be seen

All snags rectified to perfection pending jobs all completed
Handover ahead of schedule Patil happy before time, issues defeated

Proved in our work ethics we a team completely committed
Phase 2 to Zatin Parlekar Architects our efforts in complete rewarded

Atul and me for our contribution recognized
Monetarily rewarded us two we now were glamourized

One more major project in turnkey I was instrumental in roping
Global Investment Company in USD 5 Million in value of coping

Financial rewards coming my way, my confidence now surging
Prospects few more to clear my housing loan sooner emerging

141. Meeting My Old Man

Being in Bangalore an opportunity to meet my dad
50kms from the city he was, drive on a 2-wheeler tiring tad

75 years not getting any younger he a chronic chain smoker
Still pretty lithe on his feet his generation kind really a shocker

Often wondered what he did alone all by himself to kill time
Brought him to our villa to spend a few days with us in prime

Atul grew fond of him indulging him in his entertainment
But then who was not who knew his real persona in arraignment

142. Wandering Thoughts

During all this while in Becky, my thoughts would often shift
How was she in Dubai and coping up? My spirit she would oft lift
In pensive mood caught, Atul in jest will inquire, to Dubai in drift?

Becky on international call would speak for very long
Lonely in distant land emotion not alien for me but strong
Cost irrelevant, connecting just for her to talk like a soothing song

Practical reality hurt me badly all the time in playing spoilsport
Priorities first in life the perspective to dock quickly in port

Then a call from the regional director of international office furniture
Systems Flexon from Dubai to meet me for Angfin as an arbiter
Jason Waters the man in main for phase 2 he now a proposer

143. Becky and Abistha's Introduction

Sometime in June 1997, Abishta came alone
To take possession of her brand-new home

Same time a fun fair organized by the parish of Mira Road
An occasion for Becky and me together in time we rather flowed

Asked Abishta to accompany me with Becky an introduction
Mom and Abishta in quiet conference our liaison in discussion

Expectedly sis next brought a ridiculous proposition
Mother unhappy and disappointed with Becky and my relation

Your departure to leave, a certain void, Abhikya left with none to fear
Forget Becky, fishes many in the sea to make your merry with any dear

Implausibly true not surprised this was just so much like her
Respect for none games cruelly played by mom and sister

Clear her marriage an insurance in social security it was a sham
Love and companionship a farcical façade she really gave a damn

Every point in my life opportunities many came my way
Game-changing moment scuttled by very own blood in their sway

Stymied my every move with shackles in an emotional bond
Regressed into darkness for their ill conceited gains in pound

No denying as kids were brought up righteously well
Dad though astray ground rules he laid for discipline on the bell

Value dignity, self-respect in moral ethics mom always to tell

Truth uphold never hurt weak, help needy, in persona to gel

Immoral act now against other each with absolutely no scruples
Rules and values now forgotten in life now simply there no principles

Holding on threads fine hoping to bind together me an idiotic fool
Seemed to run in circles in hope of finding a broken end in the spool

Becky true in personality took to Abishta upon meeting
Body language obvious sis reluctance in her accepting

Abishta grudgingly admitted found Becky unpretentious
Humble and vivacious she was extremely very gracious

Buttressing to conceal her sour words my agony so obvious
Deep down aware my decision she superficially being glorious

144. Confession of Daring Robbery

Abishta confided in me one more development
Summer vacation time mom and Abhikya in recent
In Oman a burglary in her house a heinous event

Person to family known pull off easily such a heist in plan
House in rest intact jewelry only from safe taken by clan

Aware of exit window of apartment leading to outside
Mom on entry found bedroom door bolted from inside

Trying to force open heard noises through door
Retreated to hallway safety all quiet now on floor

Abishta dialed police immediately on helpline
Arihant informed too but tired said he was and yet to dine
Call cops it will be fine sleep I will on finishing my wine

So much for sibling love, concern or care!
But that's Arihant, couldn't care less how you fare

Reverse the plot of same calamity to befall him
Bring the house down with his mug all in grim

3rd person an outsider entry in family life always to prove costly affair
Som Chapra the culprit in constant stink an undeserving dirty player

Divided we were completely into fragments as family
Political associations of sorts as couple in joint assembly

Mom and Abishta versus me
Mom and Arihant versus me

Abishta versus Arihant to see
Mom was neutral favorite son was he

Abishta parleyed for support against Arihant from me
In support from me none but agreed wrong he had done

For in trouble with no support she was alone
If him in her place she would have certainly gone

145. Surprising Rebecca in Dubai.

Jason Waters met me at Zatin Parlekar's office on schedule
Flexon Furniture for Angfin Ph. 2 he offered a proposal in full

Presented Flexon Furniture Systems on power point
The revelation of modularity in flexibility even at joint

Numerous working variations in permutations and combinations
Worktop adjustment amazing as were fabric finishes in summation
Seating systems range of models spoilt for choice in collation

Zatin too joined us in conference room and had the same reaction
Absorbing display of ergonomically laid out office in the foundation
Convinced I was Angfin to have in phase 2 Flexon workstation

Jason Waters then threw bait in a sponsored trip to Dubai
My eyes lit up of course chance to see beloved Becky of mine
Zatin very enthusiastic an opportunity to visit Dubai for the first time

Close to Valentine's Day in thought, I hoped to spend with her
But not in the schedule as managed just 2 days missed by a whisker
Worth but each moment spent with her even if passing in a blur

Arrived in Dubai early hours in February of 1998
Warmly received by Jason at the airport and to hotel we drove straight

Freshening up after light breakfast ready for many site visit
Highly impressed on quality works Flexon already had accomplished
Leaning towards Flexon as lead designer Zatin now surely did

Breaking off for lunch discussion veered back to Angfin phase 2
Lead time to manufacture and supply in India missing the ball in cue

16 weeks unrealistic term we hit a major roadblock
For now, let us relax and catch up next day at 8 O' clock

I grabbed a moment in hand to Becky's office I made a call
Location of quarters luckily near our hotel, not an order tall

Mentally we were pretty weary needed to grab a shut eye
For me find Becky's house in Dubai bid Zatin a quick bye, bye

Those days no Google map help, only a landmark as a locator
Nothing much to go by but small grocery shop as my curator

Half kilometer alongside street I walked with no luck
Retraced my steps back yet nothing likely really struck

Really very close by strong feels in my gut
Back again in hope to find the grocery shop but

Not in main, decided to check the small by lane
Green grocery shop tucked inside off the main

Raised in hope entered in store and inquired
UR Healthcare care staff apartment location is desired

Drew a blank? Ah! In despair, my heart sank
Offices now closed past 5pm nothing in my bank

Two hours now since in operation search and seek
Entry a girl in the grocery store by chance I asked in meek

Oh, for small mercies she staff of UR Healthcare
And who may you be looking for she asked to share

Rebecca, I replied in grin wide sheer in ecstatic joy

Looked me in my eye said follow me her smile coy

Does she know you are here in Dubai she asked?
No, I replied! So, this a surprise she was so unabashed

After her, I climbed each step, stopped she then at level 1 on the floor
Rang the doorbell on left of foyer where she pointed to the main door

Look on Becky's face of shock and surprise she also eager to see
The door opened, out peered her 2 mates at me they looked quizzically

Politely I asked if Rebecca was home, I am Aarvan! Ooh!
In loud squeals both darted in calling to fetch, they were some show

And there she was finally peering from the passage towards the door
Really me, she thought? And the room lit up with her radiant glow

Her face beamed happily with her lovely smile so childlike glamorous
Holding each other in a warm hug Rebecca and I were rapturous

The evening was very special we dined and on future, we talked
On Riqqa Boulevard holding hands, we talked as we walked

Just being together we were happy not bothered on the clock
In faraway land at peace, we felt with no inhibitions to lock

When I dropped her back, it was early morning at dawn
I promised to meet her again the next evening by the lawn
Short business meeting at Flexon's office we had an early morning
Chalked out a plan on a proposal for Angfin it looked very discerning
Revert back from Flexon's office in Germany on concurring

2nd evening in Dubai an occasion to remember very special
Live band retro beats in performance in the mood we went tidal

Hardrock Café we were hosted by Jason, Zatin simply went viral
Becky and me in a perfect evening of closeness feeling very spatial
Our resolve only now sturdier for the union as one in our own celestial

Goodbye was bitter but our hopes high for this one last time to part
Time would keep us distant but unite us soon never to be apart

146. Return of Prodigal Son!

Time no more on our side in the 30s I was on its wrong side
Becky still in early, had to be in Dubai soon by her side
Latitude in time and money certainly not on our side

Yet another change in plot Arihant lands up back in Mumbai
Nothing worked out in Pune again nothing planned by this guy

Late summer of May 1998 back with the family he intends to relocate
In a solemn plea for help he asked, my dilemmas never seem to abate

My resources were thin already too much on my plate
Collected in savings for travel and stay in Dubai my date
Could not turn my back and walk away leaving him in a poor state

Lovely Poorvi now in company, new arrival in doll named Raksha
Someway to set my bro up quick my life now virtually a seesaw

Monetary rewards from work obtained now put at bro's disposal
Just ample for my needs in a 3-month stay in expense travel and local

Immediate in precedence relocation of my bro with his family arranged
Arihant had his own house in Mumbai so their shelter was unchanged

Poorvi's school admission instantly was taken care of
Bro in rival Architect's firm had him settled in a temporary job

Also gave him my business leads to help him start off
Brand new set of threads for both husband and wife to hobnob

Scan, I would every daily for anything relevant in his job profile
Chanced upon an ad post for Sales Manager just to suit his style

Belkin manufacturing a range of stationery product
A surge of hope for him in this role I felt he will surely will be plucked

However low in confidence, he was when I shared ad clip
Unsure of his chances it showed clearly in his reaction dip
I persisted in pursuance and he relented to give it a rip

Prepared a structured and detailed CV for bro
Highlighting experience, achievements in seeds to sow

Call for an interview he received and he cracked it
Set to take off all over again now in the hope he fully lit

At peace in my heart fulfilling a family obligation
Ready to fly out to Dubai my final destination

147. Dubai 1998

Headed back to Dubai finally in the winter of 1998 October
Timeline in a sequence of events to pan out life's lesson to remember

Courtesy my future wife Becky a visit visa was managed
A colleague in kindness agreed to sponsor cost her part in wage

With family on rent in bachelor shared room, I stayed
Now armed with my CV from India itself in readiness I played

4 years shy of 40 jobs to come by were for me difficult
Consultants, friends, yellow pages in hope of a quick result

Apply, apply but no reply and time was flying fast by
In person, I began in earnest calling all companies to try

3 months I had and in jiffy 2 months just flew by
Desperate times indeed a call then came out of the blue
Jatin Sha of Arcinter owner evinced interest to meet me

Next day at his office at 11am in the morning we met
Upon formal greeting company's operations, in brief, he set

Interior Decoration doubled up as local trading firm
Wood and Plywood materials to be sold in many joinery arm

Sha by everybody addressed as Jatin bhai in respect
Eloquent in his impression my CV had on him an effect

An opportunity seen in my experience for his ventures in sales to bring
In 2 diverse industry trading and projects solo me but in a duet to sing

Wood and Plywood sheet to manufacturers of Cabinetry
Concept sales in interior design to private and corporate industry

Desperate I was willing to take up any challenge but wait, not yet
Jatin Bhai to put me to test, credentials to prove myself he did bet

Booming business in demand for 3 and 5mm in Kitchen cabinetry
Wood and Plywood sheet in short, WPL volumes high in acceptability

Blanco Kitchens Abu Dhabi based company of high repute
Experts they used 3 and 5mm WPL sheet in kitchen cabinet suite

Jatin bhai for a year in trying to get their MD in an audience
Hassan divisional manager always stalled it in deferred suspence

All Banco's WPL order fulfilled by Damica from Syria
An acid test for me I asked Jatin bhai owner's name in an idea

Sharing the office number, he mentioned Mohamed Zarwan
I had to connect directly with him so a plan in me dawned

A call I made to Blanco Kitchen head office in Abu Dhabi
Arabic lady responded, an audience with Zarwan I did lobby

From India on business to meet Mohamed Zarwan
Just left his office on his mobile you may call him on

Mohamed Zarwan in his rich baritone answered humbly
Soaked every word I said in acceptance to meet him graciously.

At his office in Abu Dhabi, next day 11am it was quickly scheduled
Jatin bhai smiled in awe, bold I proved him in seizing horns of the bull

Impossible done by some quick thinking and with a bit of luck
Step one box ticked, step 2 to meet the man for orders in a truck

Dressed up in formals armed with an A4 size WPL samples
Chauffeur driven to Abu Dhabi to play one my life's big gamble

At Blanco Aluminum showroom greeted by manager Hassan
Surprised he was as I was to meet his boss and he had no information

Bit of confusion as factory in Mussafah was Zarwan's office base
Showroom I was told not an office hence we were out of place

On my insistence, Hassan kindly made the call to his boss
Asked us not to fret he'd arrive in 15 minutes in no time loss

Statesmanlike Mohammed Zarwan as humble in his look
Greeted me warmly rich in resonance he a seasoned cook

In refreshments offered kava with biscuits to put me at ease
A brief exchange in chats business then moved like a breeze

Samples studied in interest at offer price US$ 17.50 per sheet
At cutoff price provided to me deal was sealed at US$ 15.50

3x40' open top containers payment to be made by L/c
A dream home run in whirlwind romance concluded as I see

Could not believe in a span of 24 hours 3x40' containers closed
A salary of 5K AED + car Jatin bhai accepted my deal unopposed

Finally, a base for me in Dubai marking a new beginning in life
Becky and I now could together plan our future without strife

Focus for me more important always task on hand
2 entities regardless of stature can be in an alliance so grand

Attitude and approach for me always instinctive
Constantly gave me success in being very productive

In any relationship, it is not about being presentable
It is your skill in presenting yourself in a manner very able

Purchase not because of buyer's affinity to any product as a cult
In buying his trust and unconditional belief in you is the actual result
X-factor so clear in a deal with Mohamed Zarwan I could happily exult

Your attire is of no consequence
How you carry yourself is of significance

148. Jatin Bhai's Gesture of Nobility Dramatic in Act not in Reality

Things with Jatin bhai got personal in talks
Inquired about my future plans in torque

In passing briefly I talked about Becky and our priority
Ardently in chest thumping show my marriage in vow now his duty

So much for a test of abilities, for me huge luck factor in working
Mohammed Zarwan wonderful man he for me in happening

149. A New Becky in Transformation

Becky never ever alone ventured into the outside world
Now she lived all by herself the new in her unfurled

Making friends easily and many always her second nature
And in solitary moment pondering in past present and future

Overcame her worst fears in moments of solitude
Now mentally strong she a lady with plenty in fortitude

150. Ramin Davle Back in Nuisance Value

Back in Mumbai, I was, for residence visa from Arcinter in waiting
Informing Zatin Parlekar on my permanent move was bit dampening

Enjoyed my tenure also met very genuine human being
Faruk an association in blessing till date in continuing

A few days prior to my departure Ramin back in unwanted intrusion
Abhikya he in spotting at play informed on his sudden visit in brazen

None in elders; Mom, Rakshee and bro present at home
My nephew, Ramin in recognition, finely on bro and me he combed

Arihant settling in the new job was late, nor I was nowhere nearby
Missive for uncles he owns new wheels in Benz, a cheap loathsome guy

Offensive in taste meant to say, guys, I nailed you'll are losers
Dr. Jekyll and Hyde character at play in quite a dirty sadist abuser

Cracked like a glass I fumed for his deliberate obscene audacity
Opened up old wounds and bruises he did it as usual in alacrity

Spontaneously dialed his house phone his dad picked up sadly
Politely in wishing said on hearing me surprised he so pleasantly

Regrettably, statuses his son created over years me in no mood
Pleasantries far I intended to give his son telling off for good

Senior Davle unfortunate cushion in default for his villainous son
Told he no friend but pretender dishonors friendship not once

In his defense Senior replied you'll were friends as I knew;
I replied; how can he be a friend for the stew that he brews

Hooded selfish character demeans true friends in slander
To parents, spouses and among friends in a sham of banter

Selfish in action, failing in obligations, reverses word of honor
Destroyed careers and lives, ensured we are all but goners!

How can he be a friend?

He is as pretentious as he is malicious real Dr. Jekyll and Hyde
No moral right to keep gate crashing at will into our lives

How can he be a friend?

We are for a long time trying to get back on track
Tell him to stay out, he is a forgettable past if I could go back
In my life, I would erase him completely off the rack

He is nobody's friend!

Message harsh but truth not meant or intended any disrespect
Senior Davle apparently got the gist of the circumstantial aspect
That was last I thought I heard on Ramin still I was circumspect

151. Long New Innings in Dubai

And so, began my new ……. our new journey in life
Little did we know it to be loopy roller coaster ride?

A year in our lives from 1997 to 1998 we were far apart
None gave us a chance in a hope we will from each other depart
Every Birthday, Anniversary celebrated together since as a part

Soon I was going to be 37 not getting any younger
3 years in full had passed by since I proposed to her

Both families unrelenting holding on the religious ground
Both of us wished our wedding celebration with family around

But fate penned in different script something unimaginable
Never anticipated a hellish saga without Becky it was unmanageable

152. Employment at Arcinter a Nightmare

Began work in Arcinter in early 1999 beginning of another nightmare
Selling WPL to joinery units in UAE was fairly a simple affair

Delved deeper into company psyche now aware of the startling facts
First, jolt a call from Zarwan himself in dishonoring his order pact

2 months since order placed payment in L/c issued by the bank
No inkling yet, parent company Lamika in Mumbai totally drew a blank

No small matter 2 months without any information
Asked Jatin Bhai on delay in a courteous discretion

Including all parameters lead time in maximum 2 weeks
Production, Documentation, Customs and Shipping all tweaked

3 open top 40' containers in Jebel Ali by now should've long docked
Jatin Bhai called his younger bro Biren in India in reason for the block

Clarification none provided asked instead L/c to be extended
Zarwan in kindness at his cost, not usual but obliged as requested

In open office exchange of communication with Biren animated
Jatin Bhai on putting the phone down exclaimed he was disgusted

Apparently, production not taken up at all, factory in planning still shy
When asked reasons for delay answer none at all forthcoming in why

Lamika's smug apathetic, incompetent and complacent approach

Detrimental in our plan in market development without reproach

Intention to visit Zarvan to book a new order now I canned
No face to go to him for a cyclic order I got myself banned

Upset I was how one can be so lackadaisical in an export order
One year to woo Zarwan taken, now in flash a mess in disorder

153. More Skeletons out of Cupboard

Yet new story unfolded in Ajman's Hager Waufic, another factory!
Supply of WPL sheets in credit piled up US$250K a year in history

Now thrust with the responsibility to collect money in full
Attitude of owners at Hager Waufic threw amazing control tool
Implied big favor to us in buying, in a market like us many fools

Owner Elvan drove to the office in his Porche Coupe sport car
Holed up in his plush office ensure all supplier inside be barred

Newman his uncle a manager on his guarantee goods were supplied
Temperamentally short he was outrageously loud to be mollified

Act in aggression for in suppliers instill fear for meek submission
Either accept in part or return back later in hope as a concession

Monday's particular day in the week set for supplier payment
Sharply arrived at 9am in wait for an hour in 2 for holy sacrament

Newman sheepishly then asked me to return back in 2 days
6 weeks in row continual show I then drew line firm said, Just Pay!
Newman short of conceding my presence said maybe next day?

My displeasure made known in an outburst on his ethical biz practice
In trade honor pledge to suppliers on payment without any tactic

Least expecting verbose attack questioning his moral stand
Stood up went to Elvan in 10 minutes came with a cheque in hand

Newman asked if ready to supply again, for sure I said
Henceforth with a letter of credit business in fair to be played

Wily old fox two kisses on the cheek in traditional Arab greeting
Habibi in sweetheart talking, Jatin Bhai out of his hand in eating
Fell hook, line and sinker in guile agreed to his terms meeting

US$250,000 in credit line offered again! Once bitten, twice shy
…….. And in my word twice bitten and fools die! This was Jatin bhai

In retrospect strongly felt it was a class act
Uncle Newman and Nephew Elvan in a dramatic pact

A game plan they were in sync
A perfect foil for each other to hoodwink
One tyrant another victim in the link

Victim for goods from suppliers in sympathy
Tyrant in delayed payments in clarity
Uncle Nephew duo now surplus capital in their kitty

154. Jatin Bhai's Messy Business Management

Zarwan's orders alone could fulfill production need for Lamika
An entire year in sales orders like full seasoning of paprika
10 containers a month definitely a scream Eureka! Eureka!!

Most buyers' supplies direct only from Damica in prize
9'x4' a favored sheet perfect cut achieved for various size

Despite our product failing in size with an order, he did us a favor
Probably leverage us as plan B in event of any price waver

3 months now gone with l/c extended my worries just began
3 months to fulfill an order for 3 containers a wide time span

Direct in confrontation asked Jatin Bhai politely but firmly
Do we really have a factory? Looking away he fumbled guiltily
With a deep breath, he said the capacity of I container contritely

Felt now I in solitary confinement, long way yet from redemption
My face told him a story now in deaf to all his made-up confession
Any reassurance from him was nothing but a useless verbal pension

Things started falling into place only two clients to show
Blanco and Hager Waufic in these now 2 issues to mow
Collecting money and order execution both in feel I was low

Realities sank in me and with that my total enthusiasm
Rocky boat yet again in a month I was now deep in the chasm

No product to sell basically nothing tangible really to show

The job market was slow worst from 1st month no salary flow

Wedding plans of course not to be put on hold anymore
Funds in question for divine intervention only left to implore

Amidst darkness, there was one bright glow in good fortune
Becky offered a position in Dyna mount Middle East in a quiet boon

155. Glancy Rego

In the second month, I met Glancy by profession an Architect
With Archinter poor lady she too for 1 year had no salary in effect

Her first query how on earth did you join Archinter?
An obvious question it was more sarcasm in banter

Glancy on annual vacation she was at the time of my draft
License for Arcinter not issued devoid of professional in same craft

Unfortunately, she too a victim on unpaid salaries I learned
More than 1 year of her time and worth the company just burned

A single parent with two children in an alien country she a brave heart
Bright lady, simple outlook and hardworking her task was just cut out
Fortunate in Dubai strong moral support of her maternal family
Mother, sister like a rock behind in strong backing for her morally

In excess of 1 year drove her to point in sheer exasperation
Wages unpaid, rising bill, basic survival, leading to desperation

Jatin Bhai now even more evasive in eye contact a sign of deflation
Salary she now demanded completely in a feeling of sheer frustration

But he chose to blame her for unfinsihed jobs in a draft of exploitation
Receivables too he debited on her in a clever mask of manipulation

Glancy a one-woman army for design, contracts and supervision
Executed jobs through third-party vendors prudently she in wisdom

156. Losing Blanco Aluminum as Client

Sporadic supply of single container in Ply sheets in a bale
Set about looking for small opportunities to market in wholesale

3 and 5mm thick sheets to small medium enterprises in a sale
Multiples of 50 sheets in the sale too less in content for a full tale

Opportunities hardware accessories also I looked into
Hinges, door handles and knobs suppliers I spoke to

Most ready to support anything in profit for the trade
My initiative on 2nd thought inviting trouble in aid
The risk in dues to the suppliers like on my jugular a blade

As last resort to Mohammed Zarvan call in desperation I made
A new order with us can he place if in stocks he has all flayed

Nothing more shocking after what he then said
At Jebel Ali Port unloading goods full team he led

Supposed to have been 40' high cube in an open top
Bungling fools sent 40' standard in ops they were a complete flop

Manually with forklift each master pack in drop
Real-time for unloading max in 30 minutes in op

Now for this mess, it had taken 6 hours on the trot
And in thought for order, dare I pass by his office to pop?

December 1999 order placed May 2000 Delivery completed
180 days for 3 containers? From contact list, we were deleted

Chance of livelihood for all at Archinter was huge in cost
What an opportunity a chance for this huge business we lost!

157. Brave Heart Glancy

Glancy with Jatin Bhai overflowed in her cup of patience
Unpaid salary blamed for debts, he had no conscience for collection

Enough chances on releasing dues given she was now infuriated
Last resort she opted for justice in labor court in plea belated
Obvious this verdict was going to be only in one way stated

Summons to appear in court against Jatin Bhai quickly issued
Cognizance of victim a lady fast-tracked by court ruling lassoed

Verdict swift in favor of Glancy was certainly in belief
Settle overdue payments in full, justice delivered in immediate relief

100K in accumulated backlogs no choice but to pay
Week in maximum to deposit in court and no further stay

Consequences in failing action severe in flay
One final con he tried his best in usual despicable play

Purposely penned 10k instead of 100 K cheque in the tray
Caught in act court warning stern in dragging another day

Sadly, for Jatin Bhai loss of face for his constant sway
Personal presence demanded by the court in full cheque to pay
Her dues paid in full she a brave heart sure to say

158. Register Marriage

Personal priorities for me now took precedence
Marriage plans hitting roadblock major in petulance

Far away from our respective families yet
The pressure we felt was like a subtle threat

Religion to the forefront trying to crush our will
Bond with our families was a high cost in full emotional bill

Depressingly weak it made us both in forced guilt
Hurting them was never our option, for them inbuilt

Used against us as a potent weapon this weak sentiment
Depressingly feeble it made us in spirit a huge detriment
Families only were in our union a major impediment

One front my job did not provide us with any financial security
Second, in a war of nerves, I was holding my mental faculty
Beyond control over demesne forces of intangible gravity

Overwhelmingly exhaustive but every time down on the mat
My tenacity helped me rise higher and I could afford me a pat

Firmly now I pushed Becky in taking the plunge first in court
Marriage once registered enough for me in the plan to hold fort

May 18th, 1999, we went to the Indian Consulate in Dubai
Formal application filed for intent to marry and say aye

In UAE and in Mumbai in English an Ad in local daily
Dispatch to separate residences of our families mainly

NOC in approval acceding to our marriage intent plainly

Arihant in prior I called from Dubai asking him to receive the letter
Contents indicated he obliged in an understanding of the said matter

Thirty days in the time since Ad in dailies and letters to families
Thankfully no twist this time completed all procedural formalities

159. Drama at Indian Consulate

Consulate office in Dubai provided us a list of dos
Mandatory to solemnize our wedding to save last minute blues

Two witnesses as signatories in presence of Vice Consul for sign
Augustine Philip, Steve Arius both ready to pop a bottle of wine

Augustine Philip my roommate wonderful and holy guy
Steve Arius a Greek national soft spoken and very shy

22nd July Morning was D-day in our lives first in a ceremony
Becky, me with Philip drove to the consulate for our matrimony
Steve came on his own met us prior to our sworn testimony

Becky looking beautiful in traditional Indian Churidar Kameez
In a formal suit I was, a special occasion should go off like a breeze

At window for receiving we submitted a copy of our application
Vice-consul in few minutes propped his face in a solemn declaration

Aarvan Rayudu, Rebecca Alvarez on mic our names blared
Advancing to glass window he peered and simply declared

Proceedings in solemnizing this marriage will not be cleared
Our papers are in order I said, on time for vows to be shared

Next an absurd assertion he made, stunned intensely I glared
Coming from a high-ranking diplomat riled me so bad I flared

Steve Arius as witness improper as he is but a Greek National
A string of recent happening had in me pent up in combinational
Desired a fissure kindly given by vice consul in his words irrational

Exploded loud, in your list of dos clause of nationality is devoid
A month ago, in compliance names with nationality, you now avoid

No legality in your statement to be more personal than legal
Furious I was, caught him off guard; for sure nothing here is illegal

A normal cacophony of visitor crowd in the waiting area of early morn
But now just pin drop silence only one voice in angst I was torn

Issues had gone beyond simple wisdom in clarity
And from a veteran diplomat, it was simply sheer stupidity

No apparent rationality, trapped in bureaucracy's web of complexity
Personally, he made it up for witness only to be an Indian nationality

Ruckus in campus brought Consul General now in main
Expectedly as an intricacy made out of something so plain

Fairly young handsome diplomat confident, warm personality
The situation at the moment assessed a ready smile with no difficulty

Invited Becky and me to his chamber an apology offered politely
Dispelled quickly any notion of witness in matter of any nationality
Request postponement in our D-date to Sunday 25th in humility

No more surprises humbly I implored but firmly I did imply
Witnesses' formal leave of absence in offices to apply

Just for an autograph as witness time, they have to comply
Bride and groom also no exception in the system to notify
Assured me his duty to ensure our marriage is solidified

25th July 1999 assembled once again we all in a small room
Indian Consulate in Dubai the venue for bride and groom

Witnesses' ready vice consul in pronouncement to legalize
In jest, he said a final chance of freedom to reconsider in wise
The room erupted in laughter relief no more spanners in device

Finally, we Aarvan Rayudu" and "Rebecca Alvarez were united as
Man and Wife and we were now one as long-term bosom allies!

Marriage formally registered in the court of law
Destination wedding of sorts to be in awe

160. Informing our Parents in India

We both called Mumbai to inform our parents
Becky's mother only on a church wedding relented

My mother was adamant, go ahead she said fulfill your wish
Talents in making me feel miserable she will constantly dish

Displeasure in chosen girl was unlike in religion and culture
Outlook and mindset contrary to 180 degrees in a departure

161. Our First Apartment in Dubai

The first hurdle crossed now legally man and wife
Still, miles to go to please our families now a way of life

For our oncoming event in preparation an apartment a must
After hunting several, a studio near Lulu settled in just

Ideal for Becky for her company bus pick and drop
Fairly large studio apartment in location it was top

Furnished our future home from a nearby used furniture shop
Sofa, bed, dining, fridge and washing machine all in one stop

Becky as paying guest found a place to stay
For a couple of months only till our wedding day

One last time a final call to my mother earnest in pleading
With her blessing in Dubai have a customary Hindu wedding

Declined in total an excuse of leaving Abhikya alone
Planning from Dubai together I would have them flown

An event she saw more in her ego hurt for a chip in life to carry
Accepting loss in face of Becky her fictional foe she just couldn't parry

She said Abishta and Siva for our royal wedding her representatives
State banquet anyway it felt in Dubai guests were all executives

162. Trying Hard at Work

At work now six months without salary back to the harsh reality
Living on credit cards 5% minimum in payment our actual affordability

From Becky's savings, every cent on our homemaking expended
Deposit, Rent Cheque, Furniture etc. now my salary all depended

Efforts at work continued in hope of times to someday change
WPL sheets, hardware accessories, if must also the entire range

Futile it was always factory in production remained unfulfilled
Orders lost customers goodwill too, my moral was now stilled

Jatin Bhai in such, to his cabin call for a long sermon to deliver
Life has ways in its onslaught, be strong to overcome all failure
Not aware in me was veteran already in clutches of such cavalier

Informed him on our wedding date celebrations
Money in need to make all advance preparations

Assured me his best to try to pay me all my dues
Only hope to cling on, nothing finally to come true

Recalled emotional promise 6 months ago he loudly dictated
My marriage his responsibility hollow words now abdicated

163. Sivaraman's Visit to Dubai on Job Hunt

Calls from Oman from Abishta my dear sister
In the job hunt, if can proceed to Dubai her mister?

Sugar coated words in polite ask
Siva stays with me in fulfilling his task

A couple of months to try his luck
Job in Dubai to earn his buck
I said yes, its time from Oman to get unstuck

Siva did come with CV prepared in full planning
In his job quest helped him doing all his running

Employments hard to come by all his efforts were in draining
Despite his spotless credentials no single call in receiving
In month left for Oman in promise for our nuptial sure in returning

164. Jatin Bhai Renegading on Promise

Church Wedding fixed for Friday, September 24th, 1999 in date
Now 8 months in unpaid wages nothing for our nuptials in plate

The burden on Becky now also to look after my basic need
Bare minimum salary half of it now gone in our rental feed

Everything now rationed had to manage in savings minimum
Barely from Becky's salary our survival in the very early millennium

Rent, commissions, utility and telecom deposits in a disbursement
Rest on credit card our savior as well as the bane of all amercement

Choices none in our kitty for any option
Quickly assess for funds in need by adoption

Financing our wedding now no more delay
Becky to apply for a personal loan disbursed in a day

Becky's mother and brother's Hilton's visas on the list to do
Invite cards; give away gifts, wedding hall and banquet menu

Wedding gown, bands, suit, bridal jewelry, car, MC and DJ,
Photographer, centerpiece, longlist increasing in ladies say

Thursday 9th September my last day at work
Leave for wedding preparation now my mark

In one last final call asked Jatin Bhai if at all
Release my payment least in half of the install

Forty Thousand Dirhams in unpaid salary

In half at least give us, a start for some bloody Mary

But it was not to be, said he; not a penny to give
Saddened now an ominous feeling all over again to live
One more issue added in our cup of woes
Becky's personal loan added to my new low

Selflessly for our marriage her contribution in 100
Began to ponder how many concerns new numbered

Not an ideal start to new life inside me it really tore
Future alarming in thought what else more in store

165. Wedding Preparation

Alvarez's Matriarch Anna and Brother in Law Hilton
In Dubai 2 weeks prior for nuptials arrived in the city of sun

To be a mother in law huge help in planning for our nuptial
Becky and I busied ourselves finalizing guest list as a couple

Alvarez's spared no efforts in ensuring smooth sailing
Ramada Hotel for reception our venue in celebrating

Hilton I hardly knew him was my best man
Guest list mine just a few in numbers to fan

Jatin Bhai and family, office colleagues
Jason Waters and family few invites in release

Becky's cousins their family, few close friends
Office colleagues mixed nationalities in the blend
Add color and flavor to party occasion in trend

166. Our Very Own Special Day

Grand day of our wedding arrived finally
Abishta and Siva arrived from Oman on eve my only in family

At the church in my car, I arrived first with bro in law Hilton
Arius my Greek friend drove us in plenty of banter and fun

In pretty decorated limousine with roses and crafted doves
Becky moments later rolled grandly into the church threshold

Chivalrously chauffeur from the limo, door he opened in courtliness
Emerged lovely bride to be in bridal finery glowing in all her radiance

My Becky an epitome of simplicity and beauty in charm
Dazzling smile in elegance she graceful as led in Hilton's arm

Cute little flower girl Jewel with pageboy Jonas
The choir led by a brother, sister duo Ralph and Zenas

Church benches neatly decorated in roses handcrafted
Readings and Hymns arranged in folder neatly bonded

Sylvia, Becky's close friend at UR Healthcare her bridesmaid
Hilton Alvarez my bro in law my best man suited in suede

Church congregation as part of ceremony looked very natural
Hilton gave Becky's hand in mine as we walked slow and gradual
Over decorated aisles to waiting priest at altar like serene pastoral

Ceremonial formalities now completed we exchanged our rings
Pronounced man and wife our life in union now finally with wings

Photography time for memories to be etched for posterity
Many poses captured in the church courtyard seemed in eternity
Stage set for letting hair down in the glorious moment as celebrities

Into limo for couple drive to Hotel Ramada for guest reception
Arms entwined smiles in finality in each other's visual perception

Words none in exchange just a passing thought in 4 years we lost
In our time waiting just to make our families happy, for us big in cost

167. Reception an Unforgettable Celebration

On reaching the banquet hall door, cacophony of noises to account
In expectation I had none but the guest in numbers few to count

Peered into the crack of door opening stunned I was in utter disbelief
100 plus in excess for our wedding reception it was a joyful relief

Bless them all gracing an occasion for our wedding celebration
Becky's charisma in full view her entire office in the traditional fashion
Descended in strength to join in fun and feast in blissful passion

Let the party begin blared DJ Mario a three in one action man
Decorator, DJ and master of ceremonies all rolled in one

Festive mood took off to music for Bridal Wedding March
Urged and cajoled by MC crowd swelled to form an arch

Raising the toast, a gentleman called John Crow a jovial Brit
15 days only in acquaintance through Arius he a verbose treat
Recommended for my reception as toastmaster for a classic feat

Gave him tips on my profile only good side to speak in humor
Sure mate, he in laughter heard plenty on you in passing rumor

John was eloquent, fluent as he elicited me in terms so glowing
Becky concealed her laughter at stimulated hyperboles flowing

I loved it; crowd lapped it and his speech they applauded
With a wink and knowing smile, John at the bar was duly rewarded

Keeping my speech short in gratitude my first in express
Becky's mother and brother in a mention for their quiet nobleness
Their presence adding vivacity in joy our unbridled happiness

Next thanked my parents, Abishta and Siva for their presence
Having made it from Oman felt in spirit their luminescence

The most precious moment of evening bridal couple dance
Sliding in each other's arms in holding we waltzed deep in trance

To a memorable song - From This Moment On" time stood still
And that moment forever will endure in my memory till......

The evening got lively and the party had just begun
Guest couples joined us on the floor in merrymaking and fun

Reached out to my mother in law for a dance she did sportingly
Abishta and Siva too joined in celebration having fun willingly

The dance floor was full with kids too joining in
Games for kids for adults too with prizes many to win

Becky and I walked to each guest table to express our gratitude
Truly overwhelmed and happy by their presence with their brood

Jatin Bhai was there with his wife and some of my colleagues
As the evening wore on the fun and frolic reaching its peak

DJ started playing typically Indian masala songs mix
Crowd some in few drinks down went delirious for a six

One of Hilton's colleague was dancing with Becky when
Suddenly he carried my bride, tried to dance but then
Struggled for control and to her rescue, I took over amen

Carrying her in my arms grooving to song and music beat
Crowd lapping and clapping in rhythm raising tempo and heat
Gathered in a circle around us whistling in approval of my feat

Did not stop in tango till the music reached crescendo and
The applause of assembled guests put my beloved on her feet

Dave Cyler, Becky's senior in office his wife Helena asked a favor
Get her husband on the dance floor and be her party savior

Immediately Becky obliged and approached shy Dave Cyler
Gallantly on to dance floor he grooved to music in obliging her
Helena in elation joined in setting the dance floor on fire

Truly wonderful time an evening of joy and happiness
Those euphoric four hours, time stood still for both of us

Wedding celebration it was unforgettable in every part
Guests thrilled in fun and joy, till the end did not depart

An exhilarating event at international destination smart
Becky my darling was indeed the true winner of hearts
Celebration forever etched I will always cherish in my heart

168. Bidding Adieu to Alvarez

Goodbyes are always bitter and sad
Time for Mom Anna and bro Hilton to get back
Bidding adieu in tears of emotion they cracked

As a mother she only had one thing to say
My daughter, now I leave in your care

169. Filial Ties in Complete Tatters

Abishta and Siva in presence so to say was in token
Rest all were I felt in ties completely tattered and broken

Mother, Father, Abha and Arihant their family
Abha out of loop rest unconcerned even in a mere formality

Now I look back it doesn't matter anymore
Present turned past what future had in store
Only in distant time, ours will be a forgotten lore

Mother's ego bared completely in her false pride
Pleaded once to Siva's father for daughter's side
Today as a matter of convenience she had changed side

For now, she a mother from son's side
Tables turned on daughter from another side
But not interested as girl's culture from a different side

Siblings careful not in offending mother
Beneficiaries in the property so why really bother

Abishta eventually bid Oman a final goodbye
Summoned back by mom to roots in Mumbai

Abhikya's supervision needed with Hawkeye
Big lad now to be guided as his strong ally

Once back in Mumbai in no time up to her old tricks
Being nice to anybody for long as an allergy it pricks

It was a year since I left India for Dubai
Arihant with Belkon now well settled in high

Grown in stature and confidence tall reaching the sky
Work in routine was now chalk, cheese and pie

He now started traveling across the country
On business, it was for him in regular duty

Being immediate next-door neighbors now
Mother and son bonded thick and how

Arihant even spent more time with nephew
Even if Rakshee rationed his time in curfew

His affection in abundance on both his girls
Fiercely protective in his love for them possessively it whirled

Despite my telling Abishta as a family to unite in good counsel
Silliest of pretext picked a fight in my advice she cancels

Only one agenda in mind she had all along
Whisk mom away, she felt only with her belong

Intention more vested than in thought any noble
Kitchen in mom's hand plus an anchor in sum total

Matter in maturity could've been handled well
Instead, another saga of histrionics in serial like hell

Mother an equal partner in fomenting fuel to the fire
Obvious her loyalties more on demand than in desire

Duplicity to fore again in its dreaded raised hood
Manipulation at work amidst kin for each their own selfish good

Knew them all so well and their imprudent move
Bionic bond in total disconnect pieces of evidence to prove

170. Heartbreaking Start Jatin Bhai Vicious Vindictive Act

Becky and I after our wedding had a welcome break
Blissfully married now in relaxation our time to take

However, deep down a portentous feeling, I had in terrible
Distinctly something to give in soon I'd be cast-off like a feral

Sunday 10th October 1999 a month to date at work I resumed
Jatin Bhai unusually early to office sign ominous now in loom

He barely acknowledged me first sign of turbulence in room
Summoned me in his office in blunt he pushed me to my doom
Terminated in prompt effect unaffordability reason in a gloom

Snap of his fingers, just like that, emotions none in betrayal
But his eyes betrayed in seething venality of doubt in a portrayal
I knew but wanted to hear from the man a chest-thumping astral

And so, asked me for total handover by client visit to him as boss
Dubai, Sharjah and Ajman selling WPL sheets in Emirates across

Reality check on me if in any dubious deal I was linked in
Charged extra top-up margin for me deliberately I inked in

Every client we visited my work free from any encumbrances
Up to date and debt free all operations nothing left to chances

Except in Hager Waufic a key blunder only in his acceptance
Serenading song Habibie in kisses a guarantee in his advances

Suspected me in the embezzlement of company funds
Desperately wanted to nail me but in evidence none
Where was the moolah in liquidity for me getting it done?

But still, he was going sick in his mind
His body language faltering in the grind

His lips and finger in trembling convulsion
Had to get it off his chest in avulsion

Haltingly he said but in apparent definite revulsion
Managed but how funds for the wedding celebration?

He knew, if right I would not care for protocol
This his immeasurable gumptious cheap call

Retort in spontaneity I had the balls
Stolen cash from you to think you have the gall

Collection in cash for use in my party ball
How dare you think and act so mean at all

Challenged me to obtain an order
Employment offer for me you made in barter

Fulfilled criteria with 3 containers successfully
Disabled same customer in 3 months only in your folly

Open new doors with new clients in the tally
No stocks in supplies to maintain orders in a rally

What more do you expect me to do by golly
And then you think I milked your cash by jolly
Never saw you dishing out money like an ice lolly

9 months minus salary yet kept my motivation high
Tried everything within my means for the firm to survive
Despite all your vows and promises in void and sigh

Yet without any semblance of shame or guilt
In obscene audacity, you seek my confessions of jilt
Must say your timing in my termination perfect to the hilt

No right you have nor deserve to know
But since you ask for my cards I will show

My wife in a personal loan she borrowed from the bank
Just ample to manage or hopes will have then sunk

I then asked him what about my 9 months in unpaid wages?
Blandly at the road ahead, he stared his mind full in emptiness

Thanks to Jatin Bhai, what a start to our new life?
How was I going to break this news to my wife?

171. Becky's Comfort in Words

Becky and I from each other never kept any secret
Look on my face told her everything but she had no regret

Now since Ramin's time a feeling in me always
So close and yet so far horizon remained in haze

She knew I was devastated so was she in emotion
But we could ill afford to sink in hopeless desolation

She composed herself quickly to reach in holding my hand
In assurance comforting, she spoke her touch like a magical wand

172. Count our blessings

Let us one by one just count our blessings
In each other, we have a presence in expressing

We have in plenty ahead in time for progressing
Money, material wealth or assets will not be our caring
In times bad we have each other in sharing
In good times we will revel in life in joyous tearing

Having each other in loving is our wealth in blessing
Together we are only in each others gain or nothing

Blessed we are in absence in person not missing
Look around see how many hidden tears flowing

Husband, wife, father, mother and child, family in each other missing
A roof overhead, clothes to wear, 2 square meals enough in needing

All faculties in senses intact wealth anytime in earning
Body and mind whole health always a precious wealth in saving

Together we will always be each other's wealth in gaining
Profound words from my Becky gal a lesson in life for learning

Happy I am for more in all said blessings
Becky a companion for my ethos in redeeming

173. Becky's Freak Accident

An old saying, I recall when trouble does come
Unannounced in torrential force it comes by the ton

Few months into our marriage Becky had a freak accident
Whilst alighting from the bus in natural motion onward she bent

In a grating rut, on steps right heel of her shoe in between it went
Landing on left leg as she fell an excruciating pain in ankle it sent

Carried to building lobby by office colleagues she lost in senses
From home ran down on being informed mindful of inferences

Carried her back home tended trauma with ice on swelling
In severe pain, she was orthopedic attention surely telling

Took her to UR Healthcare hospital in an emergency
Dr. Abhay Sarwatte reviewed X-Rays in urgency

Broke the news he did in humor in gentle exigency
Perfect job of breaking her ankle with a minimum efficiency

Multiple fractures it was in 3 her ankle bone broken
To be operated on first early morning doctor had spoken

Good news she had company insurance in direct pays
Bad news insurance was valid until only 2 more days

New insurance policies to redeem pay first and claim later
In post operation hospital care 3 more days in stay in care to cater
Naturally, call to Jatin Bhai in money as he owed me greater

First instance despite me informing him situation critical
Simply he said no for me now an option only in a miracle

Changed tact in my posture he has to arrange for funds
No more say in this matter I was desperate in my stand firm

10% in a total bill of 5000 dirhams was all he could manage
Sad situation but through credit card avoided any damage

Becky from hospital now discharged 3 months rest she was advised
Weekly visit with the doctor for curative progress now organized

174. The Feral World of Professionals

The next 5 years I was a freelance vagabond
In the feral world of professionals, a puppet just spawned

Plied my skill in sales and marketing whosoever wished to align
Joinery and carpentry firms, trade even architecture and design

Nobody, just nobody was interested in hiring a new hand
Few paid me sincerely many used my services as a free band

One such company in the business of tiles even hired me full time
At venue on the date, HR Manager retracted their offer in sublime

Professional world a big game hunt truly feral and ruthless
If you are in part of company odds bright for businesses in access
When not part of routine a pariah as a willing mate to suppress

Jatin Bhai retained my visa all through
For he had yet to clear all my dues

Surviving only on Becky's salary and credit card
Fortunate on 5% payment minimum in times being very hard

175. Our Annual Holiday to India

Our first visit home in 2002 to visit our families hence
The show despite our worries had to go on in pretense
Ground situation in our family homes always very tense

Becky still not accepted a part of my family
Whilst I was only Becky's husband in her family

A cordial greeting from mother it was more in compromise
Arihant and Rakshee whether or not she an ally they yet to size

As told by sis on acquaintances inquiries both felt chastised
Why? Cause she not human but first as a catholic dehumanized
We both ignored this news; on sly anybody could be telling a lie

Poorvi a big girl now only too glad to see me in ages
Raksha now a lovely little girl her childhood now in stages

An invisible sword of Damocles always seemed hanging in the air
Ecology heavy and intense, to break wind always ready to dare

None from either side of the family knew of our hopeless situation
No job, no steady income source, long list of mine in citation

Living in an alien country our predicament always unpredictable
In hardships times Becky's loving support stayed unconditional

Sweetly she once said take away your stress for she doesn't care
As long as she has a job she willingly always supports us pair

She saw how I kept trying despite many times having fallen
So close to breaking wind but an unseen force over me to trodden

Blame herself, she'd for my quandary in a belief of superstition
Casually dismiss in laughter her uncalled-for madness in delusion

Mom, as usual, poured her cup of woes on Abishta
Nothing new but new saga on her and Siva

He truly loved and cared for her but was not expressive
Not his fault that's simpleton Siva humbly very submissive

He even took all taunts my sis battered him with
Smartly playing victim despite her brazen violations in pith

He still accepted her for what and who she was
Salute Siva for his courage and conviction without any clause

176. Hilton in Dubai

In 2002 Becky's Brother Hilton came to Dubai as deputized
Marine Shipping Company of US on work he was duly advised

He came to live with us in our small humble dwelling
Just a studio in partition he quietly managed in adjusting

Informed Becky in an offer to share the cost of an apartment in rent
Laughed at his offer reliving my time with Abishta in her tent

Of course, point blank I refused to even consider such an offer
Demeaning sanctity of the relationship between a brother and sister
They as siblings from childhood always very close to each other

Hilton and I still not acquainted in our basic fundamental
He soft-spoken and gentle; me sporadically temperamental

My wrong side Becky knew very well fearing consequences
Constantly in reminders, she would see me through lenses

Hilton stayed with us for almost a year
Sibling duo shopaholics in splurge without fear

Both brother and sister slept like a log
A light sleeper I was like a bloodhound dog

From bedroom hear the alarm ringing in living
Hilton so dead to world despite it buzzing

Then in raised voice call out Hill, Hill
He'd jump out of bed hearing kill, kill
Routine now for him in early morn drill

Nothing in me as a person ever changed
But Hilton's approach to me in a lot had changed

Both Becky and I were pleased for him
His stay in Dubai felt happy to the brim

177. Abishta's Unwanted Interference

Abishta always a troublemaker in the guise of do-gooder
Influence my mother's ears with brazen stories as fodder

Her house renovation at her behest achieved in my supervision
Budget allocated 100K completed in 48K in complete precision
Money saved to use in new elements for her house in the allocation

Working with Architect Zatin my access to best-skilled workers
Invested my time in meriting quality without middlemen or brokers

Now mother legally as an owner of her 1-bedroom apartment
Willed me as a nominee in records for the concerned department

Arihant never ever invited and never did mom stay with bro
His family first always yet rights in a claim with mom to and fro

Every decision on the house she ready always had me to refer
Sell both our houses together; bro tried his best to convince her

Invest jointly from capital gain in a plot of land in Pune city
Build a private villa at a fraction cost but no solid plan a pity

Vested interest there was, of course, Rakshee's family in part
Favored to stay close to them but mother warded it off

Mom aware of his covert advances as she was of his intentions
In his selfish outlook once a job is done put you in eternal detention

In 2005 Abishta tore down interior walls of mom's house
Without my knowledge or consent, suspicions it did arouse

An investment like a braggart in reason not required at all
A conspiracy next Becky a target she made an international call

Adroit use of words, surprise in waiting on a visit to Mumbai she said
Matter in hush-hush I am not to be in loop an evil intentions she bred

For work, she done claimed from Becky 300K rupees in relief
Send her money without my knowledge she was a petty thief

Savings I managed in plenty for sis in her house supervision
Pilfer from my kitty for mother's house in proxy in her blind vision

Becky point blank in refusal told her very categorical
Amid us secrets none she apprised in Abishta's historical

That was the end of it or so I thought of a deceitful play
Mom then intervened to say for her work I had to pay
Without my consent?! I declined nobody but only I have a say

178. Anand Rangadharan

4 years now Becky's stable job the only source of steady income
My contribution in bits her full salary our life support system

Desperately we wanted to start a family now a high priority
Time not on our side Becky now in her late 30s and me on 40

Among many products raised access floor I used to market
Elevated structural floor over slab creating a hollow pocket

Enabling passage of mechanical and electrical services
Antistatic tiles used in IT, data and command center premises

During one client presentation a gangly and garrulous dude I met
Tech savvy, brilliant, a sharp mind and ready wit but maverick yet

Anand Rangadharan an engineering postgraduate from IIT Delhi
A star could have been in the business world if he had it in his belly

The hunger he had but somewhere in his mind he got stuck
In bottleneck of the middle rung, he found it difficult to chuck

Politically shrewd brain just short on leadership qualities but
Conniving nonetheless he typically elite south pedigree gut

Some of the company he kept was a very dicey lame duck
Family in generations of intellectuals in places high they struck
High ranking bureaucrat his father, in trend, was Anand to buck?

Divisional Business Head Andy he liked to be called by a nickname
For large IT Company Data Beta in Dubai, he held his own in fame

In the swanky data center of a five-star hotel in Dubai our first meet
Technically sound, knowledge expanse impressive, he was truly a treat

Well read, skillful, meticulous in his work, on his own he a manual
But somewhere dark side in him lurked he was like a caged animal

His intellectual ability in contriving led to his eventual downfall
Deviously intelligent he an entrapment my chi saved me from fall

179. A Beautiful Addition
to Our Family

Mid-Feb 2003 finally for Becky and me in glad tidings
One of the happiest moments in our lives now came in binding

Becky and me soon parents to be
Ecstatic our cup filled with joy and glee

In midst of ruins came a ray of sunshine
To light up our lives we were on cloud 9

Our families were informed both mothers in joy
My father I informed who too was overjoyed

Oddly my mother to come to Dubai willingly she volunteered
For Becky's delivery, she herself enthusiastically offered

Becky for her antenatal care checked in UR Health Care
Gynecologist Dr. Vasuki monitored her in monthly welfare
Respected lady doctor always advised dutifully on motherly care

180. Prenatal Scare

Our baby doing well in mother's womb for 7 months, not a hitch
But on 8th month Becky erupted in skin rashes it was a scary glitch

Boils on her body with incessant cough in discomfort she'd twitch
In an emergency, Dr. Vasuki betrayed concern of allergy for her itch

Immediate review with skin specialist Dr. Nadir in UR Healthcare
Forgot his Hippocratic Oath refused to see Becky in critical care

Despite urgency in the health of pregnant lady voiced in dire fare
Perverse he was a doctor in noble work nor duty he did not care

Said he without prior appointment he does not indulge any patient
None he had, sitting pretty he was in time completely free and vacant

Regardless of Dr. Vasuki's plea on Becky's condition of sensitivity
Ignored his colleague and let my Becky suffer in pain in extremity

In anger naturally, I shot a letter to the Hospital Board in Management
Underlining Doctor Nadir's Apathy in ignoring 2 lives in abandonment

Nothing but just a short letter from Chairman's office in salutation
Token apology but toothless in action against Dr. Nadir in annulment

Fortunately, to another doctor referred outside UR Healthcare
Cleared Becky of any adverse reaction to mother and child fare

29th October we were blessed proud parents of a beautiful girl
Our lovely little princess, Arecca, loving, precious jewel-like pearl

181. My Mother in Dubai

For all differences with us, mother may have had
She arrived in Dubai to be with the new mom and dad

Mother looked after Becky and Arecca in care and nourishment
All was well in the first couple of months in the land of enchantment

It dawned on us differences cropped between Abishta and mom
She came to Dubai with the intention of staying put in our home

We were only more than happy to have her in our midst
Just knew too well to last soon there would be a twist

Then Abishta called, at Dubai Airport en route to Dar es Salaam
With mother in long talk applying a soothing patch up of balm

One day mother asked me to fetch some stuff from her bag
Found CD Walkman an unknown brand with a note on a tag

Mother too in dark maybe by mistake made its way she said
Abishta sent to Dubai for repairs, she was totally out of her head

In cat and mouse game craftily, she planned this deal
CD Walkman a gift for Abhikya, mom's Achilles heel

Didn't give a damn I was furious at her cheap tact
Cost of Repair = New CD Walkman a practical fact

And an unknown brand no standing in Dubai in its clan
She simply played her cards according to her plan

Told mom in no uncertain terms of her tacky act

Abhikya in the equation now, mom retaliated in strike back

Resistance in passive by ignoring Becky and the little one
Conversation she made none in the entire day she showed no emotion

As expected all went inversely with mother in equation
15 days advance in a huff she abandoned her station

At airport not once she looked back at her 60-day grandchild
Sadly, her priorities were more materialistically compiled

We called Abishta to inquire on mom reaching home safely
Intentionally all our calls went unanswered expectedly
Caller ID in her home a status quo for months held on stubbornly

Quickly we had to now find an alternative in our baby care
Started looking in close proximity for a reliable daycare

182. Happy Home Automation

Professional interactions with Andy developed steadily
Shared his dream with me of being an entrepreneur readily

Invited to join him, in me he saw a profitable strategic alliance
The concept in "Happy Homes" Automation solutions in dalliance

A novel idea literally transfers control at your finger snap
Automates every equipment in a home with just a key tap

Home Automation concept new yet to set feet in UAE
In 2004 concept uniquely niche to be really tested to see

Change is certain but resistance to change always inevitable
The concept wasn't rocket science but rocking and very credible

Big players established in the market for them inquiries on table
Happy Home a non-entity, businesses certainly not charitable

Platform desired to launch never mind big, a medium was doable
History in references key in the least degree of being measurable

Competition expectedly fierce home automation first of its kind
First to create a budgeted hands-on design that would rule over time

Andy sold himself and his pet concept to Mr. Prakasam
MD of company Regent for him this project on his lap was plum

Regent in trade of supply and install of UPS, Emergency systems
For 10 years now from a humble start, it had come to some distance

Credit to Prakasam its owner his sheer determination and grit

Evolved in repute in turnkey supplies of back up utilities in full kit

Andy's professional reputation preceded him always
At Data Beta earned his stripes in every project he had a say

No secret or surprise for any company to have him on board
Dedicated team man ability in getting best out for the desired goal

Prakasam in smart move absorbed Andy as Director of Sales
Salary of AED 18K + profit + perks both had a common tale

Regent gave Andy a free reign to develop his entrepreneur side
Happy Home a division of Regent, team composition now to decide

183. Job Offered in Happy Home

Division Head position I was offered and accepted
Reasonable salary of AED 6K + profit in total bested

My own 2nd hand small Polo I had purchased to use at work
Reimbursement on actuals on fuel and maintenance in perk

Small businesses and residential units in our radar
Sales target of AED 1.2 million a year was decent by far

Margins in gross @ 50% overheads for now just me in one
Average of 100K a month returns were more than handsome

However also factored projects, Andy, to bring in value
His brainchild this venture it was a natural lot he can do

Awarding projects on sub-contract to small MEP contractors
Once the ball gets rolling to appoint a full-fledged engineer

One small catch here automation an unfamiliar territory for me
No rocket science, common sense approach would set me free

Jan 2004 Happy Home set up for Smart Connected Home
A separate division now ready to operate within Regent Dome

Dubai all set to explode in major real estate boom
Aliens allowed title in property and now realty to zoom

Challenges to recognize automation as a concept in working
Intricacies of many products their interoperability in grouping
Compatibility in communication in brand protocols differing

Business development through architects, interior designers,
Electro-mechanical consultants and networking contractors

My responsibilities included preparing proposals and quotations
Project management too so I was an all in one augmentation

Within 3 months I had 11 projects in value AED 1 Million
Advances of 50% in kitty we were ready to rock and roll on

Plenty in kitty now to leverage business growth
5 years a feral now finally coming into my own

Steady job, stable income for my small family to support
Eventually, in time afford a decent holiday to an exotic destination port

All projects awarded for a single-handed effort of yours truly
Against rivalry big and tough yet client belief in me wholly

From here on we call Prakasam in short as just Sam
Very soon the door of opportunity on us he would slam

184. Duped by Prakasam MD of Regent

All sales orders for Happy Home under Regent auspices
Happy Home an unlisted company with Regent now with all aces

Proposals/quotes presented on Regent for there no choices
Naturally, revenue advances in cheque also under its hospices
Rest left on trust to Happy Home bank account in transferences

3 months passed no salary or fuel return to me was paid
Déjà vu Jatin Bhai now Sam too of the same coin in grade

My credit card woes in liabilities on the rise though handy
The matter was taken up with Andy who played wily and dandy

Passive onlooker, he asked me to take it up directly with Sammy
A leader I thought in pedigree but was ordinary in double whammy

Incensed I asked him what are you meant for then dummy?
Angry I was he grasped now dealing with incensed chummy

Entrepreneur claimed to be in ownership of team him a big zilch
Now in doubt with Sam, he sacrificed and let my terms rot filch

Duty in loyalty achieved his dream venture to summits from zero
Aware of my predicament in regular income he was a villainous hero

Sam not expected in office for the day
At end of my patience, I had lots to say

Mayhem plenty as I let loose cannon of dignified verbal assault

Tirade direct and swift against hierarchy for their deliberate faults

Stunned not knowing how to handle situation and me
Long in due coming, knew uproar would bring in dear old Sammy

It was then informed by an employee Regent staff too unpaid
3 months of salary in pending company business focus strayed

It was not Regent was not doing well on the contrary
Biting more than they could chew situation was scary

Sam never acknowledged me as Regent's employee
His take simple Happy Home Andy's brain and baby
Small cabin space his pledge people, not his liability

To Happy Home Account Regent never moved any money
Happy Home account never an intention with Regent in slummy
All advances poached by Sam, Andy was his Easter Bunny

Regent apparently in the liberty of bank's overdraft facility
In process of greed and over ambition built in a huge liability

Advances of Happy Home gulped in by overdraft accountability
Happy Home then began bleeding even before it reached puberty

Instead of a positive healthy financial base in progress
Happy Home spiraling down towards growth in regress

Domino effect many starting from dishonoring projects
Facing angry whiplash of clients in shock and regret

Inviting lawsuits and jail term from clients now a serious threat
Loss of time, energy and the goodwill of my sincere sweat

Sammy the boss sauntered in hardly looked worried

In pilfering our funds, he knew we were dead and buried

Closeted with Andy in his office wondered what they studied
Result predictable I was shattered and once again bullied

Something had to be done Andy his usual self-beside in rhetoric
His dream he said would live it and be my insurance in plethoric

Never whetted the process on a separate bank account with Sam
Not for a moment in suspect he on his butt kicked hard wham bam

For me now this an emotional guilt of terribly tangled controversy
Andy for all business savvy he proclaimed made this issue very messy

Money siphoned off by Sam but the trust of clients for me paramount
Andy's Plan B in seeking Venture Capitalist not that he was renowned

Slowly in realization this guy Andy had absolutely no clue
For all his worth in brilliance his network at best to the nearest loo

185. Ayaz Coatwallah the Venture Capitalist

Enter Ayaz Coatwallah seasoned impresario at core a gentleman
Successful business in office furniture with perceptive acumen

Ayaz introduced to me by Glancy Rego an ex of Archinter
Ironically, we first met at Regent Office she an arbitrator

Ayaz and Saqir his brother to discuss prospects in Raised Floor
In awe, I was to see the finished product sample called Heis Floor
Then Ayaz for UAE market offered me a position in an open door

Timing so much of essence but for only a couple of months now
Loyalty in work for Happy Home declined politely with a bow

But in parting told we will stay connected for any need in future
Thought of him as potential VC for our stuttering venture

In those few moments felt in him person genuine in nature
As fated unilaterally in huge risk he backed with his debenture

Ayaz sponsored both our travel and stay in full to Mumbai
Andy to present at their corporate our venture proposal in Dubai

Very generous host he put us up at Grand Hyatt near Airport
Personally, picked and drove us both to his office a very humble sport

Ayaz and Andy first time in meeting 30 minutes in drive and talk
Andy now in his element with his repertoire not for once did he balk

Hammer and tongs, he went his business dream depended on it

Gave it all and why not Ayaz soaked it up in time bit by bit
Impressed he was safe to say the first step it was a hit

After primers in pleasantries with 2 Directors at the corporate office
Mentor Kalpesh Gorade joined in session now rest in look were novice

Post presentation on PowerPoint Ayaz high in impression
Kalpesh his one-line query summed up his actual attention

Ownership of fund and minimum guaranteed return
This, of course, was Andy's call and totally his concern

His entrepreneurial dream, now his call-in trust to earn
This far every step I enabled now time for him to fill the urn

He retorted on both counts to accomplish he has iron balls
Just in rhetoric but soon to prove he just a loose cannonball

Destined to meet Kalpesh again as an advisor a few years later
It was then he made me privy to his decision as a neutral arbitrator

Anand Rangadharan heavy baggage in waste to carry
Best to parry, for him only too much talk in the air of glory

Ayaz Coatwallah indeed a generous man an individual
Project deserved a chance he felt his mind now in a duel

Gamble on person Andy unknown to bet on just his credentials
Ayaz to fund this venture promised Andy to fulfill all potentials

186. Left Out of Equation

Suddenly left out of equation only Ayaz and Andy in discussion
Slighted I was; among them hammered all terms and conditions

It was good in a way for my priorities was to get back on track
Salary was vital and the key to start projects, to avoid client's flak

Ayaz ready with funding of AED 300K in requirement
Mandatory to start LLC firm in Dubai minimum in acquirement

Funding on loan through his relative in Dubai
Just a call-in brief to his counterpart from Mumbai

Jabazz an owner of a respected trading firm in tools
Badruddin Trading his father in business he was a school
Destiny in time to intertwine Jabazz and me in life's pool

Funds given directly to Andy and so I no more in the loop
Andy now complete authority none on him to snoop

Ayaz now in direct call only to Andy both together in coop
Not once did Ayaz call to inform me of their sacramental holy hoop

For records, I felt one final meeting in tripartite
Financials drawn in clear terms on cost how to bite

Office set up, project funding, management at the site
New businesses, collections, likely profits to cite

Payment in need of personnel for homes to fire bright
Reporting system in loop done all in black and white

Nothing of sorts in like happened, now a disaster in waiting to strike
Once again in life, I was going to be rudely pushed out of sight

Knee-jerk plan of action put in place for a start
Andy to collect funding cheque from dear Jabazz

Provide a counter guarantee cheque for the same amount in mass
And deposit passport just in event of leaving shores by air first class

Release full amount back to Jabazz on the formation of a firm
On need basis Jabazz to release funds as in required term

Andy but had other ideas in making
Practical less, total showoff in faking

Ask for realistic opinion but veto on his taking
Team interest no priority at all in asking
Careless spending in absolute no planning

Office space new in heart of city business center
Princely price of AED 60K in needless renter
Demo center in office an undesirable expenditure

A large area reserved for him in closed partitions
Next costly furniture for conferences in mission

He on a spending splurges a work in suicidal decision
Clients to glimpse futuristic homes in his blurred vision

Small shop space around 24K per annum in prudence
Office to double up as demo center a sheer common sense
2 months pay in priority for staffs in need of expense

Sales and site personnel out on field and site 90% of the time
Secretary just one to man office, spending otherwise is a crime

Projects worth AED 1 M won without demo in work only mine

Then Andy in 60K spent in new house rental an expense in self-center
A leader he useless put himself before and the team he left in hunger

One day Andy casually dropped breaking news for me to jump
An equal partner to bring me on board thought I will be pumped
More share of liabilities built up, eventually on me he to dump

Smart cookie brought legal documents of partnership to sign
Bait he contrived as benefactor mine in his dream he designed
Looked straight into his eye without hesitation blunt in decline

187. Happy Home Not Happy Anymore

2004 during Ramadhan afternoon 2pm time to wind up
Routinely picked my infant daughter from daycare stop

Cradling my little bundle of joy in my arms my mobile rang
Ayaz mirrored on screen and heard his tone different in twang

Calm yet angry his words in an orchestra of a storm he sang
Andy has yet to return 300K loan and I haven't got a hang

Yes, I was shocked in his tale but told him I had no clue
You, I said kept me out of the loop now you call me for your blues

This news share now has me more depressed than you
You knew he said! But how? Neither you nor Andy kept me in cue

It was then I realized a few weeks back Andy to Qatar had gone
Consultant for American MNC his expertise sought to be drawn

Had to withdraw his passport from Jabazz to travel for a week long
My passport in the request he made I surrendered without any yawn

Three weeks since he was back no effort for my passport retrieval
Realized its implication, gun now on my head he in mind was evil

With my little baby in my arms, to the office, I drove back
Summoned Andy in private alone for a quiet confidential talk
Ayaz call to me had him stunned in disbelief
Squirming now he said he had in ready plan B

How much more time was he going to waste
Never did you have any plan not even in haste

But the priority for me my passport with me a must
Asked him firmly to hand his to me now in just

Evening in hand my passport I ensured first
In anguish at heavens, I looked is there left any trust?

Heavy in heart loss both fiscal and mental in emotion
Another year in my life a maverick hand in demotion
My family too for his idiosyncrasy suffering in damnation

Called Ayaz and conveyed my final decision
He realized no hand of mine at this implosion
It was time for me to cut and go in sheer resignation

All clients started calling me in desperation
Every call I answered without any hesitation

The truth I told them that I no longer in association
Happy Home no more my livelihood as the destination

188. Fate a Circle in Full

My 2nd term visa with Jatin Bhai was due to expire
Money in 6 years was still pending so I let it run to the wire

But now circumstances were extremely dire
Offer from rival automation firm in time to inspire

Went to meet Jatin Bhai expecting in his old office
Apparently no more an occupant in the same orifice

Shifted to a new location in the tower of a large edifice
He now riding in the stratum of a high street in lattice

Told him time for us both move on each our track
He then spoke in new business now please join back

Real Estate boom bandwagon he too was on it flush
Couldn't have achieved without funds in turbo plush

You are fit for a position of CEO I have foreseen
Generous in words no doubt he always has been
Live deed in action is what I have never seen

Quote your price and terms you shall have it
Presence of your now more needed than by bit

I was now in quandary on my decision
Known or unknown devil a hit in precision

Crossroads in life a junction never a miss
Always in chances who do you first kiss?

189. Another Innings with Jatin Bhai

Sword double-edged on both sides
Devil on one and deep sea beside

Decided on Devil for reasons known
Realty in new business now was in zone

How he came about funding so huge
Torrents in millions it was a deluge

Business none it was of mine to peruse
Salary in constant was my only refuge

In passing revealed investors from UK big
3 members sync in motion as a trio they swig

And so, it was I joined Par Consultants
Realty Experts in property developments

My first assignment a warehouse sale
Per square foot Price @35 to nail
Closed the deal in the first call without fail

Suddenly Jatin Bhai hiked its price
Now @ 40 for same he threw the dice

Success @ 40 too was a deal in grip vise
Next @45 and @50 in price rise
My success I felt for him was unwise

190. Change in Task Assigned

Tasked now with daily copywriting ad
Boring static work no-brainer it was bad

Nothing dynamically significant happening
The same usual story of past in sermons making

A direction in defined path none in taking
A just usual routine of ad copywriting

191. Andy Like Jatin Bhai and Prakasam

In between calls from Andy in courtesy so to speak
More in a matter of my progress in information he seeks

One day call from an unknown person called Ranjit
An engineer with Andy he for sites to handover when complete

He cried his heart out of desperation woes
Unpaid salary of 6 months from Andy his low

Asked if I could help him in another job securing
Said if I come across any I loop him in assuring

In curiosity, I asked him how he obtained my number
Said lots in good about me in ear felt a need to correct his blunder
Couldn't help but laugh at his bumper words in wonder

In a revelation, he then made Andy's on me his nasty words in snitch
Flattering words during an internal meet of my betrayal in a loud pitch
But natural rapidly in livid but in wait to have him first in the ditch

And then Andy called just to say hello
Inquired if all is well like my dear beau

Sure, I said after your smash below
Still can afford a smile in warm hello

Mouthful of invectives in blast I let him listen in jazz
In his defense said 2 legal suits against him he has

Your sinful ways and doings in curse sure you have
Called it upon yourself as well killed many innocent lives

Said wanted to meet me for air to clear
Certainly, I said place and time in chosen was familiar

On time nay before time I was there in full gear
Andy never showed up simply out of fear
That was last I heard from this wastrel peer

192. Annual Visit to Mumbai in 2005

In Jan 2005 along with our little baby, we went to Mumbai
Arecca 's first visit to our homes and her first also to fly

After mom's illogical defiance in Dubai expected aloofness
Despite uneasiness in the air, there was a token charade of goodness

Not used to new people and with a couple of new faces around
Arecca clung to Becky or me not willing to be put down

Abishta, as usual, was her friendly self on hand with a bribe
But our little one wouldn't be bought in distress with her vibe

But on Becky's mom's beckoning at sight hopped in her arms
The startling shift from our baby to our relief and grandma's charm

Gelled well with aunt, uncles and her big cousins on her doted
She only girl child in family pampered in love they exploded

Her first birthday in Mumbai in joyful celebration of gathering
Entire maternal family clan alone more than 50 in numbering

Granduncles, aunts, cousins, children and friends in celebrating
An occasion unplanned but in the fun, frolic music and dancing
Event beautiful like a dream sequence so vivid in unfolding

193. Arihant's Relocation to Pune

It was at this time I was informed about changes in bro's life
He moved on as Marketing Consultant in capability he was rife

He then moved back again to Pune this time in permanent
The disparity with mom and sis in family skirmish so apparent

It was going to be a long time before we touch base again
Strange circumstances to make contact but were to be in vain

We were by now totally disoriented and family dysfunctional
Only as convenience in the matter any contact purely emotional

194. African Safari

Back in Dubai at work after a holiday cure
One fine day in walked a trader goldsmith to lure

Met with Jatin Bhai a business project in lore
Supplier of finished gold jewelry in pure
To major outlets in Dubai souks and near

Proposed through his contacts in Africa
Purchase raw gold at 1/10th cost from the source

Partner need in finance to sponsor its inflow
Neither facts nor fluency in gold to blow

Yet decision in funding in approval to go
Jeetubhai goldsmith now a broker in tow

Yours truly in project gold as mission de attaché
Jeetubhai's language skill was as good as neigh
To Ghana in West Africa for many a gold cache

Gold a windfall at 1/10th in price only a game of con play
Alien land and lingo have you bound by law for life in decay

Sack of dust it looks gold but for your eyes only in a belay
If not quick enough to spot its switch you certain in doomsday

Tribal head called Nana a bottle of a black label for him to sway
In Backstreet alley shady joints in darkness sample only to display

A local gang in their hands your life but a pawn to throw away
Each 6 foot plus and strapping ready to have your skin flay

Two trips in all I did cover on this El Dorado wild goose chase
In 60 days only 2 shady meeting to merit in this crazy gold race

Jeetubhai contacts local for supplies only boastful bray
Deals other than gold many varieties available for foreplay

My discontent made to Jatin Bhai in communique blunt as a portray
Waste of time in resources dangerous game in this real-time broadway

Yet despite my advice ¼ million US for Jeetubhai in foolish risk
50K self-indulgence in 5 stars living the goldsmith blew in brisk

Counseled Jatin Bhai funds to guide in familiar gainful business
Venture in Modern Trade as valued supplier listed in all wiseness

In category one in baby steps proposed to begin in kids wear
Suppliers were thin, carve our niche expand the range in products rare

Completed supply chain process and sampling in chain le' four
Confirmed as a listed supplier and also my 2nd termination in the score

Dismissal second time round linked to his generation next
One of his sired 3 had a conflict of interest in personal and was vexed

A story in absurdity his progeny the office used as her own fiefdom
Make staff wait after office hours late for her chat in online kingdom

For her it was routine for rest it was family and kids in waiting
No ethics or respect nor graceful in etiquette she was unbending

Charade went on for long until her disdain I could stand no more
And I told her in manner calming yet firm for others too life is a chore

Now a director in realty firm, she tried with me her strong-arm tactic
Would try and assign a task in contradictory to her father's practice

Obvious it was for me for the basket in which to put my loyalties
Shunted then to Africa for business farcicality in gold royalty
And so, ended the chronicle with Jatin bhai in all incongruity

Once bitten Twice shy, twice bitten and fools die
1-year Feb 2005-Apr 2006 was all this association went by
This was the wannabe businessman Jatin Bhai

Nothing left now to fall back on
Everything just suddenly just gone

One time feeling on top in exhilaration
Then downward in one spiraling motion

Never in control of destiny my own
Change of good winds always only a notion

195. Call from my Chi for Me to be Just ME!

All alone at home now wound in my thoughts
What next my mind whirling round in ugly bouts

Little one her future troubling my mind in practicality
20 years now almost living in a hostile community

Friends, Siblings, Employers; my lady luck lost
Too long enduring pain of failure huge in cost

Something in me just snapped a call from my chi
Too much I had changed for others within me

My chi said it is time for me to be just me
The world can feel what they want about me
For it is only their problem but me just let me be

Changed my way I walk the talk they so insecure
Moderate my way I talk the walk for them I an eyesore

Well that's their problem they wouldn't change for me
With me an excuse for them in dealing with their complete insecurity

Altered my persona on many bits of advice on how to be
My attitude, my persona is my real strength in me

Altering or suppressing it was not the real me
In pleasing others only, I constantly was unhappy

Take ownership and return to who I was meant to be
Felt a surge of confidence rise from core within me
It is for others to accept me not as them I meant to be

196. Ayaz Coatwala my Savior Raised Access Floor

Voice in a prompt to contact Ayaz from within deep
2 years since an offer he had made now to reap

Just enough credit on my mobile for few minutes to last
An international call it was to India need to act fast

Dialed Ayaz, real gentlemen as he listened out to me
Said he was fine having me on board for markets in M.E.

Terms and condition too in acceptance in my favor did he
Asked me to call Jabazz in 1 hour to set things up to tee

Jatin Bhai said he would retain the visa status for me
On this count Ayaz and me from encumbrances free

The first day at Badruddin Trading in the hope I was excited
Greeted me Jabazz politely led me into office cabin private

My office for Heis Floor until we find an alternate
Car too he arranged a notch higher more than adequate

Raised Access Floor tangible product finally
Set going about the task in earnest zestfully

Heis Floor in quality very extraordinary
Benchmark as a product of pride it was exemplary

Made few calls to trade in flooring product range
Big firms in commercial carpet trade for tie up to arrange

197. Flooring Enterprise Official Distributor

Flooring Enterprise in Dubai was the first in my shortlist
Already contact known in past a good feel in assist

Balkrishna (BK) finance head but equally adept in sales
An aggressive hands-on approach he was to tilt the scales

Meeting schedule at Flooring Enterprise Head Office fixed
BK and me at 12 noon in a meet with feelings mixed

Confident I certainly was of Heis Floor quality in the world with any
Just the mania of Europe or US products with company's many

Pleasantries exchanged time now for Brass tacks
BK eyes lit up on presenting Heis Floor tile 1st from the rack

Cementitious steel bare face panel a series from a pack
Finishes in wood core and calcium sulfate back to back

In time I said under development, in near future in the stack
We were both in sync and moving forward right on track

However typically business compliance in the Middle East
Quality, Certifications aside Price the ultimate beast

Bargain; bargain back and forth till buyer gets least
Finally, we agreed on price terms time now for a feast

Flooring Enterprise in UAE now Heis Flooring's official distributor
An enviable partnership deal synergy in each a major contributor

198. Business in Flow

June 2006 1st week travel schedule to India in plan
Heis factory in Mumbai a visit with BK our go man

In meantime, BK initiated projects with multiple inquiries
An exercise in communication logged in our email diaries

2 months now and in plenty already in promotion
In 3rd, two containers order business now in actual motion

Teething issues in any new business always round corner
Just putting sane heads in sync for solutions plenty in armor

The factory in Mumbai apparently just enough to cater in local
Volumetric quantity from imports to cover Pan India in total

Avail benefits in manufacture purely for exports for an entire season
Pro rata gain for import quota to fulfill India market a logic in reason

Quality of Indian made Heis panel far superior to imported OEM
Proud to market the same in the Middle East more than happy I am

Many challenges to achieve many more miles to go
Documented global 3rd party accreditation a sure must in tow

Load, fire, axial, impact, overturn, air leakage test to show
3 to 6 months to achieve in a process the going now to be slow

Business has to move on a compromise to procure as OEM
Many possibilities in logistics switch B/L one of them

199. Badruddin Trading Additional Role in Onus

New Development in meantime at Badruddin Trading (*BT)
Airaa, Jabazz's better half she was him in business aiding

Lady pleasant in disposition, progressive work outlook in upgrading
A desired change in work ethos among staff sought my help in urging

Time on hand with Ayaz's concurrence accepted in agreeing
Compensated fairly for responsibility extra additional in binding

BT in the business of tools and hardware in the construction industry
Principal agencies of world-renowned names in global fraternity

BT name synonymous in tools a brand in itself in trust had grown
Jabazz after his dad plying the trade with a team now on his own

Jabazz and I familiar in person, he very shy and humble
Simple, methodical, no-nonsense, without any jumble
His work ethics traditional yet rational without a fumble

In work customary, unassuming always quiet within his zone
2 showrooms in the business district he had since made his throne

July to December transformation huge in BT rapidly in happening
Kalpesh Gorade hand in major as a consultant ecology in changing

Existing team complacent and careless, their job taken for granted
Routine in system so deeply ingrained they unwilling to be motivated

Result in a reality check for monthly revenue for chickens to peck

With supplies outweighing receivable debt burden over the deck

Personally, on onus collected more than million from debtors
Brought down all liabilities to zero P/L now looked better

Kalpesh informed Jabazz and Airaa few harsh decisions a must
For growth weed out unwanted else impacts in business to go bust

Replacement bright and diligent I hunted over networking in the field
A couple of good guys in skill I hired assured of new deals to be sealed

Now as General Manager I mentored a team cohesive and healed
Oct 2006 to Feb 2007, zero to million a month of sales huge in yield

Complete team act but one in distinct brilliant among unit a stand out
Honored to lead an upbeat team from the roof in my joy I could shout

200. Murtuza the Senior Pro Deserved His Rightful Dues

Just one but in regrets, senior personnel Murtuza asked to go
Nothing wrong for he had done his time a long time ago

Almost 4 decades in service to BT as a salesman on show
His loyalties in deserving a sendoff for his life in rest to glow

But it was not to be as Airaa in her belief had other plans in stow
End terms benefit his right by law she covertly made him forego

For an ordinary human in the evening of his life too much to let go
Hundred Thousand AED in denial a crime likes him on death row

Jabazz by inheritance a millionaire, 100K by far for him a peanut
Murtuza from his dad's era merited well rather than kick on his butt

Saddened by this I was he had told me about his son's wedding
Grand reception for him in Mumbai with this his lifetimes earning

Asked to sign an official receipt payment in full none in pending
Swore money in full will be paid in Mumbai before month ending

By this, he had signed off his legitimate claim in trust of receiving
Months to year went by but funds to him intentionally not in remitting

Airaa felt for Murtuza in sum amount huge, him not at all in deserving
His calls from Mumbai ignored or chided in angst of him harassing

Orders to vendors for the wedding in advance of 6 months in giving
In debt now, life in shambles, Murtuza old man in tears dearly sobbing

What was achieved in making a life of loyalty miserable by denying?
In fact, 10K in bonus will've reaped for them in life, amply in blessing

Simply beyond my simple principle in life and understanding
Why do any privileged deny unequal's their simple right of living?

201. Full Time in Heis Floor

From March 2007 I moved back full time to Heis Floor
Certification issues set, phase now to open new businesses door

BK now serious in planning a visit to our facility in Mumbai
Departure scheduled for last week of March 2007 from Dubai

Ayaz and Saqir in meantime made a couple of visits to Dubai
Visited Flooring Enterprise HQ met with BK and lunch in tasty Thai

Thoughts in deliberations on inventory and support in as an ally
Satisfied with outcome in preliminary returned back to Mumbai

Deliberations besides product, sampling and documentation
My role, tasks, visas, travel, offer letter an exercise in direction

Officially I had joined Heis Floor in summer of April 2006
A year now formally an appointment letter for me their HR yet to affix

Till date my salary paid by Jabazz from Badruddin Trading
But legally as an entity to move in Heis for my role in associating

Followed up in Mumbai when traveled in crisis in September'06
Saqir assured offer letter he'd ready and send it to me as quick

202. Domestic Emergency

In 2006 I could not accompany my family home on an annual trip
Told Becky to go to her mom's, mine for a start from airport to skip
Arecca fussy little one feel more in comfort in her own mother's ship

Next day with our baby neatly tucked in a dress with bow
Visit she went to pay my mom with nephew Franko in tow

Goody bag of chocolates from me fair in quantity and ratio
Bags of provision intent in civility and at night to stay in their burrow

Signs ominous Arecca in journey already loud in bawling
Becky's anxiety of my absence in migraine attack on her telling
Fears not unfounded reception in cold at sister's door in unveiling

Snubbing her at door in unkind gabble sis told mom of Becky's arrival
Becky with our baby and Franko besides in frantic wait for survival

Disregarded in full, not once was Becky asked if any help she needed
Arecca in unbridled wailing for divine succor she badly pleaded

From Dubai, my call told Becky to leave back in an apt intervention
Back at her mother's our baby happily quiet, a sure relief in tension

Few days' later calls to Becky at her mother's from my mother
In the fiery wrath of unworthy words unleashed on Becky to smother

Woman demeaning other in toxix abuse cruelly on her DNA side
Murder she claimed of her grandson, together we planned in homicide

Unbelievable it was on chocolates I gifted that she laid her proof
Expiry date 4 months to go it was just her ploy to unleash her coup

Asked Becky for me to make a call from Dubai to her direct
In the verbal assault of allegations on us, she burst like a manic wreck
Finality mom with a son in a link to end she put in immediate effect

Foul game by mother and daughter duo long since in their mind
July'06 deluge in Mumbai, moms flat in deep, had her in fate resigned

Sis talking me into selling for a one-off calamity, in the hope I will sign
Firm in resolve in telling sister lay off even in thought, I declined

Abishta basically feeling a pinch of her hand in renovation
From her funds claimed she, spent for moms flat in devotion

No right to claim back money for your unwanted intrusion
Hope she harbored to claim her cash after the flat sale in duration

She asked Becky her view on her work of art in a ratification
Becky clear in a review on her excessive self-admiration

Work well done but budget unjustified in over aggregation
Sis not in the least amused knew how to vent her vexation
Clever use of words in effect for mom to trigger ramification

Mother's decision of not selling her flat always intransigent
Abishta's one masterstroke, she signed my warrant in banishment

However, mom independently fierce always in her own right
Her thoughts and views her own to gauge in a choice of ambient light

Next beyond any sane cognition just an imaginary insight
A decision to sell impulsive out of spite with Becky in a one-sided fight

Cardinal gaffe, now she always in the shade of my sis in her plight
But she could still hold her own in event condition getting tight

She called Becky's mother, in turn to inform me of her deed
Not in possession of my Dubai number her excuse indeed

Asked me to come to India and my belongings to collect
Nothing much left besides 2 photos framed of past to reflect

Disowned by mom for the same flat I had built in her name
Abandoned now once again by covert family political games

At 44 nothing left for future for my small family to fall back on
With my wife and kid's photos in hand walked away and was gone

A final nail in the coffin they say, my mother, she hit very hard
A big part of me died that day faith and trust from now I discard

No more of sis or bro or mother for their troubles to shore
At peace with myself now no more interference I swore

Few days' later calls again received in Dubai whilst driving
Mom, it was in loud rant she just let out in caustic lashing

Arihant had just made a call to her and he was dreadfully threatening
Share in money from sale of her property he from her was demanding

Told her first to get her informer credentials right in verifying
Bro's out of touch since years now he for me in hibernating

A U-turn in immediate her words she now in reversing
Actually, a realty broker my mom rebuked, to bro he did the snitching

In solitude, by myself, I couldn't come to terms in utter disbelief
A wry smile I could afford when your own kin to scavenge as a thief

203. Dad's Call in Emergency

All through these years funding dad's expenses in regular
His troubles big no less for me to bear in every quarter

Every quarter he shifted house, in call for deposit in demand
Begged and told him to get out of that place like he in remand

Shift to Mumbai and live in my house to please understand
Every quarter in a deposit of 20K is something out of hand

One afternoon call on my mobile from an unfamiliar voice
A woman on another side in breaking news she gave me no choice

Dad's ill perhaps suffered a stroke she said the news was in pits
Requested her to the nearest hospice for dad to please admit
Arriving in Bangalore at the earliest flight I informed in quiet grit

Becky called mom, sis and bro from office to inform
Mom and sis sedate, bro said he'd try to make it by morn

Reached hospital ward in Bangalore directly on arrival
His loud voice in corridor, the nomad was on road to revival

Extremely relieved I was, he happy on seeing me at the door
In his excitement and happiness said, my son! An affection of outpour

Thanked the family of strangers who looked after my father
Unrepayable debt of humanity in making him stronger

A few days later in Dubai, he called me yet again
Told me to shift him permanently to Mumbai in a bargain

Made all arrangements for him to be well looked after
Hired hands to cook separate male nurse for his needs hereafter
Brother in law younger Lawry spent time in his company
Dad and he then would regale in each other's symphony

Hoping dad in no more indulgence of any more in adventure
At 85 he was too old now to look after himself and his needs in future

At heart but he a nomadic vagrant easily bored by nature
One day just disappeared into oblivion his normal usual feature

Only this time never to call or return back dutifully to his enclosure
In vain within my means tried to find him in the known land of pasture
Hope he at rest and peace with himself anywhere in quiet leisure

204. Offer Letter

Sep 2006 managing 2 different issues personal and professional
In crisis a fulfilled dream sold and meetings at Heis office in parallel

Important in keeping focus at work, right now stability a key
Forces unseen playing nonstop cat and mouse game with me

Meetings with Ayaz and Saqir on product and biz dev in earnest
Primer with 3rd director Mushtaq Dhagawalla, a person serious at best

Flooring Enterprise's BK travel plan to Heis's Floor factory discussed
More likely to happen in the 1st quarter of 2007 only dates to adjust

HR Head Sonali exchanged information with her on my active role
Sales, Payments, Logistics, New Markets, PR a package in whole

Standard procedures but for me a separate draft on offer to hold
Concur with Saqir to have it ready soon and sent to me in a fold
Within 1st week of October 2006 latest by courier, I was told

Global Business Manager (GBM) position for Heis Floor in making
Did evince my interest but already in shortlist one in confirming
Kanan by name soon to arrive in Dubai to meet me for 1 to 1 meeting

Pursued the matter intermittently with Saqir on offer letter
Since I was managing both BT and Heis floor left it for a bit later

Also, the process of certification ongoing on close will be better
Almost 5 months still no draft insight from a senior legislator
Afore transfer of BT tasks in Feb'07 end sent Saqir a gentle reminder

205. Teething Issues

Diplomatically broached all issues along with offer letter to issue
Swore he with Ayaz to concur with clarity on March 2nd to pursue

Plenty happening in meantime with Heis Floor in UAE Business
Orders fulfilled as OEM from Far East to maintain market fitness

Natural in a spot of bother occasionally on account of logistics
The rate in port to port transfer in speed part of biz characteristics

But stress factor mostly in human coordination to err biologic
Add fuel to fire Saqir's unilateral action deliberately neurotic

Kanan GBM suggestive in name but in aim extremely erratic
Quote in few instances for issues eventually to go ballistic

Rafat Bareiliwalla Sr. Commercial Manager for operations
Responsible for all import, export procedural documentations

However, for Heis floor exports was now first of its kind
Complication none unlike the theory of relativity by Albert Einstein

Common sense approach in a procedure like imports
Certification of the process to follow likewise in exports

206. Issues Complicated in Making

A typical environment in the corporate the buck is always passed
Fire the gun from other shoulder and blame it on a certain forecast

Order for container quantity with BK in negotiations numerous
Finally expanded to 10x20' quantity, surely it was really onerous

Request to Saqir to arrange for Pro-forma Invoice
Major order in quantity a draft to be devised

Looped in Rafat Head Commercial on Saqir advice
A draft article of terms sent for my review and revise
Satisfied with corrections reverted and apprised

Rafat Head Commercial with BK to be direct
Instructions shared with him accurately with template

Yet several a delay in a decision for action on due date
Redirect instruction for B/L via me for L/C immediate

Shipment sought at least for containers in 3 urgently
Project site ready for Raised Floor installation reportedly

BK in fervent hot pursuit on batch delivery constantly
No information from Rafat his inaction shown callously

From original date, Aug 14th cargo pushed further by 2 weeks
28th Aug now to leave, yet only 3 for rest the news seemed bleak

Logistic sense if in delay by 14 days all 10 in load to seek
Or at least get the roster in partial shipment for shippers to tweak

BK relentless now in follow up with me for information in obvious
Evident none I had to provide with accuracy or else sound dubious

Pressure from project site team looking rather inauspicious
Clearly, we at fault for all issues in mounting making us anxious

Export order by commercial team very miserably bungled
Despite many weeks in prior notice, time in shipment jumbled

Cargo stuck on arrival documents yet not released in original
Demurrage levy on Flooring Enterprise client action merited in critical

BK extremely dismayed in coordination of material deliverance
In spite managed in overcoming this mess, an awful bad experience

Passed it as one-off matter shipping line liable for any variance
But Heis floor complacency in logistics was matter of decadence

Certainly, commercial head to account for, it was his indifference
Flak I absorbed from BK for erring head's ownership in irrelevance
Absorbed demurrage on cargo overstay was BK's noble acceptance

Spoke my mind on record by email to Rafat on his compliance
Saqir of course was looped in to keep him abreast in reference

Next in immediate an email addressed to me in bad taste
From Saqir nonetheless for my email to Rafat he replied in haste

Quoted in loud his disapproval for a direct salvo of my displeasure
Mess apart made by team cost in magnitudes by a large measure

Cost to Heis Floor in many by way of in extras from our treasure
The team in the office in full strength for each role assigned in leisure

Here I was multitasking roles in variety always under pressure

PR skill I put in effect to save company face always in an endeavor

The saved extra cost in demurrage by BK's benevolent gesture
The impact of Rafat's inaction detrimental for company's future

Saqir preempted any reciprocal reply or call in his email refusal
Said poor planning from my side in his dumb unethical accusal

And further asked for reports of forecast again for his perusal
But suitably forgot my offer letter now 6 months yet in disposal

An excuse now to concur with HR in final to frame in a proposal
First Ayaz, now HR 180 days in deference for my letter not so crucial

207. Car Towing – Petty Mind at Work

On sales calls in peak summer, my car broke down on a quiet highway
The temperature in the high 40s instructed towing van to find his way

Charges nominal @AED 100 filed in petty cash for recompense
Terms clear from onset car inclusive of fuel and maintenance

Saqir refused without reason, in his act petty I felt it best dispense
Slowly getting a feel of his mentality not in dollars but in cents

208. Global Business Manager Trip to Dubai

Kanan the GBM of Heis Floor to Dubai in his first trip
Set up a meeting with BK, inquiring with me on this new flip
Spontaneous he in reaction, his intent with Kanan for meets to skip

His take since I already a point of contact so why this blip
Global Head he is, rational for a market update in a zip

Apparently I was informed by Saqir about Kanan's fetish
Night Clubbing interest in live song and dance he does relish

Well ill afford I could in matters of else's sensual fantasies
Not my style of living it up in another's frame of such dizzies

In a round to follow Saqir a Director in his statement was really clumsy
Entertainment of boss so-called, nothing left to spare to make it fizzy

It was payback time for things were really spiraling in one-way highway
Epistle terse they conveyed to me it was either their way or no way

209. Saqir's And Kanan Joint Trip to Dubai

December of 2007 both in Dubai on a business tour
Operation more to clip my wings I was in aware for sure
Ready and waiting I was, my ammo full in their cure
For any false notion, they might have me in bind insecure

Started off in the wrong foot as expected Saqir at the helm
Kanan a silent audience in reading my expression

Usual razzmatazz in his script spiced for my capitulation
Waited patiently in hearing a bombast from him for completion

Asked him politely in calm if he is done in action
Now my turn I said and would brook no interruption

This an unexpected turn of the event not in their anticipation
Duo traded glances in surprise my attitude in the least expectation

No expression of any nerves but pent-up raw frustration
Let torrent flow in a volley of outburst without any inhibition

Said I; you'll a battery in a team of individuals in the role all seasoned
Here I am multi-tasking in every role for a prime reason

Expect support staff in readiness with frontline in cohesion
You assume sales, logistics, receivables, reports across all season

Yet time allowed in procrastination for back office team in a legion
Your priorities need to be right for yours is a misplaced horizon
My loyalty to company not any single, yet dare accuse me of treason

Leadership a balancing act of righting wrong not wronging right
Here is Kanan Global Business Manager so to say he is a dire plight

Reception in waiting for him at the airport with bouquet alright
He no kid just gets into a cab and at final destination to alight

Get good sleep overnight and ready for a routine business fight
And then amuse him at the nightclub you seek my company at night

Entertain him on his stay when petty cash of 100 refused at sight
Seriously your expectations low for I decline with all my might

My salary remittance consistent in delay for 10 months now
Yet demand in reports, work in progress every time, on time and how?

Selfish style, lack of serious leadership skill your talk only hypocritical
10 months in reminders on my offer letter yet you are rudely cynical

In abeyance my appointment letter despite promises whimsical
Excuses many in concurrences with Ayaz and HR just prototypical

And it ends with your own folly as a leader in your shortcoming
Least in bother yet you have a gall to admonish my ethics in working

Stunned into silence both clear in aware their bluff I was calling
In sharp verbal duel salvo, I did fire one more sack me in daring
Timeout Saqir called for lunch and to a restaurant, we went driving

Moments of silence followed as we indulged in a sumptuous buffet
Tactics changed my need imminent for now or they in doomsday

Lauding my efforts in success in UAE Saqir broke ice, touché
Bringing Flooring's as a distributor for UAE, he sounded cliché

But still in manner wanted to in some way get me in his hold

He in compromise will fulfill offer letter as quickly me he told

But would not tolerate insubordination in any manner or mold
Depends entirely I said if our view on it of the same cast in bold

No decision in unilateral will I acknowledge in cold
Respect is earned and reciprocal not to demand untold
No more trust in anyone not in the least these 2 to behold

If I have erred job wise no hesitation in me offering an apology
But if I am failed, prompt action is taken to balance in waning ecology?
Stalemate it was for I an individual against the company in topology

210. Below the Belt Game of Politics to Fore Bidding Adios to Heis Floor

Afternoon in meeting with BK at Flooring's office on payments
The unique model put forth in a proposal in defining statement

Payments executed for a bill of exchange through term avalization
Issuing bank pledges payments on an agreed commercial transaction

Saqir accepted, now to obtain his company's bank confirmation
Obviously, his call also to loop in co-directors on this vital information

After 90 days flurry of reminders for payments from accounts
Surprised I was should have been cleared without any miscount

Called BK and appraised him, clear he was on the actual situation
Processed and cleared from his side on terms of avalization

Now verified again with accounts on our bank's confirmation
Mushtaq Dhagawalla (MD) 3rd director in a loop now in intervention
Crass worded email statement to me felt bitter pill in consumption

Crushing it felt but suspected surely crossfire of internal political war
Why did Saqir not inform Mushtaq on avalization acceptance so far?

More than 3 months since meeting with BK in covenant
Directors on board just 3 yet in 12 weeks not in appendant

An onus Saqir said he would revert on as trusted informant
This was not an errant but from Saqir in gross aberrant

Did not mince my words for too many issues now in abeyance

Fall guy I was made to be for every mishap of inconvenience

Protocol I never did bother in event of being taken for granted
Mushtaq, Saqir did not matter in least, who in my radar will be blasted

Saqir clearly in mention I did in my email very high in relevance
Now apparent it was Mushtaq did realize its source and significance

But that he was not informed and kept in complete unawareness
Reply from Mustaq of this major goof up diplomatic in despondence

Saqir a Director utterly in oddity on a matter high in importance
His ineptitude led to plenty of confusion in unwanted disturbance

Certainly, measured in amnesia resulting in hurtful discordance
Did not even bother to regret his inaction willfully in any conscience
It was clear in a subtle message of killing 2 birds in one shot license

More than 6 months since eventful tripartite in Dubai rendezvous
My appointment letter and timely salary yet in any breakthrough

Charges on transfer invariably deducted by my bank always in few
Despite bringing it to their notice accounts never acted on cue
But reports, payment, sales and forecast demand since in continue

18 months nothing tangible yet forthcoming from management
Kanan in meek held I take the blame of Saqir's fiasco in judgment

The leadership in my eyes Kanan a dunce and scored a big dud
The kind who lacked any decision ability but nip any promising bud
Very, very politically correct knowing which side to butter his bread
Character in aspirations pinning anybody as fall guy he would shred

Even in my letter of resignation a decision he abstained in dread
Concurred with Saqir in emergency and then accepted as it read

Time in June 2008 salary again delayed past 45 days yet no atonement
Response none from Kanan as GBM or head of accounts department

In exasperation, I stopped communication to ponder annulment
Kanan in panic mode his emails I ignored in any acknowledgment

Realized one-way traffic this was in a time of deep introspection
Wanted to unbind in primitive archaic restraints of domination

Never fulfilled any part, management even in mandatory obligation
Leadership more in coterie nepotism rest always in discrimination

Forced stress needless in a burden on mindset, focus but a dereliction
Delay many theirs only procedural but mine if any certain in conviction

In my experience this was typical management procrastination
Time to put plan B into action a backup I readied in anticipation

Approached global MNC of repute in building materials production
A position of Business Manager for ME tabled on detail discussion

Freedom to operate, develop the market in ownership for decisions
Accepted in delight finally in space of my own clear in direction

Lines laced with sarcasm I said he was politically correct
Saqir and Kanan lacked moral grounds of basic ethics in effect

Depicted by his rather callous and blasé remarks to deflect
Issues since 18 months to address yet continued to neglect

Never eliciting a response from either to close this topic aspect
End of benefits my rightful dues in 2 months a lot to forfeit

Without offer letter, of course, no proof and in ethics did not expect
Time to move on better than to lose sleep over and regret

The message very clear and loud I sent to Saqir and Kanan

"My attitude my strength,
In my strength you see weakness
That then is your weakness
For your weakness you want me to abandon my strength
I rather keep my weakness which is my strength
My attitude my strength"

211. Thank You Ayaz

From my heart huge gratitude and respect to Ayaz, he gave me a break
From myside all communique I forwarded him for his in total retakes
A gamble he did take when in need I was of a job extremely desperate

Even as I left there was nothing in pending or amends to make
He once in between mentioned 300K to Andy written off as take
Ayaz I will always hold in very high esteem for his unbiased sake

Ensured from my end no loose strings left to tie or leave an open gate
Everything from orders to receivables was in total up to date

Floors to continue in partnership with Heis to flourish in a spate
My best always as I left with Heis Floor biz in UAE doing great

212. Brazilian Samba A Fortuitous Journey

Supernova a 100-year-old South American MNC I joined
Became an integral part of the management team in time

Came into my own finally for my last hurrah in the sunshine
Now at 46 had to feel 26 to make up for all my lost time

20 long years in 2008 to arrive in port I had to be in my element
Maze of crossroads I had to traverse full in endless impediments
An extremely torturous heartbreaking journey of open bedevilment

35+ years of life in my professional working
5+ years in early career all for the family in raking

15 years as feral in free without any real pay in receiving
7 years since getting married no income in forthcoming

10 years late in life for my own little family in making
And this 10 not possible without my Becky in absolute supporting

Just on one salary of Becky, we were in surviving
Managed in thrifty with credit card banking

Beyond means never indulged in any useless borrowing
All debts on credit card finally we are in complete ridding

Thankfully our small family today stable in living
Many a family holiday in exotic destinations we began enjoying

213. Epilogue

Power is both strength and weakness
But in weakness a weapon extreme in meaness

People you have known a lifetime in whom you implicitly trust
In a moment they become strangers ready to have you crushed

You are their means to reach their pinnacle of glory
So cut you will and design a make-believe story

True it is the life in lies that we really live
And lies becomes what we believe to be true

String of petty crimes being ignored does not redeem a sinner
Only spurs criminal minds for conquests big as a winner

A pattern in circles as my life slowly evolved
Failure of each in relation in symbiosis it dissolved
Entrapped in a maze that just couldn't be resolved

Just as with 2 hands in a clap to beat
2 in rhythm also your dancing feet
Likewise, every relation a must in 2-way street

Each relation a chance in this story
Strength to strength to grow in glory
But not to be it had a twist in work so gory

All played dirty without scruples the game of real life chess
No rules barred making each a pawn ensuring their mess

Jungle law in extreme each a predator and prey

Willing to tear into another never mind how they slay

a. The Clergy

Comes to mind a compassionate godly kindly noble soul
The moment in mention he has been ordained in a priestly role

Shunned all worldly assets they in service of humanity whole
Guiding light from depth of darkness for all in brightness to unfold

But each turned out to be a hopelessly vindictive a terrible ghoul
Burned out the light that would otherwise be shinning gold

Religious zealot's impure deed, tie innocents in a concocted manacle
In repugnant act belying in fact, their fantasy to be in power tyrannical

On weak and gullible they stalk in their prey to assault
One that could not retaliate or seek retribution by default

Just in one stroke of madness killed an innocent life
Assault so brutal leaving an indelible scar permanent in strife

Yet another in prized time he carved away with a slash of knife
The two clergies wrote my condemning destiny in kind
In their dirty game of chess, I was but their pawn to grind

They were the alpha power all prevailing as in jungle raw
No care in nefarious indulgence they felt above every law

b. Army man

Army man in gallantry sacrifices makes his country proud
Could've been real captain in lives he providentially found

Held the flock in order true guiding light in lead

Forever grateful flock strong, for his unselfish deed

But in principles and values he in shredding
Personal agenda he bred, a real con in making

Swindle any and many in fast buck taking
Cash or kind, property or bullion in raking
From the onset, relation doomed he was in faking

Swayed himself in heart of my beloved sister
She an idealist always a romantic dreamer

Prince, she believed him to be her loving charmer
Turned out he miserable, wretched, dirty schemer

3 decades our sis he kept away from her mother
In guilt, he came when she was no more to bother

Suffered she in terminal silence until in her breath she no more
In her lifetime trauma of dignity, she pained alone in her core

She longed for once to relive happy moments with her maternal
But the cruel design of fate by her worse half sent her prior in eternal

He a cruel prince uncaring not charming her existence he made a mess
In life manipulating her cruelly like a pawn in primal game of chess

Even in her sleep finally at peace, sadness seen in serenity
Bless you dear sis may you always be happy and joyful in eternity

c. Friend

Then came along Friendship so defining

Faith in a friend always from onset blind in trust

Gave all in loyalty always company before self-first

With promises galore, he invited to join in the business midst
Bagful in goodies in real he committed to sharing in an equal fist

Created a business path as a partner for in prosperity must
But in greedy lust on his loyal friend, door of wealth he cruelly shut

Then came along another great pretender
Turned out he too a subtle chronic offender

No doubt he was brilliant in mind
But he was certainly evil in design

Used his friend's network for connectivity in fund
His own grid entirely empty and void barring none

The identity he pawned to sacrifice his own friend
Despite help received demeaned him in trend
Family too each did not spare, in lowly depths stooped to descend

Together if desired, earned to share in abundance of wealth
Built together an empire strong, a business world keen to have dealt
Killed not only a dream but many lives to be in want all for self

Denied in basic need for survival, leaving him and his family in strife
Whilst he with his filial enjoyed all the pleasures of materialistic life

In a show to world he a noble benefactor
But in cold reality an evil gruesome detractor

Theft not only in materialistic wealth
Time in friend's prime taken away in brazen stealth
In the game of chess, each piece protects another in sacrifice
But a friend first he is nice has your trust in a strong grip like vice

Then, he casts you like a dice; lucky for him you fetch a price
And then he cuts you in slice once, twice and even in thrice

Friend in friendship defining was not even an enemy at best

d. Boss

A committed leader of herd an organized platoon he drives
Gently, firmly and sometimes sternly in every situation alive

Leader true in unmitigated inspiration
Lead from the front in guiding aspirations

Exemplary in time with a focus on strategy and management
Does not demand but earns respect for his leadership dependent

Selfless always in managing his team in unison
An unbiased approach to ensuring no division

Create opportunities in making leaders of tomorrow
Freedom on decision even in mistakes assuage no sorrow

Ensure the right of privileges and perks given without reminder
Stress enough on mind to divert attention on rejoinders

Leaders of today and tomorrow in homage for his touch in effect
Now they as a teacher, in guiding light inspire gen next in same respect

But in real World?!

True Boss-like in human anatomy is an arse hole
In the business world many such in lead typically half in whole

Block dynamic real aspirant progress to stub his goal
Depends on boss whether likes your dance erotic on pole

Or being served tender or well done in life's highway toll

Self before rest is how they love to hold
Knowingly wrong but still they will not fold

Divest your privileges, perks, bonuses strike down in annual appraisal
Rewards of virtue, wielding his power, immoral way for sure in reprisal

Sermons and show cause notice on basis of a protocol
Hide their cardinal sinful crime they are one big shameless ghoul

Discourses many from holy gospel concealing his hideous esteem
Steal your time and work to earn on pretext to deprive in your dream

Praise your triumphs in motivational pretense unlimited to the moon
Drop you down 6 feet under next into netherworld in ultimate doom

His political manoeuvres cleverly worded in procedural delay
But order for the season was you lacked total performance in foreplay

Depends entirely on choice how you wield your arm
Suck, duck or buck in options of chancing your charm

Trust none but only him in self
Control by fear like an evil elf

Intimidation and threat in his corrupt ability
Coerce and extort to certify your disability
Sure, winning formula for his extended durability

Ensure he wills your loss of confidence
In paying himself rich for his incompetence

Oh! Yes, the boss just hates moment of truth or dare
His reflection in the mirror a reality in how he truly has fared

At your peril, if done the arse hole will block you without any care

The leader in you will defy, a definite threat to his order of supremacy
Only one Alpha can be in jungle of grassland, bush or corporate legacy

Only he has sole and exclusive right mate, to say Check Mate!

e. Family

Our family could have been an envious pride
A lion and lioness would have shone each in our hide

But individual virtues of greed and jealousy to guide
Outside Influence goaded and to each other, we lied

Each in our vision so myopic for outsiders enjoyed a free ride
Our union now broken like a deep gorge and chasm so wide

Vying with brethren in connivance to have each on their side
It does not matter anymore whether an ebb or flow in the tide

Family values and principles totally roasted and fried
Bond in the family in time just faded and died leaving a big void

Mother

A raincoat of every life she holds in her being
Close watchful eye over her children growing

Protect each life in her womb
Even at risk if it means her tomb

Magic, she weaves mother universal word of love
Nurtures each seed into a solid sturdy tree from ground above

One day their own in world robustly free full of love
To shelter and fill in time fruits in a treasure trove

Like mother bird she watches her brood of fledglings
Working hard in fetching needs in their nourishing

To face the tough headwind, exercise their wings in strengthening
Now her resilient young all grown ready to fly on own in daring

But somewhere along in turbulent weather change
A difficult choice in make she had to take

She would hold her favorites close to her bosom
And rest unfortunately abandon to fate

But a mother she would always be to us in guiding light
Protected us from every harsh onslaught of any forceful might
Taught us everything to be strong to face the cruel world beyond sight

Mother, Oh Dear Mother, love you always for my identity bright!

Father

The root strength of family united
Bark of a tree against an all-weather onslaught protected

Fiercely possessive of his pool of pride
With patience in diligence, he teaches with you besides

Through all darkness, he is a firm guide
Fear in none dare any touch his little ones, them in half divide
In mistakes for their good, he does sternly chide

But slow and steady he builds in them
Making each strong as in time he bides

Naturally, like real mentor he hones
True bright shine on each their hide

In time his pain will bear sweet fruits
Proud head of the family all willingly abide

But if the head of the family is a lone hunter
Gambler, vagabond and nomadic punter

The plant will wither away no tree to shelter
Pride no more, in fear of outside pack run helter skelter
Many villains in waiting to rain havoc as cruel pelters

Father, Oh Dear Father If only you were beside our Mother
This world never even laid their eyes to have us in a bother

All of us would be united never to be singled out to smother
One huge strong solid tree we would all have been in one gather

Siblings

Siblings older wiser they were now in years
If only held fold together in each their pinky fingers

Despite many pleas to the family to restore healthy root
Siblings selfish in conceit each outdid other to uproot

3rd front an outsider took advantage of the team in disarray
Fueled dissension ensured the entire team would go astray

One now in nirvana she sips nectar from sacred cask
Two the bohemian lass today just like an empty flask

Three the prodigal still finding his radar in a task
And yours truly finally did all his nemesis unmask

If only together braved every onslaught of hostile weather
Yet not budged in the faith of trust in each other

Legacy in values of inspiration
In cohesion for many future generations

Strong foundation laid for future brighter
Their flock's grown many folds solid stronger

But;

Tree in constant abuse withered and dried sadly, I saw in slow pain
No matter water in plenty also sunshine but no more in love to gain

Parasites and awful pests together destroyed it to pore
Now its just only a dried withered and hollow empty core
Fertile ground once in bountiful of promises now no more

Devoid in nutrients of plentiful affection, dutiful in care
Soil dangerously acerbic, saline and now a toxic lair
Sadly, not even dead in it in dignity will ever really fare

The relation in sacred no more to fork
All but over in one brutal stroke

Yours Truly

We live in a make-believe world of ethics
Principles and values neither thin nor thick

In reality a dangerous jungle out there
No kin or kith nor friend or foe all's fair

In love and war to grab your share
Strip you for sure they will completely bare

Drag you out even from your hidden lair
Bull or Bear if only we could willingly share
But in fraud we only clandestinely snare

And I saw it all happening before my very eyes!

Every relation in hold coddled in a wholesome brutal purge
Connived willingly all and sundry stealing others in a gorge

Tried in every ploy to halt their manic attack
Counseled too in gentle sometimes in a firm tack

Alas it was to no avail they all firm in their track
Snigger at me for sure, they felt a fool I was watching their back

Red flags in caution many at every step
Still at my own hazard dared my instinct instead

Wallowed then I did in huge self-pity
Nobody cares to notice this silly emotional deity

Our is jungle law civilized in extreme aboriginality
Like predators, we stalk our prey in all originality
Parents, Siblings, Friends or in Corporates all in brutality

Grassland or bush all maze of squares like in chess
But rules in game none, in choice anyway you may onward press

In a constant game of survival as a pawn, you are in a mess
Attack and counter-attack none to be spared even in a cess

Family grown could have been abundantly big and strong
Yet in time totally dysfunctional and disintegrated in wrong

Philosophy of life is so simple on every mantle
Yet Homo Sapiens in greed will simply dismantle

A lesson for us all as in past one more so truly a sad story
For in time it will lie buried in a heap as any in distant history

Fortunate I am, in life many chances could afford to take
Wealth gathered as experience far too much I could make
Still, my precious time in prime I lost huge for me to forsake

The moment on road in life I traversed as an entity
Came into my own to have my very own identity

Realized too late emotions to use in play as decoy in ruse
Fools one too many will fall, for you to recycle after use

Principle, values, ethics and morals only inspirational rhetoric
In the real world these are for rooted minds, deeply prehistoric

Constitution, Rules, Clauses, By-laws, Amendments all encourage
Crime sans proof an escape route whilst you are collateral damage

Finally, Faith in Trust just a gamble if must
In life, I did just that, gambled my Faith in Trust

Russian roulette or poker and flush
A lesson in life for me in a seasonal gush

Faith in yourself first, Trust in you a Must
Rest does not matter not even in Trust!

Binding us all in the Cosmos

I have been around when there was nothing
All evolved and I witnessed it happening

Countless came and unaccounted went
Some left their footprints behind others simply spent

Who are you an identity you seek to build
Many questions yet remain unfulfilled

It does not matter to me who you all are
But in all of you, I am but the significant czar

Many greats have come and gone
Monarchs, messiahs, philosophers and seekers
restless in their quest of a new dawn

Empires Flourished, Dynasties Perished
Brave and their bravado in moments embellished

Fame and Fortune too fade away into oblivion
However I am indispensable will remain your custodian

Without me you all are absolutely nothing
Subservient to none I am with respect abounding
Even most powerful in cosmos to me is acceding

None could however much they tried to accomplish
Could hold, pin or dictate my power to diminish

For I am the one that binds the universe
Never for once do I stop to look behind in remorse

For better or worse in small steps I traverse

I am who I am you seek me out always
I am TIME!

If I could change something then….
I wish to have back my lost good time

I wish to have back my lost good time
Did you not hear alarm chime?

Time in life is like fine grain of sand
Pick but still many slip from your hand

Little that remains is your prime
Rest never will be your time

Choices made like grains of shifting sand
Pick another scoop in your hand
This will be your new time in land

What falls off can never be your time
Grains of sand your pain and gain in rhyme

Life in this world like a plant in arid sand
Nourish with water and plenty of sunshine
Healthy in growth and sweet fruits in time

But vermin and parasites plenty in grime
Weed out unnecessary or simply waste time
Keep them too long only you will lose shine
Precious time lost memory could've been fine

Many beings will cross path in your time
Family and friends will make it a rough grind

But it is your time and it will not rewind
Time no relation, no friends or blood line
Just moves on without looking behind

Yesterday in history, Future a fantasy in mind
Today an event unfolding yours and mine
Time unbiased motion, every step is a sign

I wish to have back my lost good time……..

My Incredible Anchor

All felt lost then along arrived Jessica, my dear,
Sailed together the rough seas despite many fears

With a hand held out in anchoring me to her
Many, our strong hold in vain they tried to shear
But never let go of me she held me dear

Without you I just another wannabe hero
An epitaph in bold inscribed, me just a big zero

And came the moment of reckoning on spine
Abandoned by every single person called mine

And alone you stood by my side kept the shine
Unconditionally like a rock, you were fine

Helped me weather every rain and storm
With our arms in each other entwine

Many calls in life I made went wrong
Yet your faith in me was ever so strong

Gave me courage and will as you walked along
And help me reach for destiny I truly belong

Every moment in our lives from then on a prom
Sashaying to beat and rhythm of trumpet and drum

Truly humbled in my life's successes in glory you etched
Many milestones like lyrical musical you helped me fetch

And so glad I was you said aye in grand
In graciousness when asking your hand

In journey together, we will waltz in loving band
As equals conducting maestros waving the wand

Sometimes in a stupendous symphony
And occasionally in a sheer cacophony

In sync, we tune gracefully in eternal duet
And walk in perfect harmony towards our sunset

Thank you, my darling Jessica,

Lightning Source UK Ltd.
Milton Keynes UK
UKHW041940240219

337804UK00016B/164/P